HANDEL'S Messiah

A Musical, Historical & Theological Study

Gretchen Simmons Brown

HANDEL'S MESSIAH: A MUSICAL, HISTORICAL & THEOLOGICAL STUDY

Copyright © 2010 Gretchen Simmons Brown
ISBN 978-1-886068-43-8
Library of Congress Control Number: 2010934184
Published by Fruitbearer Publishing, LLC
P.O. Box 777, Georgetown, DE 19947 · (302) 856-6649 · FAX (302) 856-7742
www.fruitbearer.com • info@fruitbearer.com
Graphic design by Candy Abbott; cover illustrations from istockphoto.com
Edited by Fran D. Lowe

By author preference, pronouns for the persons of the Trinity are capitalized throughout the text; however, the style of deity pronoun capitalization in Scripture quotations and other referenced material retains the original source as a matter of accuracy.

Musical Excerpts

Musical excerpts are taken from *George Frideric Handel's* Messiah *in Full Score,* Alfred Mann, ed. Copyright © 1989 by Dover Publications, Inc., used by permission.

Scripture Quotations

Scripture quotations without translation references are taken from the actual score written by Handel and Jennens.

Scripture quotations marked KJV are from *The King James Version of the Holy Bible,* public domain.

Scripture quotations marked NKJV are from *The New King James Version.* Copyright © 1982 by Thomas Nelson, Inc. Used by permission. All rights reserved.

Scriptures from *The New Oxford Annotated Bible,* copyright © 1973, 1977, by the Oxford University Press Inc. Used by permission. All right reserved.

Scripture quotations marked RSV are taken from *The Oxford Annotated Bible,* copyright © 1964, by the Oxford University Press, Inc. Used by permission. All rights reserved.

Scriptures taken from *The Harper Study Bible,* Revised Standard Version (RSV), Harold Lindsell, Ph.D., D.D., ed. Copyright © 1946, 1952, 1971 by Zondervan Corporation. Used by permission. All rights reserved.

Scriptures marked CEV are taken from *The Contemporary English Version* © 1991, 1992, 1995 by American Bible Society. Used by Permission.

Scriptures marked TLB are taken from *The Living Bible, Paraphrased,* copyright © 1971. Used by permission of Tyndale House Publishers, Inc., Wheaton, IL 60189 USA. All rights reserved.

Scripture quotations marked MSG are taken from *THE MESSAGE.* Copyright © by Eugene H. Peterson 1993, 1994, 1995, 1996, 2000, 2001, 2002. Used by permission of NavPress Publishing Group.

Scripture quotations in *The Everyday Life Bible* (notes and commentary by Joyce Meyer) are taken from *The Amplified Bible* (AB) and are used by permission of the Lockman Foundation and The Zondervan Corporation. Additional text copyright © 2006 by Joyce Meyer; Amplified Bible copyright © 1954, 1958, 1962, 1964, 1965, 1987 by The Lockman Foundation. All rights reserved.

The author has researched attributions to the best of her ability and is not responsible for the accuracy of the source of quoted material.

Printed in the United States of America

for Rod,
my favorite musician

You've got tickets to hear Handel's *Messiah* this year! How awesome is that? Will it be your first time? When those of us who have performed *Messiah* hear the piece mentioned, we are already singing "Hallelujah, Hallelujah!" in our heads. Regardless of the number of times we hear the masterwork, *Messiah* is always exciting. The influence of this oratorio to draw people closer to Christ is far greater than even the memories that it brings to mind. The piece is an old favorite that is somehow comfortable and reassuring, almost a liturgy in itself—a worshipful experience. As an audience made up of believers and unbelievers, we are all united in God's universal purpose for our existence.

This book begins discussing the first movement of *Messiah*, referred to as "The Christmas Portion." Part the First juxtaposes various biblical texts from Advent and Christmas, including the prophecy and realization of God's plan to redeem humankind by the coming of the Messiah. Advent is the prediction and expectation; Christmas is the birth and incarnation of Immanuel, who is "God with us."

The "rest of the story" (Parts the Second and Third) continues with the resolution of God's plan (His story), and is referred to as the "Easter Portion." This masterpiece that was conceived and composed as a total unit ideally should be performed as such. If the entire *Messiah* were to be performed at one sitting, it would require about two and a half hours, so find a comfy seat.

Part the Second is the telling of the mighty work of redemption featuring the passionate sacrifice of Christ, which involves the events leading to His death and triumphant resurrection, ending with the most famous song in the oratorio: the "Hallelujah Chorus."

Part the Third continues with the effect of the resurrection: Christ's ultimate victory over death is extended through faith to all people. It contains a thanksgiving hymn for this final defeat of death. The oratorio ends with a four-minute "Amen" chorus. Whew! After sitting for all three parts, we would be physically and mentally exhausted, yet exhilarated.

The author's intent is to place Handel's great masterpiece squarely in its musical, historical, and biblical context. Any diligent performer or discerning listener should be able to find just what they're looking for if they have questions about the score, the Scriptures behind the music, or the composer. Because this volume is intended to be a handbook or a study guide, some of the information in a few chapters may be redundant. This is in case a soloist may be researching only a particular solo piece or movement.

Messiah is a truly stimulating piece to masses of people. Handel himself must have been genuinely inspired in order to be able to wed the text and music together so beautifully. What a gift he had to be able to express the spirit of the Word of God through gorgeous music.

This book has provided its author with the opportunity to combine her two passions: music and the Scriptures. Singing anthems, motets, spiritual songs, hymns, and oratorios are a great way to put Scripture passages to memory. When someone hears a Scripture read aloud, the jingle of that musical phrase just pops into his or her head and the entire Bible verse comes alive.

Handel's *Messiah* is an annual event, a seasonal favorite that we love to revisit. Those of us who have participated as chorus members get so excited when we hear the piece mentioned. We immediately start singing "And He shall purify" or the "Hallelujah Chorus" with all the gusto that we had displayed previously when singing the oratorio on the stage. This time, as we study *Messiah* together, let us hear God's words and Handel's music as never before . . . in a strikingly new way.

Acknowledgments

The inspiration for this book began 30 years ago when I was invited to teach a Bible study on Handel's *Messiah* at Fairfax Baptist Church in VA. God has nudged and prodded me through the whole journey and provided a symphony of support:

My heartfelt thanks goes to my husband, Rod, and to my dad, my daughter, my son, and my two young grandchildren for their continual support and enthusiasm from beginning to end. A special thank you to my mother who introduced me to *the* Messiah.

Friends, too many to mention, have supported me in this endeavor, but Norma Locher has shared this journey with me since we were ten years old. She and I first experienced Handel's *Messiah* as sopranos in high school where we donned our choir robes and sang together.

What a joy it has been to work with my publisher, Candy Abbott, of Fruitbearer Publishing. I thank her for her tender care, cheerfulness, and creative ideas. She truly orchestrated this beautiful final product as we worked side-by-side in harmony.

Thank you to Fran Lowe for her professional diligence in editing and wordsmithing the manuscript over and over again until we got every thought just right.

I am grateful to Bob Hill and Will Lockwood, two of my early readers, who encouraged me at the halfway mark.

Dover Publications has graciously allowed me to use excerpts from the *Messiah* score. Special acknowledgment also goes to Abingdon Press who published the twelve volume series of *The Interpreter's Bible*, from which I have quoted extensively.

A warm and hearty thanks to all my readers. When Handel completed his oratorio and was complimented that he had "entertained his audience," he replied, "My lord, I should be sorry if I only entertained them. I wished to make them better." I do hope this book speaks to you on a personal level and encourages you in your enjoyment of Handel's masterwork.

Introduction

On the right day in London of the 1740s you could see him walking down Brook Street in the vicinity of Grosvenor Square. An elderly gentleman, neatly dressed in his lace coat, ruffles and three-cornered hat, he would proceed at full steam, talking to himself as if the problems of the nation were on his shoulders, and then pause abruptly to contemplate his surroundings. The people he passed often noticed that he spoke a mixture of German and English, and he was overheard one day to mutter, 'He is ein damn scoundrel, and good for nothing!' This was none other than George Frideric (as he spelled it) Handel.[1]

Handel was born on February 23, 1685, when his father, a conservative elderly barber-surgeon, was already sixty-three years old. His father desired a legal career for George, the second child of his second marriage, so he would not let young George have access to a musical instrument. In spite of such a severe restriction, the boy still managed to learn to play the organ and the spinet. One story says that George, aided by his sympathetic mother, smuggled a clavichord up into the attic of the house, where he could slip away and practice quietly after smothering the strings with strips of cloth to avoid discovery by his father![2]

Recognizing, perhaps reluctantly, his son's apparent natural talent, the elder Handel took the ten-year-old George to play for the reigning Duke Johann Adolf of Saxe-Weissenfels, at whose ducal court he was

---

1 Jay Welch, jacket cover to Columbia Records album, *Handel's* Messiah, The Philadelphia Orchestra, Mormon Tabernacle Choir, Eugene Ormandy, Conductor, n.d.n.p.

2 Milton Cross and David Ewen, *An Encyclopedia of the Great Composers and Their Music*, Vol. 1 (New York: Doubleday, & Co., 1953), 328.

employed as a surgeon. Somehow, at one of the Sunday services, young Handel managed to play for the duke, who was so greatly impressed that he filled the boy's pockets with gold and advised his father to provide him with proper lessons.

The boy's father gave his consent grudgingly because he had no alternative. To refuse meant displeasing the duke and endangering his lucrative business. The teacher chosen was Friedrich Wilhelm Zachow, organist of the Halle Liebfrauenkirche (Lutheran church), who was quick to recognize that a genius had come into his hands. Young Handel made rapid progress and was even able, at the age of eleven, to substitute for Zachow as church organist upon occasion.[3]

By the time Handel was seventeen, he was an accomplished musician, organist, harpsichordist, and violinist, as well as a composer. Skilled in harmony and counterpoint, even at this young age, he was determined to make a mark in the larger arena of secular music. After beginning his musical career by playing in the Hamburg opera orchestra, Handel learned the opera business so rapidly that he then made a crucial decision which would shape the rest of his career. He tried his hand at writing Italian opera—a style of opera immensely popular in England—with his first full-scale musical work, *Almira*, in 1705, at the age of 20. He also frequently traveled among the various Italian music centers, where he met Italian composers Arcangelo Corelli and the two Scarlattis (Alessandro and his son Domenico), from whom he would develop his use of warm, luxurious melody and harmony.

Handel then took London by storm in 1711, when the twenty-six-year-old arrived there to produce his first opera seria, *Rinaldo*, followed by his *Giulio Cesare*. The Italian operas he wrote proved to be the most colorful, sensuous, stirring entertainment the bustling city had ever known. In Handel's heyday, between his first visit to London in 1710 and his death there in 1759, he wrote about forty operas in Italian. Being known at this time as an operatic composer, he also became quite a successful musician. Handel was, however, huge in size (often called the "Great Bear"), not very polished in manner, and frequently strode through the streets of London muttering to himself.[4]

Established around 1719 to present Italian opera, the Royal Academy of Music was supported by many wealthy patrons of the arts, even the king of England. Handel, appointed the musical director, went to Europe to persuade some of the leading soloists to visit London to participate in this artistic venture. Unfortunately,

3 George Lucktenberg, ed., *Handel: An Introduction to His Keyboard Works* (Van Nuys, California: Alfred Publishing Co. 1973), 3.
4 Cross and Ewen, 333.

the Royal Academy of Music ran out of money due to mismanagement in 1728, so Handel had to look for a new venue where his operas could be performed. The "Great Bear" would not accept defeat.[5]

Regardless of such resolve, however, by 1737 the bottom fell out of Handel's endeavors. Financially devastated, he decided that he had to change his creative approach. What could he do to appeal to more people and make a living? About this same time, the public was becoming fickle and growing tired of operas, especially the serious ones. A new era was dawning, one virtually symbolizing a major social change in both music style and preference. Handel would have to find a fresh way to appeal to a rising middle-class public.

But respond he did. In 1738, Handel turned to writing large, dramatic vocal-orchestral works known as "oratorios," usually based on Old Testament Bible stories. He knew then that he had found a new medium for his genius—and for him, the greatest medium of all.

In this same period, the fifty-three-year-old Handel had suffered what might have been a stroke or an attack of severe rheumatism. Partially paralyzed, he made a journey to Aix-la-Chapelle to take advantage of the healing baths. Perhaps his amazing recovery contributed to the fervor with which he began the writing of his oratorios.

Actually, Handel turned to composing church music in order to pay the bills. Beginning in the late 1730s, he wrote a series of approximately twenty dramatic oratorios on biblical themes in English. Among these oratorios are *Jephtha, Belshazzar,* and *Israel in Egypt.* According to Matthew Gurewitsch of *Connoisseur Magazine,* "What they sacrificed in spectacle, they easily made up for by the new addition of Handel's tremendous choruses, which swept the action to the visionary heights of epic."[6]

After all, Handel was, of necessity, both a businessman and composer. If the tide turned in a different direction, he would turn also. So from Italian operas, he now wrote oratorios, which were popular with the general public and had the advantage of being allowed to be performed during Lent, when the opera was closed.

When Handel moved from opera to oratorio, however, he was not really moving that far. The Handel oratorios are really Handel operas without scenery or costumes, but performed in the English language. Although filled with deep religious feeling, they were not written to be church music pieces. They are monumental choral dramas built out of *recitatives* and *arias* of the greatest lyrical variety, since Handel was

---

5 Ibid., 334.
6 Matthew Gurewitsch, "Hallelujah for Handel," *Connoisseur Magazine,* February, 1985, 95.

no longer constricted by the necessity of writing for specific voices. The basic difference between operas and oratorios is that the drama for the oratorios is projected in mighty choruses, cathedral-like in their majesty. In writing these choruses, Handel brought not only the fullest resources of the polyphonic art, used with such lucidity that its complexity often eludes the ear, but also a wealth of humanity and compassion.[7] The Handel scholar, Paul Henry Lang, insists that the oratorios are not devotional religious works at all; rather (with perhaps some overstatement), "They are dramatic works on biblical subjects, completely divorced from the church."[8]

What a pity! "Completely divorced from the church"? Whether or not Handel meant his oratorios to be a religious offering, they were considered as such by the public. The April 1813 issue of *Chester and North Wales Magazine* had this to say: "The music of Handel, is, indeed, admirably adapted to fill the mind with that sort of devotional rapture which, with the commemoration of our blessed Lord and Saviour, as men we ought to admire, and as Christians, to feel."[9]

It was at this time, in 1741, that Handel, at the age of fifty-six, wrote his immortal masterpiece, *Messiah*. An invitation from the Lord Lieutenant of Dublin, Ireland, came to Handel to prepare a work for a charity performance. Handel conducted this first performance of *Messiah* as a benefit performance for a jail and hospital in Dublin, and it was well received. The orchestra for this Dublin performance consisted of modest instrumentation, having mainly strings and *basso-continuo* but no oboes, bassoons, or brass.

A year later *Messiah* was performed in London at Covent Garden, March 23, 1743. This time, the presentation was a distinct failure. The nobility called it dull, while the clergy condemned it as irreligious and were appalled that it would be presented in a place of worldly amusement. Seven years later, however, it was performed in London again, this time proving very popular. Handel knew that with oratorios, he had found a new medium for his genius. Two decades later, it was performed in America at George Burg's Music Room of the New York City Tavern and has been performed thousands of times since in every corner of the world.[10]

7 Cross and Ewen, 339.

8 Harold C. Schonberg, *The Lives of the Greatest Composers,* 3rd edition (New York: W. W. Norton & Co., 1997), 46.

9 Ibid., 47.

10 Cross and Ewen, 335.

TABLE OF CONTENTS

PART THE FIRST

❦❧

PART THE SECOND

PART THE THIRD

Part the First

Chapter One

Overture

As the first chord of the Overture is played, we leap right into the somber setting marked "grave" (Italian for slow or somber). This chapter describes the French style in which the overture was written and takes the reader through the fugue-like ending. It also discusses the orchestration of the Baroque era.

George Frideric Handel

When Handel sat down to write *Messiah*, he actually began the overture first, as the autograph (the original copy of the score) shows us. Handel begins his *Messiah* with a haunting orchestral melody, largely scored for strings. The stately, slow dotted rhythm is unsettling, and this feeling is heightened due to its somber key of E minor. Choral expert Leonard Van Camp says, "And yet, there is a certain lightness in feeling since brass instruments have been omitted in Handel's orchestration. The heaviness in tone is not a heaviness in sound."[1]

Handel's modest orchestra consisted of violins I and II, viola, violoncello, double bass, and harpsichord (with brass and winds added for particular pieces). This "A" section opens with a dynamic marking of *grave* (Italian for slow or solemn) and great pomposity. Handel uses imitation of a short motif, with its leaping sixth and *fortissimo* on the high G. Observe the opening musical score:

---

1 Leonard Van Camp, *A Practical Guide for Performing, Teaching and Singing* Messiah (Dayton, Ohio: Lorenz, Roger Dean Publishing Co., 1993), 27.

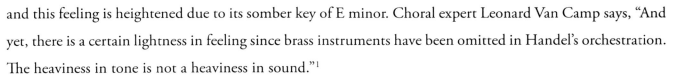

No. 1 SINFONY

Grave

VIOLIN I
Oboes I, II

VIOLIN II

VIOLA

BASSO CONTINUO

G. F. HANDEL
begun Saturday, August 22, 1741

This 12-bar section is repeated, beginning softly, *crescendoing* (increasing in loudness) to its final chord in the dominant V, B Major, moving from a minor to a major tonality.

The overture, called "sinfony" in the original score, was written in the French style that was developed in the court of Louis XIV. Normally, this style has an AAB form composed in two sections: a repeated passage of the slow, pompous introduction (A) using a dotted rhythm, followed by the *allegro moderato* (B), using imitation of a short motif.[2] In Handel's overture, however, we hear a stately "A" section that is followed by a *fugue*, "B," only then to return to the slow, dotted rhythm of the "A." Thus, the ABA form is used for the overture.

The second section comprises a lively three-voice *fugue*. This is imitative counterpoint in which the theme is stated in each voice of the polyphonic texture. The theme, first presented alone by one voice or instrument, is then imitated or answered usually in the dominant (the fifth note up on the scale) by a second voice. The third voice enters on the tonic note again. The motif is bounced among the voices for quite some time. All voices move nicely together, conversing in counterpoint. Then, twelve measures from the end, the opening motif returns very strongly in *fortissimo* (loudly). The piece ends with a high E *piu lento* (more slowly), falling down the scale to resolve on an open E minor chord, just as it began.

---

2 Don Michael Randel, ed., *Harvard Dictionary of Music,* 4th edition (Cambridge, Massachusetts: Harvard University Press, 2003), 338.

HANDEL'S *Messiah*

Let's look at the *fugue*-like theme of "B" below, which is picked up by the violins in a lively *allegro moderato* (still in E minor). This motif sounds like a shepherd's pipe, moving rapidly with busy eighth notes. The opening motif is joined by its other voices. In later performances of *Messiah*, when the main theme was repeated, the oboes and bassoons were added to the strings. In Leonard Van Camp's *A Practical Guide for Performing, Teaching, and Singing* Messiah, he suggests that conductors "hold the strings back a tad, so they don't push the tempo."[3]

Fugues and *fugal* passages are to be found throughout the works of Johann Sebastian Bach as well as in those of Handel, most significantly in the choruses of his oratorios. Van Camp continues, "For both Bach and Handel, the *fugue* provided the best means for the realization of powerful musical ideas; generally, in the works of these composers, the *fugue* represents a climax of musical intensity."[4]

In the Baroque era, composers thought in terms of the "line," or melody. Each instrument, then, may actually be playing the same line or melody, yet appear to sound in counterpoint. So, the composers desired to use instruments of the same color or timbre. This was the birth of the art of orchestration. But even while this art was still in its young stages, Handel chose his instruments based on their several colors; he knew that what you heard was what you got. He selected carefully from the differing tones of the instruments available to him: the recorders, the wooden flutes, and the *viola da gamba* (leg viol) with their gut strings. These were the instruments that were accessible to him in his day.

In Handel's orchestra, no instrument except the violin (and occasionally the trumpet) played a solo part. The solo players were called the *concertino*, and a larger group of supporting players was known as the *concerto grosso*. The *concerto grosso* passages, then, created a dialogue between the solo instruments and the *tutti* (all others).

---

3 Van Camp, 27.
4 Ibid., 218.

The oboe and the bassoon do not appear at all in Handel's original score, even though these instruments participated in the performance (as was proved by a later discovery of orchestra parts written for both of these instruments, adding their voice to the strings.) The oboe and bassoon, which belong to the double-reed branch of the woodwind family, were added for textural depth. The oboe has a distinctive spicy, nasal "honky" sound and tends to stand out from other instruments in its tone color (timbre). Its sound is especially desired for pastoral music. Although less nasal than the oboe and relatively neutral in tone, the bassoon adds fullness by doubling the cello line.[5]

During the performance, Handel sat at the keyboard—usually a harpsichord, but sometimes an organ—from where he was in direct eye contact with the other musicians so they could see his signals, "up close and personal." No dynamic markings were indicated in early Baroque music, so it was very important for the musicians to watch Handel as he directed.

Also, problems with bowing could affect the *legato* or *marcato* passages played by the strings. Technical considerations, such as the need for down-bow or an up-bow at various places, were so necessary to achieve the general effect Handel desired that it was vitally important for the instrumentalists to watch him. Such communication affected not only the dynamics and tempo of the music itself but also provided the unity in appearance that Handel surely regarded as important.[6] During his lifetime, Handel conducted the orchestra from a hand-copied score. The first full score edition appeared in 1767. Oh, how fabulous it would have been to have heard Handel playing *and conducting* his own music!

5 Kent Wheeler Kennan, *The Technique of Orchestration* (Englewood Cliffs, New Jersey: Prentice Hall, Inc., 1952), 85.
6 Ibid., 86.

CHAPTER TWO

"Comfort ye, My people"

(RECITATIVE FOR TENOR)

This chapter delves into the reason why the prophet Isaiah is making a passionate cry, pleading with the priests to treat the people with compassion and urgency. This urgency is explained by "eschatology," a biblical term referring to a great divine event that is about to happen to mark the decisive end of the age. The doctrine of election speaks directly to Israel's unique higher calling in divine history to further God's purpose of universal salvation. This chapter also defines "recitatives" and "ad lib." And were there three Isaiahs, or just one?

George Frideric Handel

Following the beautiful and mournful overture in E minor is the first vocal presentation in the key of E major. This shift from a minor key to a major key is a small indication of hope, and it strikes the dominant mood for the entire *recitative*. The contrast between keys and the movement from one key to another is an essential element of musical structure. According to composer Arnold Schoenberg, "This modulation from one key to another is a change of scenery."[1]

After about five minutes of orchestral music in the overture, we now hear the first voice: the tenor who represents the prophet Isaiah, singing his *recitative* on the words, "Comfort ye, My people." This *recitative*

---

1 Joseph Machlis and Kristine Forney, eds., *The Enjoyment of Music,* 6th edition (New York: W. W. Norton & Co., 1990), 122.

is played *larghetto* (very slowly) and softly in a deliberate four-beat rhythm. In the first chord we hear the violins tapping on the G. (To hear the third tone of the chord on top is quite unusual.)[2] The scene opens in the council of Yahweh, where the prophet is addressing the priests and elders, telling them to speak gently, kindly, and tenderly to the hearts of the people.[3]

"Comfort ye, comfort ye my people,"

saith your God.

"Speak ye comfortably to Jerusalem."

(Isaiah 40:1-2 KJV)

Why was this glorious Scripture text chosen out of the entire Bible? In these verses of Isaiah, there is the prevailing dominance of the single thought of "comfort" throughout the strophe. Handel had asked his friend Charles Jennens, a poet, librettist, and wealthy patron of the arts, to study the Scriptures and give him a libretto from the Bible on his chosen theme—the imminent redemptive plan and deliverance of God's people. Jennens must have known the Bible very well, because the book of Isaiah is highly dramatic and a perfect choice of text to set the scene for God's action in history of exerting His divine will and purpose. Perhaps this passage was chosen because it places a strong emphasis on Israel's call and election, her mission in the world, and her task as a witness to God's grace.

This concept of the "doctrine of election" of Israel is better viewed not so much as divine favoritism but rather as part of a broader concept regarding God's purpose of universal salvation. As a historical narrative, the Old Testament gives a clear description of the Hebrew faith, primarily the story of what God had done, how the people had responded or should respond, and what God was yet to do. In Yahweh, Israel observed a unique redemptive work in progress; therefore, they became the people of Yahweh.[4]

Israel's special election by God had become readily apparent through the exodus. When God heard the cry of an oppressed people in Egypt, He delivered them from oppression by His mighty acts of power and made them into a nation. This deliverance was an unmistakable sign that God was more powerful than any

---

2 Leonard Van Camp, *A Practical Guide for Performing, Teaching and Singing* Messiah (Dayton, Ohio: Lorenz, Roger Dean Publishing Co., 1993), 29.

3 James Muilenburg, "The Book of Isaiah," chapters 40-66, *The Interpreter's Bible*, Vol. V (New York: Abingdon Press, 1956), 424.

4 Ibid., 385.

HANDEL'S *Messiah*

human or natural power and had shown pity on this defenseless people, choosing them for His own. Israel was called to a higher destiny. This election cannot be explained: it is a mystery of God's divine grace that can only be accepted in faith and gratitude.

The text for this *recitative* begins with an imperative urging the prophet to "comfort ye, My people." The tenor sings this phrase, holding the opening note until he runs out of breath! The word "comfort" is sung tenderly three more times, for God is begging the prophet to tell the people. This "comfort" is a plea, a command, and a call for compassion—yet with urgency, because Israel's imminent redemption is expected.

In the musical measure below, Handel has marked his score with *ad lib*, meaning *ad libitum*, which gives the performer complete freedom of improvisation.[5] The *appoggiatura, trill, mordent,* and the *turn* are ornaments that allow the musicians to "decorate" the melody line with a small embellishment (typical of the embellished Baroque era), as well as serving as a way for the performers to express themselves individually.

Handel insisted that these ornaments not be used merely to show off one's voice, but to promote the melody or expression of the text. The typical accompanying instrument of the Baroque era was the harpsichord, which allows for no shadings of soft and loud, as the piano of today allows. Handel himself was a widely acclaimed organist, so he was essentially giving himself freedom to improvise because he was so inspired during each performance. Musically, the tenor singing these words exudes compassion as he embellishes the phrase and holds the syllable "com-" for almost three long beats on a high E.

This passage is followed by an ascending sequence for "saith your God"—with strong chordal accompaniment, showing great confidence. "Saith" is pronounced as one syllable: "seth," not say-eth.[6]

---

5 Don Michael Randel, ed., *Harvard Dictionary of Music*, 4th edition (Cambridge, Massachusetts: Harvard University Press, 2003), 14.

6 Van Camp, *A Practical Guide for Performing*, 29.

"Comfort ye, *My* people . . . *your* God" are Old Testament covenant words reminding us of Israel's special place in the heart of God. Israel is the people of Yahweh, and Yahweh is the God of Israel. The dialogue reflects the intimacy between God and His people in the Old Testament.

Isaiah was a literary craftsman, clearly both a poet and prophet—a master of form who especially used alliteration and parallelism ("Cry, cry;" "saith your God, saith your God"). He proclaimed the Word of God with such elevation and urgency, and his every thought was of God and His imminent coming in world history.[7]

The prophet's remarkable capacity for participation in the event that had been disclosed to him in the heavenly councils taxed all his powers of thought and feeling. His compassion created some of the most moving lines in the entire Scriptures. His lyrical verses were always supported by his profound faith, which has given them their power.

Isaiah discerned through the earth-shaking events of his day a depth of meaning in suffering and pain that no one before him had understood. A great pessimism concerning any resolution of the divine will within history, along with a very passionate and intense faith in the coming of the divine kingdom, were always at the forefront of his writing. Prophecy had developed into apocalyptic thought, which sees more deeply into the tragic perplexities of history.

Let us now look at a more recent translation of the Bible for a current interpretation of these verses. (If only this easy, understandable version had been available for all of us when we were growing up, how many more of us would know the Scriptures?) The *Contemporary English Version* of the Bible, in its "user-friendly" vernacular, paraphrases Isaiah 40:1-2 as follows:

> "Our God has said:
> 'Encourage my people!
> Give them comfort.
> Speak kindly to Jerusalem and announce:
> Your slavery is past;
> Your punishment is over.
> I, the LORD, made you pay double for your sins.'"

---

7 Muilenburg, 386.

HANDEL'S

Handel's text continues as an emphatic exhortation with these words from the next stanza in the *King James Version*:

> "And cry unto her,
>
> that her warfare is accomplished,
>
> That her iniquity is pardoned . . .
>
> The voice of him that crieth in the wilderness,
>
> Prepare ye the way of the Lord,
>
> Make straight in the desert a highway for our God."
>
> (Isaiah 40:2-3)

After the tenor has "spoken comfortably to Jerusalem," he leaps an octave and passionately cries on a high F-sharp: "And CRY unto her that her warfare is accomplished." This climatic verb "cry" is an urgent imperative. This F-sharp is a crucial note, and the tenor falls down a five-note pattern on the phrase, "unto her." There is a triad of imperatives (comfort, speak, and cry) and objects (people, Jerusalem, and her). This commanding mood dominates throughout the passage; and the poem grows in urgency as it is sung, for the music accentuates the emphasis and mood of the words.[8] It is pure genius when the text phrase and musical phrase coincide, as they frequently do in Handel's work. Professor Joseph Machlis and Kristine Forney remind us that, "A fitting climax to a piece may be a high note sung at a peak of intensity, as we hear in 'Cry unto her' . . . the crucial note is on 'cry.'"[9]

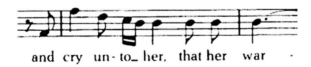

and cry un-to_ her, that her war

The original score didn't have the *grace note* E between the F-sharp and the D-sharp, which has subsequently been added. Handel often made changes to his score after many performances. Perhaps this was one of those times when the performer just fell down the scale with a five-note pattern and Handel liked it, so he added it into the score. Often singers rearrange the text words if they are awkward to sing, and the line can be strengthened by the change, such as this:[10]

---

8 Muilenburg, 423.

9 Machlis and Forney, 122.

10 Alfred Mann, ed., *Handel's* Messiah *in Full Score* (New York: Dover Publications, 1989), 214.

"And cry unto her that her warfare is accomplished,

That her iniquity is pardoned."

(Isaiah 40:2 KJV)

The prophet proclaims to the priests of the nations these two solemn disclosures—that Israel's warfare is accomplished and her iniquity is pardoned. The holy city of Jerusalem, like the nation of Zion, has a unique status as the place where God has established the Davidic line. And now, her time of service is ended and her iniquity pardoned. She has suffered enough and is now forgiven.

This phrase, "that her warfare is accomplished, that her iniquity is pardoned," is eschatological in nature. "Eschatological" is a big word implying that a great divine event is about to happen to mark THE decisive end of the age.[11] This means that Israel's time of service, similar to that of a soldier, had come to an end. The old age was passing, the new age was dawning; the Babylonian age was ending, the Persian age was dawning. At this closing of the Babylonian age, Israel no longer was a kingdom, and Judah was languishing in Babylonian exile. Cyrus, King of Persia, was sweeping over empires in western Asia in the sixth century BC, bringing about the imminent fall of the Babylonian empire. The prophet predicts the military successes of Cyrus, observing that "it is in God's will."[12]

Author John Gugel observes, "The people were a people who were in exile—far from home, aliens in a foreign culture, lost, feeling forsaken by God, cut off from familiar surroundings, struggling against enormous odds to keep alive the memories of Jerusalem, the Holy City, the place where they worshipped the Almighty God on its lofty heights."[13] Even today, the victims of hurricanes have experienced this feeling of being in exile as they have been forced from their homes to live in foreign surroundings in shelters. In other words, this is a prediction of the end times: What would it mean to be in exile? How would it feel?

In the musical phrase, "that her iniquity is pardoned," the word "iniquity" is given emotional emphasis with an augmented fourth, a difficult interval to sing. The words announce the expiation of guilt. These sufferings of Israel must be accounted for in the purpose and sovereignty of God, a concept radically different from that of just being moral. Instead, it involves viewing the destiny of Israel as God's Chosen called to be a servant. The tenor continues singing the following:

---

11 Muilenburg, 399.

12 Ibid., 425.

13 John Gugel, Messiah: *Daily Meditations for Advent and Christmas* (Fenton, Missouri: Creative Communications for the Parish, 2003), 5.

HANDEL'S *Messiah*

The voice of him that crieth in the wil-der-ness: Pre-

"The voice of him that crieth in the wilderness" sounds like an approaching stampede with its accent on the second word of the note pattern and the marking of *forte* (loud): Ta-TUM, ta-TUM, ta-TUM. Years later in biblical history, "the voice of him that crieth" would be John the Baptist, the New Testament wilderness man who would use these very words "prepare ye" as he also exhorted the people of his generation to turn to God and prepare their hearts for Him. This phrase in Isaiah 40:3-5 of "a voice crieth in the wilderness" is quoted in Matthew 3:3, Mark 1:3, Luke 3:4-6, and John 1:23. All four Gospels, or evangelists, refer to John the Baptist, the son of Zachariah and Elizabeth (the cousin of the Virgin Mary) as "THE one crying in the wilderness."[14]

Even Malachi 3:1, 4, and 5 quote these same verses. They all confirm that John the Baptist is the one who was spoken of by the prophet Isaiah, and it was he who was the fulfillment of these Malachi passages, as well. This was the very man who wore a garment of camel's hair and a leather girdle around his waist and lived off of locusts and wild honey. (This sounds pretty much like a "nature boy" from the wilderness to me—the wilderness being east and southeast of Jerusalem.) He was bold enough to rebuke the Pharisees and Sadducees who were coming to be baptized by him in the river Jordan: "You brood of vipers! Who warned you to flee from the wrath to come? Bear fruit that befits repentance" (Luke 3:7-8 RSV).

Isaiah, the messenger, will first prepare for the "day of God's coming" by purifying the priesthood: "Make straight in the desert a highway for our God." In this grandiose and impressive scene, the prophet is telling the people to prepare a processional road through the desert for the appearance of GOD HIMSELF. In that day, there was the practice of preparing roads for the victorious advance of a conqueror or king by clearing them of obstacles. What obstacles in your own life must you clear away to prepare for the advancement of the Lord?

---

14 Muilenburg, 427.

Just picture in your mind a highway through a desert on which the very glory of the Lord Himself will be revealed to all people. Isaiah's portrait of God is that of a mighty conqueror returning from his conquests over Israel's enemies, a king about to inaugurate his kingdom, a righteous judge adjudicating the inequities of the past, and a solicitous shepherd who gathers the lamb into his bosom. Perhaps this is an allusion to the exodus road from Egypt. In Babylonian culture, there were many great processions honoring gods. This was a time when cultic worship was practiced, and gods such as Marduk and Ishtar were worshipped. Surely, it was a time in history when Israel must have been tempted to abandon the God of Abraham. Yet Jerusalem has a unique status as the place where Yahweh dwells and has established the Davidic line of genealogy.[15]

The *Contemporary English Version* of the Bible, in its understandable text, says it this way:

> Someone is shouting:
> "Clear a path in the desert!
> Make a straight road
> for the LORD our God."
> (Isaiah 40:3)

The complete libretto of *Messiah* is a magnificent unification of assorted Scriptures taken from the entire Bible. In choosing his verses, Jennens took some of the text from the Old Testament books of Isaiah, Haggai, Malachi, Lamentations, Zechariah, and the Psalms. Much of the Old Testament had its origin in words that were spoken rather than written. These spoken words definitely come alive with music, and this synergy between the sound and meaning is the essence of their poetry. These prophets engaged in not a personal drama, but a social one.[16]

Jennens also chose texts from New Testament books, including Matthew, Luke, John, Hebrews, Romans, 1 Corinthians, and Revelation. Some scholars doubt that the librettist even compiled the text at all; instead, they suggest it was the work of his secretary, a clergyman named Dr. Pooley. Jennens was thought to be a friend of Handel, but he appears to be a pompous and conceited aristocrat who had the nerve to write to a friend:

---

15 Ibid., 424.
16 Ibid., 385.

HANDEL'S *Messiah*

I should show you a collection that I gave Handel, called Messiah, which I value highly, and he has made a fine entertainment out of it, though not near so good as he might and ought to have done. I have with great difficulty made him correct some[17] of the grossest faults in the composition.

Moreover, some scholars even doubt that Isaiah was the real author of these texts taken from this Old Testament book. Some biblical scholars rather believe that this portion of Isaiah was not written by the same prophet who penned the first thirty-nine chapters, but by a later unknown writer, a modest poet who was content to be just one prophet in a group of messengers. This person, or group of writers, has been called "Second Isaiah" or "the prophet of the exile." He attracts no attention to himself; instead, he remains "the voice of one crying." In this same line of thinking, there is even a "Third Isaiah" for chapters 56-66.

This theory of the different Isaiahs evolved due to the fact that there are discrepancies in the records of the historical events. This particular section of the Scriptures, for instance, speaks as if the exile was already happening. Also, the literary style and theological viewpoint are slightly different, some say, from the original Isaiah.[18] This is thought to be further substantiated by the use of the name of Cyrus, mentioned a full century prior to Isaiah's time. Oh how the winds of scholarship are always changing. The Book of Isaiah, with all of its possible authors, is a book of unusual interest and value, both literary and religious,[19] and now, thanks to Handel's *Messiah*, is being read and sung by thousands!

What does this text say to us today? In a post-9/11 world, we may be the audience for whom the words "Comfort ye, My people" are addressed. We may be those who "weep with those who weep," and cry for those who don't know peace. The tenor soloist may as well be singing to us.

---

17 Jay Welch, jacket cover to Columbia Records album., *Handel's* Messiah, The Philadelphia Orchestra, Mormon Tabernacle Choir, Eugene Ormandy, Conductor, n.d.n.p.

18 Note taken from *The Holy Bible*, Scofield Reference Edition, Oxford, 1967, 745.

19 Muilenburg, 383.

This musical style that the tenor uses to set the scene is called a *recitative* (pronounced "res-e-ti-TEEV"). What is a *recitative*, and how does it differ from an *aria*? An *aria* (Italian for "air") is a lyrical piece that may be removed from context and performed solo, usually expressing an emotion with ornamentation in the repeats. In contrast, *recitatives* are usually wordy or conversational, moving the plot ahead by taking us from point A to point B.

Recitatives imitate and emphasize the natural pattern of normal speech. *Recitatives*, as in the Italian operas written at the time, were of two forms: *secco*, or "dry" (unaccompanied), and "accompanied," as "Comfort Ye" is.[20] In his *recitatives*, Handel frequently stated *da capo*, meaning "to go back to the beginning and repeat the opening section." Thus, the form of a *da capo recitative* would be ABA, or the "sandwich form," (as in two slices of bread with bologna in between). This vocal piece actually begins as an *arioso* (which draws out one or two thoughts), but it changes along the way and is definitely a *recitative* at the end because it makes rapid progress in the text.

This piece (chapter two in the oratorio) ends in a perfect *cadence* (a sense of resolution) from D major to A major. Chapters two, three, and four of the oratorio are linked in thought and should continue, one into another, with no break.

---

20 Randel, 891.

HANDEL'S *Messiah*

CHAPTER THREE

"Every valley shall be exalted"

(ARIA FOR TENOR)

This chapter explains "aria," "melisma," "figured bass," and presents "tone painting," a technique used by Baroque composers to word-paint with their music.

George Frideric Handel

Handel intended for us to move immediately into this tenor *aria* so that the effect of the sunny change to this key of E major would not be lost. The same tenor soloist has just told us that the Lord is coming, and the noticeable sound of the E major key is fresh, alive, and promising.

In the previous chapter, God is entering upon the stage of world history, and we've been told to get out there and "prepare His way," because He's coming to lead His exiles home. What a comforting thought in today's world, as the desire for peace weighs so heavily upon our minds! It is reassuring to know that God hasn't given up on His creation, although we've given Him every reason for doing so. Now, The tenor begins singing in measure 10, imitated by the orchestra.

In this text, we hear that God is active again in creation by leveling the mountains and hills, making straight what is crooked, and raising every valley. What a study in contrasts! These words are spoken by the "voice in the wilderness"[1]:

> Every valley shall be exalted,
> and every mountain and hill made low.
> The crooked straight,
> and the rough places plain.
>
> (Isaiah 40:4 KJV)

This is the first *aria* of the oratorio, continuing with the text in Isaiah 40. In opera, the *aria* (Italian for "air") is welcome since its important function is to temporarily relieve the dramatic tension of the action; it literally "gives a break." The form, however, has been criticized because some think it is a purely musical expression that is generally rather long, often at the expense of the text.[2] It is as if the singer is saying, "Chill out, I want to sing my song."

1 James Muilenburg, "The Book of Isaiah," *The Interpreter's Bible*, Vol. V (New York: Abingdon Press, 1956), 399.

2 Don Michael Randel, ed., *The Harvard Dictionary of Music*, 4th edition (Cambridge, Massachusetts: Harvard University Press, 2003), 54.

Scholars tell us that in the era of history taking place at the time of Isaiah 40, Israel had long ceased to be a kingdom, and Judah was now languishing in Babylonian exile. Cyrus, the king of Persia, is twice mentioned by name, and there are a number of other passages in which he is clearly on the writer's mind. His great military campaigns are mentioned, and the fall of Babylon is believed to be imminent.[3] Isaiah 40 is a text composed of flowing words, warm and passionate rhetoric, much repetition of key words, and strong contrasts. The words of Isaiah, from which this text comes, are written in a highly lyrical mood, giving us a very dramatic scene.[4]

Baroque composers developed an impressive technique called "tone-painting," or word-painting, in which the music vividly mirrors the words and ideas expressed. The composer is figuratively painting a picture, reinforcing the message of the words. Such textural usage of phrases as "the arm of the Lord" as an instrument of His deliverance, as well as the use of mountains as eschatological imagery,[5] are examples of tone-painting. Movement, such as running and leaping, was represented by the comparable movement of the melody and rhythm. As an obvious example, tone-painting would use a rising melodic line to illustrate the resurrection. If the words refer to leaping, then there is the use of ascending notes, and the music literally leaps. Sorrow might be represented by a stepwise descending bass line. Look at the shape of these melodies in this tenor *aria:*

In Handel's phrase, "the crooked straight," he has actually written the melodic line crooked. It literally jumps around! In his exegesis of this text in *The Interpreters' Bible,* James Muilenburg suggests that "uneven" is preferred over the word "crooked" as a translation of the Greek, for "it is not the winding road, but the unevenness of the surface that is referred to."[6] In contrast, the words "straight" and "plain" are sung smoothly, and they are held forever (or at least for four beats).

---

3 Muilenburg, 382.
4 Ibid., 388.
5 Ibid., 385.
6 Ibid., 427.

Embellishing, or decorating the note in music, is similar to the embellishment of the furniture, art, and architecture of the Baroque period (1600-1750). In Baroque music, we sometimes find a motif that "just won't quit." With this *aria*, the tenor sings an exaggerated expansion of the word "exalted." This is a *melisma*, a musical style in which many notes are sung to one syllable of a word. Key words are extended over several notes or phrases, almost stretched beyond recognition, which is similar to the ornate style characterized by the highly decorated pieces of furniture of the Baroque era.[7] Notice how many notes are used for the word "exalted" in this *melisma:*

Did you count those notes? (I counted 48, not including the tied notes.) Singing this phrase requires the voice to exhibit tremendous control, flexibility, and agility to enable the phrase to sound fluid. It is definitely *virtuoso* passage work, requiring a great deal of practice for the tenor who sings this *aria.*

---

7 Randel, 498.

HANDEL'S

The *Contemporary English Version* of the Bible for this text uses these words:

> Fill in the valleys;
> flatten every hill and mountain.
> Level the rough and rugged ground.
>
> (Isaiah 40:4)

The valleys will be leveled, the mountains will be lowered, and steep heights and rough ridges will be filled in to create a smooth plain. Again, in his article in *The Interpreters' Bible,* Muilenburg tells us that "the poetry of the metaphors should not be linked with topography,"[8] even though it is a natural assumption. These mountains and valleys simply represent difficulties that are political, psychological, and physical in the exiles' lives. They are also metaphors for *our* trials in life, the vicissitudes of *our* daily existence. We know that it is the pebbles which cause the most trouble by getting in the way, making us stumble and fall. God can certainly write His purposes right with a crooked pencil. With God, impossible barriers will be conquered, and the King of Glory will come again.

Let us live with an air of expectancy, an air of confidence about some impending event, and an air of anticipating the profound change that is about to take place. It is hope that rises above the seemingly insurmountable truths of reality. God seeks to help each of us weary and wounded travelers. This thought is inherently democratic: it's open to all. What are your obstacles of today that get in the way of returning to God? What mountains do you find insurmountable, or valleys too low? What rocky roads are tripping you up? What are the giants that block you from overcoming your personal mountains of fear, doubt, and worry?

This is eschatological imagery. A big word . . . eschatology. This word even sounds "other-worldly," or "in the future." The eschatological orientation of the verses suggests these themes of creation, history, and redemption; and the pictures are extremely powerful. Nature is being transformed at the divine event, with the hills and valleys participating. God is the central figure from the beginning to the end. Israel's life and destiny are dynamically involved in the *events* through which God manifests Himself. The purpose of God is the dominant motif in these words, and there is tension until His will is ultimately fulfilled. We are near the END of our own ways and the beginning of His rule for us. When we perceive this dominant theme, the intent becomes apparent.[9]

---

8 Muilenburg, 426.
9 Ibid., 388.

Near the end of the *aria*, in bar 73, emotional prominence is given to this three-note phrase:

These three notes make a statement. A quarter rest follows the *fermata* (meaning "to hold"), allowing silence to become a presence. Rests, in music, seem to be waiting for something. Rests, or quiet periods, can be frightening, uncomfortable, or even threatening. Yet rests can also be times to be silent and wait upon the Lord. Haven't we heard that phrase, "Silence is golden"? In this case, we need these periods of silence to allow time for us to hear the voice of God.

Baroque music usually displays a homophonic texture, in which the upper voice has the melody over a bass line. This bass line (thoroughbass, *basso-continuo*, or figured bass) is an instrumental bass line with the inner parts improvised chordally above it.[10] These harmonies are indicated by numbers written above, below, or beside the bass notes, such as in this example:[11]

This technique implies that Handel wrote the bass line as a foundation, with its harmonies all underneath the melody. Handel's genius was composing bass-line structures with clear chordal implications. His chord progressions are a delight and tend to surprise the listener. Instead of moving down one note, he might go up a fourth to create more interest. Handel sat at the keyboard and enjoyed changing these chords at sight, since he knew and obeyed the established rules of classical harmony.

---

10 Randel, 86.
11 Ibid., 890.

HANDEL'S *Messiah*

These figures in the thoroughbass refer to the Arabic numbers specifying the intervals above the bass note. Perhaps we could call this a "harmonic shorthand." The pitches can be played in any register and doubled at will, though even here rules of harmony and voice-leading apply.

During his performances, Handel was usually sitting at the harpsichord playing the chords, while a melody instrument—such as the cello or *viola da gamba*—played the bass line, exactly as written. Handel was a performer whose mind quickly connected with his fingers to play the harmonies indicated by the chords. If Handel was at the harpsichord, he had considerable improvisatory freedom in playing his chords and rhythms, while the instrumentalist playing the cello was strictly playing what was written. As intriguing as we may find this concept, thoroughbass practice was no longer the dominant compositional technique by the late nineteenth century.[12]

What have we learned from these passages? For God to be effective in "His story" (history), He calls all of us, His created nations, to come together for an encounter with Him. During Isaiah's time, these nations failed to answer God's questions, which prompted Him to turn to His chosen and called servant, Israel, in whom He had revealed Himself from the beginning to Abraham. Now Israel is indeed called to a higher destiny.[13]

The major command for Israel was often expressed in terms of the Holiness Code found in Leviticus 17-26, which essentially said, "Be holy, even as I am holy." Therefore, Israel's uniqueness was expressed in her holiness as a chosen people. Even though Israel was a particular group of people, her calling (or uniqueness) was intended to be a beacon for universalism: there is only one God, even one covenant God, for all peoples.

The teaching of the prophet Isaiah can be both universal and particular. Yahweh is the God of all, yet He is also the covenant God of Israel. His redemption is not confined to His own people; rather, it is all-inclusive. God's purpose was to establish His redemptive sovereignty over all the earth, but He had chosen Israel as His special agent through whom this aim was to be accomplished.[14] Was Israel waiting for this? Are *we* among the waiting people?

These latter chapters of Isaiah describe a turning point in world history; indeed, their very thought is eschatological. The end of all warfare has come, and now the glory of the Lord shall be revealed. A new exodus, greater than the first, will usher in the kingdom of God.

---

12 Ibid., 891.
13 Muilenburg, 385.
14 Ibid., 354.

Isaiah looks back at the history of Israel: 1) the exodus; 2) the wandering in the desert; 3) the promise to Abraham and Israel's election; 4) the flood; and 5) creation itself. What is now happening in Cyrus' career must be understood in the light of these major events in the past. Isaiah is profoundly convinced that the meaning of all history—past, present, and future—is realized in the purpose of God.[15]

What have we learned from Isaiah in this passage? We've been presented these major motifs in God's story:

1. The Lord is coming.

2. His entrance upon the stage of world history is imminent.

3. The way of the Lord must be prepared.

4. God is still active in nature and creation.

5. The universality of one God for all people is made clear.

6. The divine reconciliation and redemption of Israel is offered.

7. The Word of the Lord stands forever.[16]

15 Ibid., 388.
16 Ibid., 385.

HANDEL'S *Messiah*

CHAPTER FOUR

"And the glory of the Lord"

(CHORUS)

This chapter, presenting the first choral piece in the oratorio, relays the important role the chorus plays in the overall drama of the story. It also contrasts "oratorio" with "opera," and entertains the reader with "confessions of a choir member."

George Frideric Handel

So, what is an oratorio, and how does it differ from an opera? Sometimes operas can appear "over the edge" because they are performed on a stage with lavish costumes and scenery. An oratorio is tame in comparison and might be called the opera's concertized cousin.[1] Their commonality is in the subject matter, which can be either secular or sacred. The primary difference between an opera and an oratorio really lies in the function of the chorus. In an opera, the soloist is the protagonist, and the chorus simply has a decorative function. But in an oratorio, the chorus—represented by a group of people—plays a major role in the center of the drama, acting as the protagonist.[2]

Oratorios also require no stage acting; the chorus is given the role of figuratively acting and reflecting upon that action. The soloists who sing the *arias* and *recitatives* are merely serving as individual voices, or

---

1 Jay Welch, jacket cover to Columbia Records album., *Handel's* Messiah, The Philadelphia Orchestra, Mormon Tabernacle Choir, Eugene Ormandy, Conductor, n.d.n.p.

2 Joseph Machlis and Kristine Forney, eds., *The Enjoyment of Music,* 6th edition (New York: W. W. Norton and Company, 1990), 166.

representatives, for the group. Handel's *Messiah* is unique, even for an oratorio, in that there is no dramatic conflict and the soloists are more contemplative than dramatic, taking a backseat to the choir.

In 1720 the Bishop of London forbade the representation of biblical characters in a theatre. Defiantly, Handel responded by writing an oratorio, *Haman and Mordecai*, and announcing in an advertisement, "There will be no acting on the stage." Oratorios were a way of getting around the bishop's puritanical censorship. Handel's oratorios opened the door for middle-class audiences to enjoy dramas that had religious themes, without the costly scenery, costumes, or highly-paid actors.[3]

The first chorus of Handel's *Messiah* opens with these reassuring words:

> And the glory of the Lord shall be revealed,
> and all flesh shall see it together:
> for the mouth of the Lord hath spoken it.
>
> (Isaiah 40:5 RSV)

These words, a continuation in Isaiah 40 after the tenor's two solos, declare that God surely has the power of carrying His plan into action and achieving His purpose. The first chorus, "And the glory of the Lord," is also the first major pillar of the oratorio. In musical composition, if the chords can be called "pillars of sound," then the choruses could be called the "pillars" of the piece. In their book, *The Enjoyment of Music*, Joseph Machlis and Kristine Forney say, "The great chorus becomes the pillar of an architectonic structure in which the *recitatives* and *arias* serve as areas of lesser tension."[4]

The *recitatives* and *arias* are placed between the larger pillars of choruses, acting as the melodic arches. They could be shown this way:

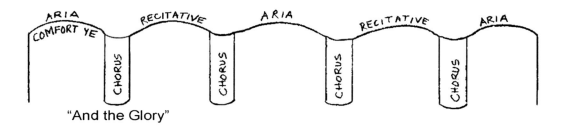

3 Ibid., 165.
4 Ibid., 160.

HANDEL'S *Messiah*

"And the Glory," written in a triple meter in a vigorous *allegro* (moderate tempo) in A major, should be conducted in a quick waltz-like ¾ tempo (like a festival waltz). After a ten-measure introduction, the chorus, as the protagonist, enters with this first structural pillar of the oratorio.

In choral singing, there are basses, tenors, altos, and sopranos (the highest voices). Here, the altos begin singing with a commanding "And" pronounced "ah-nd," the more beautiful singing tone of a broadened "A." This pronunciation came naturally to the British singers of Handel's day. Modern-day chorus members are taught to "drop the jaw," allowing more resonating space for the rounded vowels in order to give a richness to the sound. A good choral conductor particularly works on this shaping of the vowels in the mouths of the singers because it determines the tone and color of the chorus. As the altos enter singing "And the glory of the Lord," the listeners in the audience appear to be joyfully invited into sharing the music.[5]

The choir is also instructed to pronounce the word "Glory" as "GLOW-reh," and to sing it as three quarter notes, not two eighth notes followed by two quarters, as shown by these examples:

The choir members are instructed to stagger their breathing, to carefully release tiny amounts of air, similar to letting the air out of a balloon, and not to all breathe on the commas at the same time, unless directed to do so by the conductor. Famed musicologist John Tobin says, "Handel used the technique of 'broken word distribution' by breaking a sentence in the middle in order to give greater emphasis to the words by repetition and to obtain greater impetus in the drive to the climactic ending."[6] The opening of this first chorus is a clear example of this technique.

The tempo of the piece is a lilting three-beat pattern. In music, rhythm is the arrangement of time—a pulsation, or beat, accented and strong. In triple meter, as in this piece, there is one strong beat followed by two weak beats (like the waltz and minuet): ONE-two-three, ONE-two-three. In this first chorus, the contagious swing rhythm whirls us along, combining the melody with its harmony.

---

5 Leonard Van Camp, *A Practical Guide for Performing, Teaching and Singing* Messiah (Dayton, Ohio: Lorenz, Roger Dean Publishing Co., 1993), 33.

6 John Tobin, *Handel's* Messiah, *A Critical Account of the Manuscript Sources and Printed Editions* (London: Cassell and Co., 1969), 147.

Being a member of a chorus is great fun. Regardless of whether we participate in a high school, college, community, or church choir, we all enjoy being part of a combined effort in making music. Over the years, we have carried our pencils to choir rehearsals in order to write in dynamic changes or breath markings that the conductor has strongly suggested.

In my old hand-bound score of Handel's *Messiah*, my penciled note, as instructed by the conductor, for this chorus suggests that the altos sing this phrase "punchy," or at a crisp tempo. This score came from my college days, when I was privileged to be a member of the Westminster Symphonic Choir, singing under the direction of conductor-maestro Sir Colin Davis. What an experience for a young woman at the beginning of her professional musical career—to sing under such great leadership!

Sir Colin Davis came to Westminster Choir College in Princeton, New Jersey, to rehearse us on the Tuesday of the concert week. Back in those days, the ladies of the choir wore nice skirts, blouses, stockings, and black shoes to the rehearsal, while the young men wore coats and ties. We were taught to be as professional as possible by "looking the part." After being trained for weeks by our own conductor, placed in the hands of Sir Colin for one rehearsal on campus, and given one final rehearsal with the New York Philharmonic in New York City at Lincoln Center, we then presented the performances!

Each conductor has his or her own individual interpretation of a score. Here, Sir Colin thought that this first chorus should be "punchy," as he directed the four-part choir with our *fugue*-like entrances. We tossed the themes from alto to tenor to bass, and back again, all coming together at the end to join with the sopranos to declare that the "mouth of the Lord hath spoken it."

There are four main themes in this first chorus: 1) "And the Glory," sung by the altos; 2) "shall be revealed," sung by the tenors; 3) "And all flesh," sung by the altos; and 4) "For the mouth of the Lord hath spoken it," sung by the basses. (Handel was very democratic in his allocation of themes, emphasizing balance among the voices. The basses, for instance, sing the main theme again later.) The pencil-marking from my college score indicates that Sir Colin instructed us to sing this chorus "fully, and don't let down!"

Let us examine the text critically. Isaiah's thoughts are definitely eschatological, for he sees the coming of the end of Israel's historical warfare. He declares, "The glory of the Lord shall be revealed, and all flesh shall see it together." A new exodus, greater than the first, shall usher in the kingdom of God. Verse 5 of Isaiah 40 stresses the revelation of God's glory: "For the mouth of the Lord has spoken it."

Henry Sloane Coffin, the late president of Union Theological Seminary in New York City, observed:

> There was a common belief during the time of the exile that the glory of the Lord had *left* the temple at the destruction of the city of Jerusalem. In Ezekiel 1:28; 10:18; and 11:22-23, we are told of the departure of the glory from the temple. Now, we are told it will return for all people to see. The significance of the glory of the Lord is the mark of the presence of God. Reflection upon this ending of the glory prompts Isaiah to revisit the many other moments in Israel's history when Yahweh God *has* appeared: 1) to Abraham and the patriarchs, 2) to Moses in the burning bush, 3) to Israel on Mt. Sinai, and 4) to the Israelites in the Sinai desert with the gift of manna. Yahweh was to appear on the great and terrible Day of the Lord when He would come as victor. The people in exile knew that the "glory of the Lord" had left the temple at the time of the destruction of the city of Jerusalem, and that it would return at a time of God's own choosing.[7]

Coffin expounds later on this theme:

> The presence of God is for most people a fleeting consciousness and experienced in a tenuous feeling. These words "the glory of the Lord" seem to be a symbol of the restoration of the relationship of grace in which Israel stands before a transcendent deity.
>
> To experience the glory of the Lord is to be flooded with radiance. Glory is the "theophanic word par excellence." The Hebrew word for the glory of the Lord is "Kabhodh," and it means "to shine," to reflect light or become as light as in "let there be light," declared in the creation. Isaiah, in this Scripture, is describing the final and decisive epiphany, because this time, when the glory of the Lord appears in its final glory, *all* flesh shall see it together.[8]

Take note of the superlative, "*all* flesh," that Handel uses. Handel marked SATB entrances (soprano, alto, tenor, and bass) with the word *tutti*, meaning "all" (soloists and choristers). This meant that all the tenors, altos, sopranos, and basses would sing the phrase together. Perhaps the composer saw the universality in word and music: "And all shall see it together." In other words, this event will be a universal and all-inclusive awakening, which will be the fulfillment of the divine purpose in history. As modern-day Christians, we look expectantly for the Second Coming. We can only imagine what it will be like when the Lord appears on that last day!

---

7 Henry Sloane Coffin, "Isaiah," *The Interpreter's Bible,* Vol. V (New York: Abingdon Press, 1956), 428.
8 Ibid., 697.

Yahweh is depicted as both a mighty warrior, as well as a tender shepherd. The all-great is the all-loving, too. He is coming to restore His people to their proper role in His plan. The good and gentle shepherd will "gently lead and carry" them back to Him, as later sung by the soprano soloist.[9]

The *Contemporary English Version* of this same Scripture says:

> Then the glory of the LORD will appear for all to see.
> The LORD has promised this!

What a promising text! For God hasn't abandoned the exiles; instead, He is going to appear. This happy chorus gives us the feeling that God is close, so we should sing our hearts out and be delighted that God has called us His own. What beautiful and reassuring words these are, for the listener and chorus member alike.

I recently heard *Messiah* sung at the Riverside Church in New York City. When the choir members opened their mouths to sing, "And the glory of the Lord," a beautiful sound filled the huge cathedral space. Glory was bouncing off the walls, and as a listener, I felt as if I were in the middle of that circle of glory. No other word but "glorious" could describe that feeling.

As the scholar Jay Welch writes:

> Picture Handel sitting at his desk in the front parlor and putting notes on paper with remarkable speed. For the next 23 days, he wouldn't leave the house; his manservant would bring his meals. Then on September 14, after about three weeks of feverish work on the manuscript, he would shut the completed *Messiah* in his drawer where it would stay practically untouched for the next seven weeks. He must have felt desperate to finish; yet it was his nature to work quickly. Contrapuntal patterns came to him almost spontaneously. Perhaps he had already worked the movements out in his head for months.[10]

When his manservant came in at the end, he found Handel's eyes filled with tears, and he said, "I did think I did see all Heaven before me, and the great God Himself."[11]

---

9 Ibid., 428.
10 Welch, jacket cover to Columbia Records album.
11 Machlis and Forney, 167.

HANDEL'S *Messiah*

Perhaps, he too, felt that "glorious" feeling that I mentioned. Peter Jacobi is quoted as saying:

> We could call Handel a religious man, a baptized Lutheran, who gave many benefit concerts as a means of giving something back to society. But to call him religious might be stretching the point. Handel's mother had been a Lutheran; he himself was not particularly devout but was religious and enjoyed setting the scriptures to music. It could be said that he was a man with a simple, uncomplicated faith. *Unbelief does not praise the Almighty.* Music is its own language; it speaks to our souls. Only that which is lofty and pure can elevate.[12]

Surely the composer had to be profoundly affected by his own work. Handel looked upon himself as a dramatic composer—a popular composer for the masses. And let's face it, he was a man smart enough to know what was going to bring in some money. The fact that *Messiah* is entirely from the Bible does not mean that we should call it liturgical church music. The Handel scholar, John Tobin, writes, "*Messiah* was not conceived as church music, not even as non-liturgical church music. Handel gave his sacred and secular subjects the same stylistic treatment; he dealt with them as non-sectarian, as a humanist glorifying no ecclesiastical doctrine but rather the universal validity of just and moral action. Religious, Bach; but Handel, not quite."[13] Handel performed his oratorios in music halls, theatres, and hospitals, even though churches were available to him; and this really infuriated the English clergy.

Many times, I have known the joy of lifting my voice among others in the soprano section of a community choir, dressed in my robe and black shoes, and holding my black folder covering my score. The rewarding experience of choral music *is* community, bringing all of us in the choir together every week to work on the difficult passages. This is particularly true in the case of *Messiah*, only to be able to perform it twice a year for Christmas or Easter! We all share a common passion for music, but it is the conductor who has the major role in a musical performance. He or she teaches the masterwork with enormous conviction and profound insight. The conductor sets the tempo which indicates the shape and character of the piece, and encourages the blending of all the voices for a cohesive whole.

---

12 Marshall Cavendish, *Greatest Composers: An Illustrated Companion to the Lives and Works of the Celebrated Composers* (Sercaucus, New Jersey: Chartwell Books, Inc., 1989), 37.

13 Tobin, 150.

In classical music, a four-part chorus is signified, as mentioned before, by SATB. As chorus members, we earnestly try to follow a conductor waving his arms around, as he ultimately brings forth a very finely-honed sound. It's amazing to hear the rich contributions from all of the singers, many of whom are volunteers with untrained voices. We've worked together to stagger our breathing so that the passage can sound like one long phrase. We must have one eye on the conductor and the other on our music (unless it is memorized, which is preferred). The conductor has worked with us so that we can learn his techniques and interpretation of the piece. As a voice teacher, I realize that the conductor must also diagnose the physical adjustments needed to fine-tune our voices as instruments. For the chorus, intonation and balance are essential.

Writing in four vocal parts is demanding. Literally hand-writing every line of his music, as well as arranging and writing the orchestration, must have been taxing on Handel. Imagine writing out all the orchestral parts without the availability of a copier machine! Back in 1716, Handel had returned to Ansbach, Germany, where he met an old university friend, Johann C. Schmidt (anglicized as John Christopher Smith), and invited him back to London to be his copyist and secretary. It was Smith who first read the master's musical "shorthand" from his original score, and revised the copies later on. At least now Handel would have help in producing copies of his music.[14] The original autograph manuscript is located in the British Museum. Perhaps his original could be considered a first draft as he made many, many changes. Imagine that Handel may well have been within shouting distance with Mr. Smith who was busy correcting or adding to the score!

Singing the highest voice part, soprano, requires a clear radiance and great agility to move over notes lightly. Sometimes, ideally, the sopranos experience singing "in zone." The tenors also must have a fresh urgency because their line demands a command of tone in order to move through many dynamics ranging from a strong, polished *forte* all the way down to the softest *pianissimo*. Likewise, the altos and the basses must also sing with richness and beauty. Handel's Baroque chorus was small, with approximately twelve to twenty-four singers. Today, we have an average of forty to sixty singers in a choir, and we call that small!

The actual premiere performance of *Messiah* took place during Lent on April 13, 1742, in Dublin, Ireland, for the relief of prisoners and the support of Mercer's Hospital in Stephen's Street and the Charitable Infirmary on the Inn's Quay. It was well received. Dublin cooperated with Handel by supplying its fullest resources for the presentation of this new work. An excellent orchestra had been assembled and placed under

---

14 Antony Hopkins, *Great Composers* (Secaucus, New Jersey: Chartwell Books, 1989), 35.

HANDEL'S *Messiah*

the leadership of one of Ireland's outstanding orchestral conductors, Matthew Dubourg. The entire chorus was male: two professional choirs of men and boys had been enlisted from leading cathedrals in the community, with the young boys singing the choral treble parts. The male soloists were two countertenors, Joseph Lambe and Michael Ward; the tenor was James Bailey; and the bass was John Mason. The only female soloists included Mesdames Christin Maria Avoglio, soprano, and contralto Susannah Cibber, two of the most highly respected artists of the time.[15]

The audience attendance for the premiere broke a record with seven hundred persons packed into "Musick Hall in Fishamble Street," a venue designed to accommodate only six hundred. Room for the additional hundred persons was made by the audience members' cooperative response to a newspaper notice requesting that the ladies "leave their hoops at home and the gentlemen leave their swords."[16] Handel presided at the organ, along with approximately twenty-four other musicians.

About a year later in March 1743, the piece was first heard in London's Covent Garden (which Handel rented) in the presence of King George II. The people who first heard *Messiah* may not have been impressed, but the king certainly was. Legend has it that the king was so excited by the stirring music that he rose to his feet at the sound of the Hallelujah Chorus and stood during the entire section. When royalty stood with the possibility of exiting, the entire audience rose with him, out of courtesy. What began as a spontaneous gesture became a tradition. We have that custom today: audiences still rise to their feet during the singing of the Hallelujah Chorus.

According to author Peter Jacobi, some people "resented a work about the Omnipotent presented in a public theater, and regarded *Messiah* as sacrilegious. Others disliked the use of prose, instead of a poetic text."[17] The initial reaction of the British to *Messiah* was unfavorable, so the piece was not performed again until 1749.

In 1749, Handel arranged a benefit performance for the Foundling Hospital (for orphaned children) of London, and the piece was greatly appreciated. This time, it was presented under the title of *Sacred Oratorio* to avoid attacks from the clergy and others who felt that "any work about the Omnipotent should never

---

15 Welch, jacket cover to Columbia Records album.
16 Harold C. Schonberg, ed. *The Lives of the Great Composers,* 3rd edition (New York: W. W. Norton and Co., 1997), 67.
17 Peter Jacobi, *The* Messiah *Book: The Life and Times of G. F. Handel's Greatest Hit* (New York: St. Martin's Press, 1982), 45.

be performed in a playhouse."[18] That same year, Handel had presented to the Foundling Hospital a new organ, which he dedicated on May 1, 1750 with a performance of *Messiah*. For the next nine years, Handel directed annual benefit performances of *Messiah* at that hospital. These performances helped to establish the overwhelming success of that work, at least in London. *Messiah* continued to be performed for charity; rarely, however, did it make money for Handel himself.

So, the chorus "And the glory of the Lord" comes to an end as the forward stride of the bass never slackens. Following the words, "The mouth of the Lord," is a dramatic pause on the words "hath spoken it." The penultimate D major chord in the cadence adds great tension to the drama.[19] Look at the following music:

18 Milton Cross and David Ewen, *Encyclopedia of the Great Composers and their Music,* Vol. 1 (New York, Doubleday & Co., 1953), 333.

19 Jacobi, 46.

HANDEL'S *Messiah*

The sound of this chorus is powerful—a warm account of the anticipated glory. Participating in the performance of this masterwork is great, but the feeling of actually creating the music is fabulous. As a choir member, one feels lost in the music, communing with the spirit of Handel. When you hear this music sung by the chorus, you realize that the performers sound as if their lives are being changed by this experience. As in any loving relationship, we search for a deeper meaning when we are passionate about something. So it is with our relationship with Handel's *Messiah*—this fabulous chorus being no small part of that appeal, to be sure!

Chapters two, three, and four, the first three singing movements of Handel's *Messiah*, should be taken as a group, since all their texts come from Isaiah 40:1-5. Dr. Coffin remarked, "These poems of Isaiah exhibit a mastery of form and literary craftsmanship, and seem to indicate that they may have been written as a poem, rather than spoken."[20] The bright A major of this chorus gives way to the somber D minor in the next bass *recitative*, "Thus saith the Lord."

Prepare yourselves for what lies ahead!

---

20 Coffin, 429.

"Thus saith the Lord"

(Accompanied Recitative for Bass)

The ground shakes as the bass sings of God's judgment upon sinners . . . thank goodness, we have the reassurance that the Day of the Lord is coming!

For thus saith the LORD of Hosts, Yet once, it is a little while and I will shake the heavens and the earth, and the sea, and the dry land; and I will shake all nations, and the desire of all nations shall come.

(Haggai 2:6-7 KJV)

The Lord, whom ye seek, shall suddenly come to his temple, even the messenger of the covenant, whom ye delight in: behold, he shall come, saith the Lord of Hosts.

(Malachi 3:1 KJV)

George Frideric Handel

In this booming bass *recitative*, we envision the actual shaking of the heavens and the earth. If we let them, these notes of the soloist really shake our very foundation. God is speaking, so we'd better listen. Only when we listen and pay attention to His words will we know His blessings for us. These words of Haggai remind us of the terror on the day of wrath, which is similar to the expected terror on judgment day of the "Dies Irae"[1] in many a "Requiem."

The texts for this *recitative* and the next two movements are taken from a different part of the Old Testament—Haggai 2:6-7 and Malachi 3:1-3. These men prophesied approximately 520 BC. From around

---

1 D. Winton Thomas, "The Book of Haggai," *The Interpreter's Bible*, Vol. VI (New York: Abingdon Press, 1956), 1038.

the year 605 BC, Judah had been under the dominion of Babylon. Her rebellion had finally led to the destruction of the temple that Solomon had built, along with the burning of the city of Jerusalem. Seventy years of captivity had ensued. Then, under an edict of King Cyrus of Persia, a remnant (actually, forty thousand people) returned to the land. They began to rebuild the temple in Jerusalem from its foundation upwards, which was Haggai's main theme throughout his months of prophesying.[2] This restoration concept must have been why the librettist, Charles Jennens, chose this text, since we know almost nothing else about the obscure minor prophet, Haggai, except his name.

In Haggai's lifetime, two historical events played an important part. The first involved the widespread revolts that broke out in the Persian Empire when Darius I succeeded Cambyses on the throne of Persia in 522 BC. To Haggai, these rebellions seemed to be part of the final world catastrophe that would precede the coming of the messianic age. The other event was the appointment by Darius of Zerubbabel, a Babylonian Jew from the royal house of David, as governor of Judah. These events made the prophet really believe that the world cataclysm was happening at this time, for he knew these things would be a prelude to the coming of the messianic age. With Zerubbabel's appointment, Haggai saw the hope of the Davidic kingdom restored.[3]

Haggai was indeed a minor prophet, but in Handel's score he played a major role. Haggai, as a prophet of God, was urging the people to obey Him by rebuilding the temple. His words were addressed to Zerubbabel, the civil leader of the community, and Joshua, the religious head. Under the leadership of these two men, the rebuilding of the temple was begun. In 516 BC, four years after Haggai first made his appeal, the temple was completed, according to the biblical history recorded in Ezra 6:14-15. Haggai was assuring the people that God's Spirit was with them. As we heard in the earlier Scriptures from Isaiah, it had been thought that the Spirit of God had abandoned the temple when it had been destroyed.

The timing of this Scripture is a little fuzzy. According to some scholars, the temple had been rebuilt. (As we just read, the rebuilding of the temple was completed in 516 BC.) But the glorious kingdom for which the Jews looked had not yet come. Times were tough with drought, famine, blighted crops, and a bad harvest. The people had experienced all the "rough and tumble" of communal living. Because they had insufficient food and water, as well as inadequate clothing, they were not in a very good state of mind. All of their energy

2 Ibid., 1046.
3 Ibid., 1039.

CHAPTER 5 *Thus saith the Lord*

51

had gone into supplying their daily needs. The Hebrews' only concern was supplying roofs over their own heads, not in the temple.[4]

The people had been indifferent to the rebuilding of the temple, so they had excused their apathy and indifference and exhibited spiritual lethargy. Haggai saw all this as the curse of Yahweh upon His people for neglecting the house of the Lord. The *Harper Study Bible* says, "They doubted the love of God and wondered whether there was any divine justice. Since the wicked prospered, they questioned whether there was profit in walking penitently before God and obeying His commandments."[5] Haggai's thought was, "If only the people would shake off their indifference, there would be an end to the hard life. Then they will experience the blessing. God will shake the nations and then fill His house with His glory. This new splendor will be greater than the former. If one is obedient, the blessings will follow. That's usually the way it goes."

It is interesting to note that Handel's original score had a different opening for this piece. The composer's first opening was not as vehement as his revision and was even marked *piano* (soft). He originally had interpreted the text from Haggai as an expression of majesty and compassion rather than anger. The change, now marked *forte* (loud), implies anger as the booming bass voice enters on a high D. Note the difference in the following examples:[6]

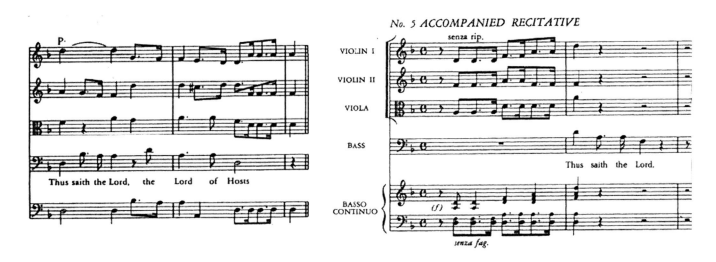

---

4 Note taken from *The Harper Study Bible* (Grand Rapids, Michigan: Zondervan Bible Publishers, 1962), 1422.
5 Ibid., 1423.
6 Alfred Mann, *Handel's* Messiah *in Full Score* (New York: Dover Publications, 1989), 215.

HANDEL'S *Messiah*

For this declaration in D minor, the bass sings the oracular formula, "Thus saith the Lord, the Lord of Hosts." This new beginning of the recitative sounds like thundering horse-hooves approaching—da-DUM, da-DUM, da-DUM.[7] Handel himself was a big, burly man, and we can only imagine his *hopefully* strong bass soloist singing the "shake" in terms reminiscent of Micah, Hosea, and Isaiah: "Yet once a little while, and I will shake the heavens."

Handel uses *melismas* to shake off the indifference of the people. *Melismas*, as you remember, are florid expansions of words, and a single syllable is sung on a group of notes.[8] In this case, the word "shake" is expanded so much that it is stretched beyond recognition. By the time the bass sings the "k" on the end of the word, we've forgotten about the "sh." It is through the vowel "a" in the middle that goes up and about and round and back again, covering twenty-four notes, shaking all the way, that we understand the context and are moved by the word. (A word of advice to the bass soloist: the breath capacity can be taxing, so save your breath as you sing the *melismas*.) This is a fine example of the use of expressive imagery, or tone-painting, on the word "shake." Handel takes an *arpeggio* and musically shakes each note, illustrating the basic idea of this text:

As the bass soloist is "shaking," Handel gives the singer an operatic accompaniment, with the instruments playing dotted rhythms and repeated chords. The violins are even using a characteristic of the French string

7 Leonard Van Camp, *A Practical Guide for Performing, Teaching & Singing* Messiah (Dayton, Ohio: Lorenz Corporation, 1993), 38.

8 Don M. Randel, ed., *The Harvard Dictionary of Music,* 4th edition (Cambridge, Massachusetts: Harvard University Press, 2003), 498.

technique with their repeated down-bows on many chords,[9] emphasizing the chordal progression. This *recitative* appears to be half talking and half singing, as it continues:

> The Lord, whom ye seek, shall suddenly come to His temple,
>
> even the messenger of the covenant, whom ye delight in;
>
> behold, He shall come, saith the Lord of Hosts.
>
> (Malachi 3:1 KJV)

This *recitative* takes its words from the prophet Malachi, who writes as a man of intense spiritual force, speaking with the authority of God's Word. He tries to answer the question regarding why the righteous suffer such hardship by replying that the people of God have been disloyal by neglecting Him.

The preceding verse in the Scripture text ends with the prophet asking, "Where is the God of justice?" A skeptical spirit seemed to undermine the prophet's faith in a righteous God who rewards good and punishes evil. The people felt that sin was prospering while their striving for righteousness seemed to be useless. Malachi argued that even though the present day seemed evil, God was coming to correct the iniquities.[10]

The *Contemporary English Version* of this text says:

> I, the LORD, All-Powerful, will send my messenger to prepare the way
>
> for me. Then suddenly the Lord you are looking for will appear in
>
> his temple. The messenger you desire is coming with my promise,
>
> and he is on his way.

The use of the title "messenger" has also been attributed to John the Baptist as the forerunner to the Messiah. The messenger will straighten out the abuses and restore the golden days of old, when worship was offered to God with dignity and a sincere heart.[11]

---

9 Mann, 215.

10 Robert C. Dentan, "The Book of Malachi," *The Interpreter's Bible*, Vol. VI (New York: Abingdon Press, 1956), 1137.

11 Ibid., 1139.

HANDEL'S *Messiah*

Are we spiritually indifferent to God today? It's interesting to think about the spin that we could put on Haggai's and Malachi's words today. Do we want to just shake God and ask, "Why?" Today, there are plenty of factors causing moral restlessness and anxiety. But when people turn their hearts toward God by obeying His laws, then they will prosper and know that God is truly with them.

The well-being and future of a society rest upon that society's concern for spiritual values. Indeed, for the ancient Jews, the temple was meant to be the outward, visible symbol of such devotion. But what if they built this beautiful temple, and yet there still was a hollowness? Haggai's metaphors illustrate this idea. Both texts deal with the making of a pure vessel in which the Lord may dwell.[12]

The piece ends as it modulates to A major, concluding with a *tierce de Picardie* that prepares the way for the message of the next two movements whose texts are still in the Book of Malachi. (A Picardy third is the use of a raised or major third of the tonic as the final chord of a piece that has been, up until the end, in a minor key). [13]

---

12 Dentan, 1139.
13 Randel, 583.

CHAPTER SIX

"But who may abide"

(ARIA FOR BASS OR COUNTERTENOR)

We are all being refined. But . . . are we ready for the Refinery? Who will be able to survive the day of His coming? For He is like a refiner's fire. And what in the world is a "countertenor?"

This ominous *aria* in D minor begins in *largetto* (meaning to be played broadly or slowly) in 3/8 time with the bass soloist's voice accompanied only with the *basso-continuo* (with bassoon added at times). The strings echo each phrase that the bass sings, as well as imitate his mournful rhythm. Usually one of the leading roles in each of Handel's operas (even Julius Caesar himself) was written for a *castrato*, a male singer who had a masculine body and lung power but a feminine vocal range. Castrati are just what the name implies—castrated males. They were more common in the Baroque era and even appeared in the service of the popes in the twelfth century. Women's voices had been banished from the church, and the castrati replaced them after being officially admitted to the Sistine Chapel in 1599.[1]

The American classical music critic Harold C. Schonberg observes:

> A great castrato was the vocal wonder of all time; a singing machine, virtually a musical instrument. Even before Handel's time, the castrati were idols. They were spoiled, pampered figures of great wealth and vanity, and even greater eccentricity. They were the first performers in musical history to achieve star status.[2]

---

1 Harold C. Schonberg, ed., *The Lives of the Great Composers* (New York: W. W. Norton and Co., Inc,., 1997), 63.
2 Ibid., 64.

This male voice sounded more like a soprano or alto of exquisite virtuosity. Handel wrote most of his higher vocal parts for castrati. In today's productions, these roles are usually assigned to tenors, countertenors (naturally high-voiced men), or baritones who sing in a higher register; or they may be sung in the original register by a woman singer (usually a female alto in male costume).[3] In an article he wrote for *The Opera Guild Magazine* entitled "Rebel with a Cause," Mark Ketterson said, "Modern audiences sometimes have trouble with the countertenor, the young hunk who comes on and sings like a soprano."[4]

In Handel's day, the castrato was either a member of the men and boys' choir or a special soloist who also sang with the choir. One famous castrato, even before Handel's day, was Baldassare Ferri, and the famous castrato for the premiere performance of *Messiah* was Giovanni Carestini. Castrati had the skill to sing a wide range with fluidity and remarkable power, yet their voices never deepened. What the castrati were proud of was their incredible breath control and ability to negotiate any kind of complicated figuration without a break in register or any evidence of vocal strain.[5] Their sound is produced by flipping into the falsetto, the upper register of their range.[6]

In 1750 Handel rewrote this *aria* "But who may abide" for the male castrato Gaetano Guadagni, who came to England as a member of an Italian troupe of singers. This *aria* had started out as a simple *recitative*, but that wasn't enough to show off Guadagni's voice; therefore, Handel transposed it and added several more notes, including the whole second section (the flashy bit about the "refiner's fire"). Guadagni made it a big hit.[7]

The text of this *aria* is taken from Malachi 3:2 (KJV), in which the prophet daringly asks the question:

> But who may abide the day of his coming?
> and who shall stand when he appeareth?
> For he is like a refiner's fire . . .

American audiences are used to hearing "But who may abide" sung by a bass soloist with a rich, mellow voice. After the slow phrase of the "A" section, "when he appeareth," we hear the strings immediately sound

---

3 Joseph Machlis and Kristine Forney, *The Enjoyment of Music,* 6th edition (New York: W. W. Norton & Co, Inc, 1990), 137.
4 Mark Ketterson, "Rebel with a Cause," *The Opera Guild Magazine,* Metropolitan Opera Guild Publishers, Vol. 71, No. 2, 39.
5 Schonberg, 64.
6 Don Michael Randel, ed., *Harvard Dictionary of Music,* 4th edition (Cambridge, Massachusetts: Harvard University Press, 2003), 305.
7 David W. Barber, *Getting a Handle on Handel's* Messiah (Toronto, Canada: Sound and Vision Publishing Limited, 1994), 72.

as if they are agitated—going mad—by playing rapid sixteenth notes in every measure—*prestissimo*, as if in a fury. The tension is mounting as the bass continues singing: "For he is like a refiner's fire." Observe the music below:

The notes appear to jump around like sparks of a fire with flashes of red, yellow, and orange leaping in the air, climaxing with the question, "And who shall stand when he appeareth?" Wow! The libretto seems to cry out for music of such fierce energy. Look at the shape of the violinists' notes: they look like fire themselves with their dancing flames:[8] Notice, too, the *piano* (soft) and *forte* (loud) markings below:

Malachi reassures the people that the Messiah will surely come, bringing judgment upon the sinners and blessings for the penitent. God is truly like a refiner's fire. The day of the Lord is coming when the wicked shall be consumed, or refined, as if passed through fire a thousand times, and the righteous shall be rewarded.

---

8 John Tobin, *Handel's* Messiah: A Critical Account of the Manuscript Sources and Printed Editions (London, England: Cassell & Co., 1969), 150.

"But who may abide" may be a bit ominous; but just you wait until the judgment day, and then, surely, doubt will give way to hope.[9]

After this fast and furious pace, we return to the *larghetto* "A" section to hear the repeated question, "But who may abide the day of his coming?" sung more slowly this time, with great poignancy. Pouncing quickly again into the raging fire of the "B" section, we feel the heat of passion once more, and the music ends with an exhausted *adagio* (slowly) on the words, "For he is like a refiner's fire." The instruments race to the *prestissimo* (loud and clear) like a house on fire!

The piece seems to fluctuate between a relentless tempo driven very hard and the slower yet strong question asking, "Who may abide?" This gives us a chance to hear the warning that essentially says, "Who can survive under such great scrutiny?" In terms of musical structure, Handel has given us a mini-masterpiece even in this one *aria*.

Many passages in the Old Testament are concerned with the problem of reconciling God's supposed justice with the obvious inequalities of life. Malachi assures us that God is coming soon to correct life's injustices. The distinctiveness of Malachi's eschatology is that it involves two acts: 1) the coming of the messenger to purify the temple and the priesthood; and 2) the coming of the Lord Himself to His purified temple to judge the people. The purpose of the preliminary coming of the messenger is to purify the temple and its priests in preparation for the full advent of God the judge. God won't come until His house is set in order. His messenger will straighten out the abuses and restore the golden days of old, when worship was offered to God with dignity and in sincerity.[10]

The *Contemporary English Version* of the Bible translates the text this way:

> On the day the Lord comes, He will be like a furnace that
> purifies silver or like strong soap in a washbasin. No one
> will be able to stand up to Him.
>
> (Malachi 3:2)

---

9 Robert C. Dentan, "The Book of Malachi," *The Interpreter's Bible*, Vol. VI (New York: Abingdon Press, 1956), 1123.
10 Dentan, 1137.

Jennens brilliantly chose the texts for all of Handel's *Messiah* "from a rich source of supply. Its unity was implicit in the Christian purpose of the work from the very outset."[11] The continuity of spiritual and musical thought throughout the oratorio is incredible, and the librettist must be given credit for his unity in conception. In this *aria*, the bass exemplifies Handel's genius by transporting us through the refiner's fire to the theme of the next chorus, "And He shall purify." Later, similarly, Handel moves us from "Take His yoke" to "His yoke is easy;" from the Christmas recitatives to the "Glory to God." This synergy between spiritual and musical content is remarkable.[12]

As the librettist, Jennens arranged the texts of most of the "scenes" to climax with a chorus, usually approached through an ascending sequence of a *recitative*, followed by an *aria*. There is a careful structuring to the placement of choruses within the whole picture and an ingenious use of tonalities by Handel that makes better sense when they are in the correct context. Leonard Van Camp reminds us that "All of these things are disturbed when cuts to the performance of *Messiah* are made, to shorten the performance, or to choose the more familiar choruses."[13] Even the sequence of the many moods is shifted when the piece is "cut and pasted."

In this *aria*, the bass has warned us of the refiner's fire, as in a refinery where the heat burns off the impurities from the ore to make precious metals. When gold or silver is refined, the dross, or waste product, rises to the surface, separating from the purified metal. Just like the sons of Levi we'll hear about in the next chapter, we become more Christlike when our impurities are burned off. May we all strive to live in the daily expectation of the Lord's coming. Now, on we go to the next chorus, "And He shall purify."

---

11 Stanley Godman, *Goethe and Handel*, Vol. XXIII (England: Goethe Society, 1954), 82.
12 Tobin, 151.
13 Leonard Van Camp, *A Practical Guide for Performing, Teaching and Singing* Messiah (Dayton, Ohio: Lorenz Corporation, Roger Dean Publishing Co., 1993), 8.

CHAPTER SEVEN

"And He shall purify"

(CHORUS)

Why was King Ahaz asked to make a pure offering in order to restore the purity of worship? This chapter defines "fugue," "tessitura," the "Neapolitan sixth," and the use of counterpoint.

And he shall purify the sons of Levi . . .
that they may offer unto the Lord an
offering in righteousness.

(Malachi 3:3 KJV)

George Frideric Handel

Who are these sons of Levi? And why did they need to clean up their act by offering a gift to the Lord in righteousness? The name "Levi" is commonly understood to be a vivid personification of the priestly order of the Hebrews. Historically these sons of Levi acted as priests and had faithfully discharged their duties of giving "true instruction" concerning ethical attitudes (not so much about performing the ritual of sacrifices or following liturgical practice.)[1]

We've learned from Deuteronomy 33:8-11 that the priests were in a covenant relationship with God, and protecting that bond was their chief concern. God had promised them life and peace; in return, the priests were expected to perform their duties with reverence and awe, as well as to teach God's laws to Israel.

1 Robert C. Dentan, "The Book of Malachi," *The Interpreter's Bible*, Vol. VI (New York: Abingdon Press, 1956), 1132.

Being a priest was, and is, a very serious responsibility, because he or she is *the* messenger of the Lord of Hosts. In these verses, Malachi is accusing the priests of actually contributing to the spiritual depression and moral weakness of the community. Woe to those priests! (Woe to those ministers and clergy today in this same category, who are accused of contributing to the moral weakness of our communities!) Malachi looks deeply into their hearts and only sees their contempt for the symbols of religion and morality. He feels that God is very concerned about these sins. Even though the priests may have fulfilled their responsibility (of bringing the people around) according to cultic requirements of the earthly temple, the people are fully aware that they are "not fit to be in the presence of the Lord God."[2]

The gulf between God and man, between the holy and the unclean, is created by an ultimate distinction between supreme ethical holiness and the corruption of human nature. Like Isaiah and his people, we are reminded with startling clarity that however well we "might have kept the accepted rules of morality in the presence of a holiness exalted in righteousness, we and all others are unclean, yet we know that we can be cleansed by a sovereign act of grace. The reality is that there exists a divine act of forgiveness made possible by Isaiah's awakened consciousness of the nature and power of God's holiness and of the real and dreadful condition of moral uncleanness in which we all stand."[3]

This chorus "And He shall purify" is the second "pillar of sound" in the structural organization of Handel's *Messiah*. In the very first measure, with no orchestral introduction, the sopranos jump right in on the second half of the second beat in this 4/4 meter piece. They seem to be attacking this music just as assuredly as their words seem to be attacking the sons of Levi.

In Handel's score on the next page, we notice that he included the phrase *senza ripieno*. This meant that only a small ensemble of leading orchestral members would play, rather than a fuller orchestra, perhaps because Handel wanted the voices to have prominence. Notice also at the bottom of the following example his use of the words *con fag.*, meaning "with bassoons." Their proper Italian name, *faggoti*, was used instead of the word "bassoon," since bassoon could be confused with the word "bass."[4]

---

2 Dentan, 1137.
3 James Muilenburg, "The Book of Isaiah," *The Interpreter's Bible*, Vol. V (New York: Abingdon Press, 1956), 209.
4 Alfred Mann, ed., *Handel's* Messiah *in Full Score* (New York: Dover Publications, 1989), 216.

Handel's *Messiah*

The basses catch the theme from the sopranos on the dominant of the key (a fifth higher), and seem to sink into the depth of their *melisma*. The altos and tenors then enter into the fray, since all the voices must sing the tricky *melisma* on the word "purify." The sopranos and tenors' *melismas* last as long as forty notes! Count them yourself below:

This is a *fugal* chorus in G minor whose rhythm is that of a very fast dance. Handel borrowed music from himself; he had used this melody before in an earlier work ("L'occaso ha nell'aurora"). Perhaps, we could say he was an ingenious recycler. The word *fugue* comes from the Latin word *fugere*, meaning to "flee," suggesting the flight of the basic theme from one voice to another.[5]

The *fugue* is a rather free form based on imitative counterpoint that combines the composer's technical skill with imagination, feeling, and exuberant ornamentation. This type of composition may well count for one of the supreme contributions of the Baroque era to the world of music.

Usually the subject of the *fugue* is stated in the home key, which is called the tonic. The answer is given in a related key (the dominant) that lies five tones above the tonic. There may be modulation to other keys in the course of the *fugue*, which builds up tension against the desire to return to the home key. The Baroque *fugue* embodied the contrast between home and contrasting keys, only to become one of the basic principles of the new major-minor system.[6]

This transition from the medieval church modes to major-minor tonality was one of the most significant changes in all of music history. As music during this period turned from vocal counterpoint to instrumental harmony, it demanded a simplification of the harmonic system. The various church modes gave way to two standard scales: major and minor. With the establishment of this new major-minor tonality, the thrust to the keynote, or tonic, became the most powerful force in music.[7]

Now, let us return to the score of "And He shall purify." The *tessitura* of these passages is very high and generally stays in the five-note range from high D on up to a high G. The word *tessitura* means "the particular range of a vocal part that is concentrated in one part of the scale."[8] In this piece the *tessitura* seems awfully high for both the sopranos and tenors. As the previous score example shows, the *coloratura* passages of running sixteenth notes seem to continue forever, without giving the singer a chance to take a breath. As singers, when we are fully warmed up and singing "in zone," we feel a ringing in our heads, and the sound just flows. The sopranos in this chorus must be fully open and prepared as they surf along on top with several high G's.

Instruments and singing voices have intriguing similarities. The range of an instrument is a major factor in deciding which instrument shall play or sing a particular line of music. Violins only go as low as the G below middle C. Likewise, violas only can play as low as the low C. In a four-voice composition, the first

5 Don Michael Randel, ed. *The Harvard Dictionary of Music,* 4th edition (Cambridge, Massachusetts: Harvard University Press, 2003), 336.
6 Joseph Machlis and Kristine Forney, eds., *The Enjoyment of Music,* 6th edition (New York: W. W. Norton & Co., 1990), 185.
7 Ibid., 133.
8 Randel, 739.

HANDEL'S

violins would play the melody, the second violins would play the alto line, the violas would play the tenor line, and the cellos would be the lowest voice. The double bass would play the same written part as the cellos, but they sound an octave lower. The Baroque composer used the natural qualities of musical production to create inherent dynamics: rising phrases naturally became louder (*crescendos*); falling phrases became softer (*decrescendos*). The Baroque composer chose specific instruments for their tone as well as their different ranges of pitch.

So, in this *fugue*, the basses, tenors, and altos all make their grand entrances after the sopranos. All four voices seem to be running after each other, and even the music itself appears to be out of breath.

These counterpoint independent lines all flow alongside one another—having their own rhythms, but harmonizing with the other voices. This creates the texture of the piece and is called polyphonic music, as opposed to homophonic music (when a solo singer carries the tune against his harmonic accompaniment). Handel was a master of this musical form of polyphonic music, and his attention to the texture and inner voices is certainly his strong point.

Finally, all four voices come together on the words, "that they may offer unto the Lord an offering in righteousness, in righteousness." Up until this point, the voices have been playing a cat-and-mouse game with driving energy.

In measures 23 and 24 below, the sopranos and basses sing a syncopated rhythm that is different from the inner voices. This syncopation gives special emphasis or accentuation to the word "righteousness." This use of syncopation allows a weak beat to function as a strong beat, as Handel shows us in the following score:

Handel made several changes in his score over the many months of performances of *Messiah*. One such change appears in the following measure, which shows the altos singing a different rhythm from that of the basses. Previously they sang the same rhythm as the basses, but Handel changed the altos' rhythm to the strict rhythm of two eighth notes, as opposed to the dotted eighth note followed by a sixteenth note that was sung by the basses.[9] This is the rhythm that we know today—one which Handel used to excite his listener. In the music below, compare the altos' rhythm in the top line with the basses' bottom line:

Another modification appears in the following score, in which we have a major note-leading change for the alto line. Harmonically, Handel made several adjustments in order to avoid writing parallel fifths between the alto and bass parts, a serious problem in composition:

In this measure, we find that Handel used the "Neapolitan sixth." During the eighteenth century, except in France, the international style of opera was called Neapolitan, whether it was performed by natives of

---

9 Mann, 216.

HANDEL'S *Messiah*

Naples or not. This Neapolitan sixth, a lowered second scale degree, (in this case, the B natural) was decisively used at this point to change the tonality to make our ears desire for the music to resolve on the dominant. It's a brilliant use of chord progressions to effect a change. Handel had spent three years in Italy, and many historians feel that he is the greatest composer using the Neapolitan style. From his vast experience, Handel had united the traditions from many countries: from the Italians, beautiful vocal melody; from the Germans, contrapuntal genius; and from the English, tremendous choral tradition. Many historians would agree "that Handel's thirty years of work in London have never been surpassed for nobility of style or profundity of dramatic insight."[10]

In the following example, observe the way in which Handel keeps the strings busy, especially driving toward the end. The music is exciting to listen to as the rhythms become more complex, as well as faster and faster, even separating into the nanoseconds of a beat. Between the *melismas* and the speed of this piece, the chorus members are challenged with a high-powered work-out.

10 Dale Cunningham, *Music and Its Makers* (New York: Sterling Publishing Company, 1963), 31.

The *Contemporary English Version* of the text says:

> The LORD will purify the descendants of Levi as though
> they were gold or silver. Then they will bring the proper
> offerings to the Lord.

Again the eschatological element appears, "as God will put right all that has been wrong. God will purify His people in order for them to be in a right relationship with Him. For His kingdom is at hand."[11] In the end, God's purpose will be fully realized. The Book of Malachi is the very last book of the Old Testament canon. As we read it, we feel that the age of the prophets is drawing to a close. Let us look at this chorus as one of those pillars of strength, in both text and composition, upon which the masterwork *Messiah* is supported.

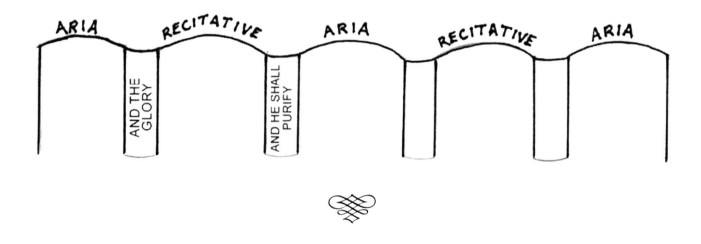

---

11 Dentan, 1138.

HANDEL'S *Messiah*

CHAPTER EIGHT

"Behold, a virgin shall conceive"

(RECITATIVE FOR ALTO)

Indeed, the Lord has given us a sign . . . this chapter presents the doctrine of the Virgin birth, and an early heresy, called Docetism.

George Frideric Handel

The whirlwind of the last chorus has stopped for the time-being. We have just heard of the "purification of the sons of Levi" and have been reminded of our own need to purify ourselves and make a right offering of ourselves to the Lord. Then boom! . . . a calm prophetic word is announced: "A virgin shall conceive."

> Behold, a virgin shall conceive and bear a son,
> and shall call his name Emmanuel (God with us).
> (Isaiah 7:14; Matthew 1:23 KJV)

Handel originally wrote this *recitative* for a countertenor, the adult male whose voice range is higher than a regular tenor. But today's audiences normally expect to hear an alto with a rich and mellow voice sing this beautiful *recitative*.

The text of the oratorio has returned not only to the Old Testament book of Isaiah, but also to Matthew, the first New Testament book used by the librettist. The tone has changed from the agitated "Purify" chorus to this calm, soft, movement that seems to interrupt the entire sweep of *Messiah*, Part the First. The alto is singing as if she were the angel Gabriel, announcing that "this is going to happen": a baby will be born.[1] The one-line *recitative* is so short that it can be shown here in its entirety:

In his craftsmanship of composing, Handel has successfully navigated his listeners through the change in keys, from the minor keys of the last two pieces to D major. At the end of these six measures, the music has modulated to A major (the dominant of the following *aria* in D major). Handel's clever use of modulation has prepared the listeners' ears to anticipate the resolution, or the key of the next *aria*, "O thou that tellest." (Composers use modulation to add variety and interest in sound to their compositions.)

In the music score example above, notice the words, *senza faggoti*, which again requests the bassoons to not "play along with the *basso-continuo*." The figured bass in the *basso-continuo* shows which shorthand notes should be played on the organ or harpsichord. In the example above, notice the numbers 7, 4, and 2. This refers to the seventh note, a C, to be the top note played; the fourth note, G, next; and under that, the second, an E. In their book, *The Enjoyment of Music,* Joseph Machlis and Kristine Forney call this "the most successful system of musical shorthand ever devised."[2] With his quick mind, Handel could decipher this shorthand to play the appropriate notes and chord progressions at sight.

This short *recitative* has two major theological themes: (1) the virgin birth; and (2) the fulfillment of the Messiah-prophecy. Let us expound on the words, "Behold, a virgin shall conceive." In order to understand the text, we must look at its context, not only in Isaiah 7, but also in the preceding sixth chapter of Isaiah. This dynamic pronouncement of the virgin birth follows Isaiah's original commission to proclaim the utter doom of a faithless and hard-hearted people. These verses continue with the prophetic teaching of apostasy and doom, culminating in the purification and existence of a remnant linked with the Davidic Messiah.[3]

---

1 Joseph Machlis and Kristine Forney, eds., *The Enjoyment of Music,* 6th edition (New York: W. W. Norton & Co., 1990), 133.
2 Ibid., 134.
3 R .B. Y. Scott, "The Book of Isaiah," *The Interpreter's Bible,* Vol. V (New York: Abingdon Press, 1956), 212.

HANDEL'S *Messiah*

In Isaiah 7, the prophet Isaiah has a word from the Lord to give to the hysterical King Ahaz, who is frantic about the nation's defense. The actual text is preceded by the words, "Therefore the Lord himself will give you a sign." These words are spoken to Ahaz because the king has refused to believe that Judah will be saved from the present attack by Syria and Ephraim. This text is distinct from that of Isaiah 6 in that it becomes a third-person account of outward events in which Isaiah is participating, along with King Ahaz.

The scene occurs in the court or council chamber where Isaiah is confronting Ahaz and exhorting him to have courage and faith. King Ahaz apparently doesn't have faith in God that is strong enough. Because of Ahaz' refusal to believe that Judah will be saved from the attack, the deliverance the Lord has promised will be followed by a far greater disaster, deemed necessary to make him realize that God is speaking to him.[4]

King Ahaz is beginning to understand; but no matter how the story ends, the issue is in God's hands, with His purpose in mind for His people. Isaiah offers King Ahaz and his people a sign—an event that will soon happen to prove to everyone that the Lord has indeed spoken through His prophet, Isaiah. (For a more detailed history of the situation, please read 2 Kings 16:5 and 2 Chronicles 28, which give a summary of the account of the attack on Jerusalem).[5]

From this Scripture passage, we are reminded that it is only through faith in the sovereign love of God that we can courageously endure the frustrations and defeats of life, tolerate the discipline that results from them, accept even unanswered prayers, and still trust and obey.

What's the sign that the Lord will give Isaiah, Ahaz, and even us today? Isn't it amazing that we demand more signs, more proof? The sign is that a "virgin shall conceive and bear a son, and that son will be called 'Emmanuel' (God with us)." All of the predictions and historical events are part of the signs of God's coming as Emmanuel (or Immanuel). Thus, God is the "greatest communicator" to His people.

Written seven centuries before Mary was even born, this text in Isaiah 7:14 appears to point to the young maiden, Mary, and the prediction of the birth of Jesus, the Messiah. The prophet Isaiah profoundly influenced the gospel writers of the New Testament. However, when Matthew wrote his gospel, he used the LXX, the Greek Septuagint, which some say is a mistranslation and not a translation from the Hebrew. All kinds of inaccurate translations of the Hebrew word *almah* have caused many technicalities in today's

---

4 Ibid., 216.
5 Ibid., 218.

exegesis. Some scholars translate the word as "virgin;" others say, "maiden;" and still others say, "young woman of marriageable age." Scholars feel that "virgin" is an inaccurate and controversial translation of the Hebrew text. If Isaiah had wished to make clear that he had in mind a miraculous "virgin birth," he would have had to use the specific word, *bethulah*. But he used the Hebrew term *almah*, which signifies "a young woman of marriageable age," possibly a virgin or not, and its usage is questionable.[6]

The narrative birth stories function as a test for beliefs about the Bible. In his gospel, Matthew tried to show that the Old Testament foreshadowed the life of Jesus Christ. To confirm his story, Matthew seized upon this connection with a "sign" as evidence of a prophetic expectation of the virgin birth of Jesus the Christ. It was especially appropriate because of the name "Emmanuel," which he correctly translated "God with us." (Incidentally, in *Messiah*, Handel's incorrect spelling in his original score was "Emanuel" and was copied by his scribe, John C. Smith. Later, it was corrected by Handel himself to be the correct spelling of "Emmanuel.")

Christians prefer the general term "maiden" and adopt the messianic interpretation in the light of the expectation that was widespread in the ancient world: a human mother would give birth to a redeemer baby who would supplant the reigning king. As Emmanuel, Jesus embodies God's presence with His people. Protestants and Roman Catholics, of course, espouse this messianic interpretation. Jews challenged Matthew's gospel assertion that it fulfilled a prophecy in Isaiah for the Messiah to be born of a "virgin." (Isaiah's word is translated "young girl.")

The division that arose in the first century between the new fellowship of believers and the Jewish church from which it was gradually separated sometimes led to what was in danger of being a disparagement of the old religion. The fact that the Pharisees were condemned created the impression that Judaism, in general, also stood condemned. But it must be remembered that it was out of the heritage of Israel that Jesus Himself came. Moreover, there was a spiritual force in Judaism that would produce people who were accounted righteous before God.[7]

Matthew's account presupposes the virgin birth: the gospel writer interpreted Isaiah 7:14 as the "Incarnation" that says, "For unto us a child is born." Of the four gospels in the New Testament, Matthew and Luke are the only two that mention the virgin birth. The gospels of Mark and John do not tell about the

---

6 Sherman E. Johnson, "The Gospel According to St. Matthew," *The Interpreter's Bible*, Vol. VII (New York: Abingdon Press, 1956), 255.
7 Scott, 218.

nativity at all. The apostle Paul even teaches a high Christology without referencing the virgin birth. Thus, the doctrine of the virgin birth was not really part of early primitive Christian thought.

The only small references to this doctrine in the New Testament are found in this passage from Matthew 1:23 and the nativity passages in Luke. In Matthew, the angelic annunciation is made to Joseph, while Luke's is to Mary. In Luke 1:34, when the angel Gabriel tells Mary that she will bear a child, her response is, "How can this be since I have no husband?" The angel goes on to tell her that the Holy Spirit will come upon her. Also, Matthew 1:18 mentions that Mary was found to be with child *of the Holy Spirit*. This suggests the all-creative power of God.

The Old Testament records many births that took place only through divine intervention, as we have learned from Genesis 21:1-3, Genesis 25:21, and 1 Samuel 1:4-20. But this story differs in that Jesus had no human biological father. (The Holy Spirit's role in conception began to be recited in the Christian creeds by the second century.) During the time of the early church, there was a heresy called *Docetism*, which proclaimed that Jesus was totally divine and only "appeared" human. (Read more about this in Chapter Six).

The Rev. Jack Hayford, in his book, *The Mary Miracle,* says:

> There is not any hint of the doctrine of the virgin birth in Mark's gospel, the letters of Paul, nor in the gospel of John. They all assumed that Joseph was one of Jesus' parents; several times Luke even refers to Jesus as the son of Joseph (Luke 3:23 and John 6:42). The real significance is that God had intervened by choosing a virgin girl as the avenue through whom He would give us His greatest gift. This was a real child born of Mary. Heaven came down to us, so God is with us. The real significance is theological: THAT GOD HAD INTERVENED.[8]

Early Christian theology declared what had been the faith of the church from the beginning, which was that God had come in human form for our salvation in Jesus Christ. Luke, in his gospel, was writing for a church that was already disturbed by schismatic and heretical teachers. The previously mentioned Docetists denied Christ's humanity, instead declaring that He had not actually taken our flesh upon Himself, suffered, nor died. From the time of Ignatius and the framers of the Apostles' Creed, and possibly as early as Luke's

---

8 Jack Hayford, *The Mary Miracle* (Ventura, California: Regal Books, 1994), 79.

day, the doctrine of the virgin birth asserted that Christ was truly man as well as truly God. The Son of God had been conceived by a human mother, a virgin in accordance with Old Testament prophecy, as the church interpreted it in the LXX text of Isaiah 7:14.

The second major theological theme of this *recitative* is packaged in the words, "and shall call His name 'Emmanuel' (God with us)." Today, we choose names for our children for various reasons—one being the pleasing sound, or because we just like the name. But the Hebrews chose a name for its spiritual meaning in God's kingdom. The name "Immanuel," or "Emmanuel," is translated "God with us." Some people reject Matthew's connection of "Immanuel" to "Messiah," claiming that the name "Immanuel" means "God is for us," not specifically "God is with us in this particular child." They object to Matthew's interpretation because they feel that the term implies that any baby could have this name, not the very one who was the actual Deliverer. "Emmanuel" is a name with a huge meaning. By this name, Isaiah's thought was "the deliverance will be so striking that a mother *will give her child this name.*" The term "savior" means "one who delivers from danger." Matthew believed that Jesus fulfilled the words of Isaiah, so he quoted the prophet in his gospel (Isaiah 7:14).[9]

Jesus gave new meaning to all the titles applied to Him. He was no mere deliverer of the nation from bondage; He was also a re-creation of human nature. His kingship was rooted in divine compassion. Jesus was the fulfillment of all Jewish hope and prophecy. It was significant that the Messiah must be born in Bethlehem because it was the ancestral home of King David, and there was a tradition that the great and future king of Israel would be descended from David. This is the point of the famous passage in Micah 5:2 (RSV): "But you, O Bethlehem . . . from you shall come forth one who is to rule in Israel, whose origin is from of old, from ancient days."[10]

The *Contemporary English Version* of the Bible paraphrases the Scripture passage for this *recitative* in its user-friendly wording:

> "Listen every one of you in the royal family of David. You have
> already tried my patience because of your unbelief. Now you are
> trying God's patience by refusing to ask for proof. But the Lord
> will still give you proof. A virgin is pregnant; she will have a son and
> will name him Immanuel."
>
> (Isaiah 7:13-14)

9 Hayford, 80.
10 Marcus J. Borg and N. T. Wright, *The Meaning of Jesus: Two Visions* (New York: Harper-Collins, 1990), 182.

So the Lord's promise came true,
just as the prophet had said,
"A virgin will have a baby boy,
and he will be called Immanuel,
which means "God is with us."

(Matthew 1:22-23)

What does this mean for us today? Even if we can't comprehend the significance of these words, we can still allow expectation to come into our hearts. We can receive and believe the gift we have been given through the miracle of Christ's incarnation and work of salvation. Redemption is God's reclaiming of the lost, forgiveness of the sinful, and then fulfillment of His purposes in each of us. This forces us into a confrontation with the truth. Mary was simply the instrument of God's grace while He was waiting in the wings to come onto His stage.

Mary was similar to you and me: she was human, ordinary, and a sinner. She hadn't been born through the act of immaculate conception herself. She didn't need to be sinless to become the bearer of the sinless Savior. This didn't hinder the workings of God because nothing is impossible for Him. God is the One acting here in His story.

The gospel of Luke shows us the story from Mary's perspective when she questions God, "How shall this be?" (Luke 1:34). But she quickly acknowledges, "Behold the handmaid of the Lord; be it unto me according to Thy word" (v. 38 KJV). Do we, like Mary, question God and fail to acknowledge His activity, or do we have faith and confidence in the power of the holy God of Israel? For love of us He came, and for love He still lives within us today. Matthew 28:20 (KJV) tells us, "Lo, I am with you alway, even unto the end of the world." Jesus Christ came so that we might know the length His love would go for our redemption: "Immanuel, unto us is born a savior." The evidence is clear that Jesus fulfilled the prophecies, promises, and hopes expressed in the Hebrew Scriptures. This text forces us into a confrontation with truth.[11]

---

11 Johnson, 255.

The Reverend Jack Hayford continues:

Only a begotten son of God, sired from outside Adam's race, yet begotten within it, could become the holy Lamb for sacrifice. The Son of God had been conceived by a human mother. She even asks, "How can this be?" If the birth of Jesus was not by a physical miracle, then Jesus himself is NOT the less miraculous because ALL birth is a miracle, and the supreme miracle, in any case, is the actual entrance into the world of One who in mind and spirit completely expressed and embodied the reality of God. The important thing is faith—an act which is the negation of all activity (because in it, it is God who acts). Faith is our quiet surrender.[12]

---

1 Hayford, 79.

HANDEL'S *Messiah*

"O, thou that tellest good tidings to Zion"

(ARIA FOR COUNTERTENOR AND CHORUS)

Breaking News! A call for Jerusalem to be a witness on a high mountain in proclaiming the glory of the Lord.

O, thou that tellest good tidings to Zion,
    get thee up into the high mountain;
O, thou that tellest good tidings to Jerusalem,
    lift up thy voice with strength;
Lift it up, be not afraid; say unto the cities of Judah,
    Behold your God!

             (Isaiah 40:9 KJV)

George Frideric Handel

Arise, shine, for thy light is come, and the
glory of the Lord is risen upon thee.

             (Isaiah 60:1 KJV)

This expressive melody in flowing 6/8 meter is one of Handel's happiest inspirations—a cheerful tune, yet sincere and reverent. Zion (Jerusalem) is being addressed as an official "town crier," and she is commissioned to proclaim the good news of the Lord's coming. The scene, taken from the passage in Isaiah 40 (which was also used in chapters two, three, and four at the beginning of *Messiah*), has shifted from the celestial council in heaven to earth, specifically to Jerusalem.[1]

---

2 James Muilenburg, "The Book of Isaiah," *The Interpreter's Bible*, Vol. V (New York: Abingdon Press, 1956), 431.

Handel wrote this *aria* to be sung by either a countertenor or an alto. A countertenor is a male alto who can sing falsetto, a distinctly lighter quality that extends his upper range. Today's audiences normally hear a female alto sing this lilting piece, usually the same woman who sang, "Behold, a virgin shall conceive," the previous *recitative*.

After a twelve-measure introduction by the orchestra, the singer enters the happy melody, heralding the coming glory of the Lord, with only the violins echoing the singer's phrases. Observe the music below.

The prophet Isaiah is telling Zion that she must ascend a high mountain so that she may be seen by all the people, and then she must shout with a loud voice that her words may be heard by everyone: "Lift up thy voice with strength!" She must announce the coming of God whose glory the whole world will see—His conquest and His victory; the ushering in of His kingdom; the institution of His sovereignty; and above all, His act of justice. The way is prepared for the eschatology (the end times).[2] So the countertenor, or alto, sings:

> O, thou that tellest good tidings to Zion,
> get thee up into the high mountain;
> O, thou that tellest good tidings to Jerusalem.
> (Isaiah 40:9 RSV)

---

3 Ibid., 431.

HANDEL'S *Messiah*

The *King James Version* uses these words, "O Zion, herald of good tidings," yet the RSV text is more adaptable to a melodic line. In the Septuagint, the clause "that brings good tidings" is expressed by the word *euaggelizo*, which in the New Testament is the verb often used for declaring good tidings, or preaching the gospel. Our words "evangelize" and "evangelism" are derived from this Greek verb.[3]

Rich in symbolism, the name "Jerusalem" represents the nation in covenant with God, a nation that has played a major role in His plan for the world. Jerusalem was God's chosen messenger to whom He had revealed Himself: He was disciplining her as a unique service to all people, and He was now affectionately speaking to her, entrusting her with a very large mission:[4]

> Lift up thy voice with strength; lift it up,
> Be not afraid; say unto the cities of Judah,
> Behold your God!

> (Isaiah 40:9 RSV)

Jerusalem is commanded to tell the cities of Judah (her mission field) to prepare themselves for God's entrance. Her immediate joy was here at home, but she would soon have a wider horizon, and all "flesh shall see it." Handel brilliantly combines this text with music that literally lifts up:

This phrase is a series of intervals of perfect fourths, rising by whole steps, figuratively lifting up, just as the words suggest. "Lift up thy voice" implies a commission to evangelize. Perhaps the first commission of its kind, this has become a decisive development in religion ever since, particularly in some denominations. As

---

4 Note taken from *The New Scofield Reference Bible*, Oxford, 1967, 746.
5 Muilenburg, 432.

Americans, we are a people with a Christian heritage and trustees of a gospel desperately needed by the world today. We are being told to "behold our God." God is coming as king to His people; the way is prepared for the vast panorama of history and eschatology that is to follow. Jennens chose to omit the next two verses of the biblical text from his libretto:

> Behold, the Lord comes with might,
> and his arm rules for him;
> Behold, his reward is with him,
> and his recompense before him.
>
> (Isaiah 40:10-11 RSV)

The very next verse, "He shall feed His flock like a shepherd," is used later in chapter twenty of Handel's *Messiah*, when the soprano sings her solo. Isaiah 40:9 is the third strophe from the original text that culminates in the announcement of the imminent appearance of God upon the stage of world history. This three-fold "behold" was a rhetorical device that Jennens used to his advantage. It is interesting that the next strophe of the *aria*, and the text of chapters ten and eleven of *Messiah*, are taken from the end of Isaiah's prophecy, chapter 60:

> "Arise, shine for thy light is come,
> and the glory of the Lord is risen upon thee."
>
> (Isaiah 60:1 KJV)

The *Contemporary English Version* of the Bible places these verses under the title "Your God is Here!"

> "Your God is here! There is good news for the city of Zion.
> Shout it as loud as you can from the highest mountain.
> Don't be afraid to shout to the towns of Judah,
> 'Your God is here!'"
>
> (Isaiah 40:9)

> "Jerusalem, stand up! Shine! Your new day is dawning.
> The glory of the LORD shines brightly on you."
>
> (Isaiah 60:1)

HANDEL'S  *Messiah*

In her timidity and lethargy, the church needs this prophet's summons: "Get yourselves up to a high mountain, and in the sight of all, boldly assert your gospel for them; lift up your voice with strength, affirming the presence of the redeeming God. Lift up your voice; don't be afraid to say, 'Behold your God.' The prophet's aim is to elevate the people to be more confident in their faith. The Christian cause will not grab the attention of the world until the glory of God is revealed in the righteousness of a nation. Only then will Zion be flooded with the radiance of the risen Son."[5]

As the new age is about to dawn, Zion is addressed with urgent imperatives to arise and reflect the brightness of the divine glory. We heard "glory" mentioned already in chapter four, "And the glory of the Lord." The central word heard again in this verse is "glory" (kabhodh), the transforming and radiating effect of living in God's presence. (The word was originally associated with the revelation on Mt. Sinai when God appeared in a cloud.)

The eschatological significance of the verse allows us to imagine the sun rising over Jerusalem, lighting up the whole city; the city becomes a new Jerusalem where His glory dwells. This is a case in which the literal and the symbolic connotations join forces and the prophet is allowing us to see the eschatological event as having already occurred, as in "The glory of the Lord has risen upon thee."[6] These words are sung in a rising, stepwise motif, just as the words imply.

After the soloist finishes singing, "is risen upon thee," the theme is picked up by the entire chorus. (See the following score.) While the soloist has been singing, a very small ensemble, marked *senza rip.*, has been playing; but when the chorus appears, *tutti* is the marking, indicating that all instruments, including the oboes and bassoons, play *forte* (loudly). One can almost see the chorus members' bodies swaying as they move in time with the 6/8 meter. This rhythm is a rollicking swing with its strongly marked two-beat accents on the first and fourth beats.

The sopranos (and oboes) jump right in on the sixth beat of the same measure that the soloist has just finished. Handel's original autograph score bears the notation *attacca il Coro*, meaning, "Let the chorus attack,"[7] or *Let it rip!* The chorus sings the same basic melody, just sung by the soloist, with a few exceptions.

6 Ibid., 434.
7 Ibid., 435.
8 Alfred Mann, ed., *Handel's Messiah in Full Score* (New York: Dover Publications, Inc., 1989), 215.

CHAPTER 9 *O, Thou that tellest good tidings*

What is wonderful is that the emotion projected at the beginning by the individual soloist is now experienced by the chorus, representing the world as a whole, as it punctuates the dramatic words. The differences in the melodies are slight; the sopranos' second note goes up to a D instead of down to a lower D, as the soloist did. Also, the sopranos stay on the F-sharp on the phrase, "tidings to Zion." Find the *attacca* and the *tutti* in the following example:

HANDEL'S *Messiah*

What makes Handel's compositions so successful is that his part-writings are even interesting from a linear or melodic standpoint and pleasing within themselves, and they don't seem to "muddy" the texture when combined with other voices. Handel pays particular attention to the color and movement of the inner voices.

At the end of the piece, the violins swing us out with a full twelve measures' worth of sixteenth notes, as if they too are lifted up and the last note is suspended in air. The piece begins and ends in D major, but the tonality of *Messiah* turns to darkness with its B minor in the very next recitative, "For behold, darkness shall cover the earth."

CHAPTER TEN

"For behold, darkness shall cover the earth"

(RECITATIVE FOR BASS)

This chapter introduces Handel's genius use of chords in portraying the striking contrast between darkness (minor key) and light (major key).

For behold, darkness shall cover the earth,
and thick darkness the peoples;
But the Lord will arise upon you,
and His glory will be seen upon you.
And nations shall come to your light,
and kings to the brightness of your rising.
(Isaiah 60:2, 3 RSV)

This bass *recitative*, along with the following *aria*, are both beautiful examples of tone-painting—the imagery of light shining in the darkness. The theologian Marcus Borg tells us:

The symbolism of light and darkness is ancient, archetypal, and cross-cultural. It has many rich resonances of meaning. Darkness is associated with blindness, night, sleep, cold, gloom, despair, loneliness, chaos, death, danger, and yearning for the dawn. It is a striking image of the human condition. Light is seen as the antidote to the above and is thus an image of salvation. In the light, one is awake, able to see and find one's way; light is associated with relief and rejoicing that the night is over; in the light, one is safe and warm. In the light there is life.[1]

---

1 Marcus Borg and N. T. Wright, *The Meaning of Jesus: Two Visions* (New York: Harper-Collins Publications, 1999), 183.

This recitative begins in a B minor key with the gloomy, downward chords in the *basso-continuo*, suggesting the ominous sadness of the setting. The violins and viola play their sinister eight-note pattern of seconds, which sounds similar to the music in the movie *Jaws* when the shark is approaching in the water:[2] "da-dum, da-dum." Observe the opening musical pattern for the violins and viola below:

Even the strings seem to tremble as the bass soloist booms, "For behold, darkness shall cover the earth." These somber words are under the heading of "Poems of Glory of Jerusalem and of God's people," but what seems to be a hope*less* lament eventually is hope*ful* as it bids the fallen Zion to rise, shine, and reflect the glory of the Lord.[3]

> For behold, darkness shall cover the earth,
> and thick darkness the peoples.
> (Isaiah 60:2 RSV)

---

2 Leonard Van Camp, *A Practical Guide for Performing, Teaching & Singing* Messiah (Dayton, Ohio: Lorenz Corporation, Roger Dean Publishing Co., 1993), 5.

3 James Muilenburg, "The Book of Isaiah," *The Interpreter's Bible*, Vol. V (New York: Abingdon Press, 1956), 697.

The bass soloist enters on measure five:

Upon hearing the bass sing the words above, the listener is jolted into picturing darkness—even thick darkness—and imagines groping in that darkness. The darkness symbolizes judgment and unrighteousness, as well as life apart from God:

> But the Lord will arise upon you,
> and His glory will be seen upon you.
>
> (Isaiah 60:2 RSV)

God has called Israel, His covenant people, to bring light to the nations, who are groping in the darkness of ignorance. Handel's use of tone-painting portrays a somber tone; however, it is one that is not filled with pain, but hope. The whole verse accentuates the contrast between Zion and the rest of the world. In the thick darkness, God sheds forth His light upon Zion first.[4] The downward chords of the first strophe are now beginning to rise, coming up in a scale-like pattern on the word "arise," with the dawning kingdom of God. Again, Handel is brilliant in his use of the rising contour of the vocal line.

This is proud music, as the notes rise step by step, and the bass sings a *melisma* on the word "glory." Glorious light is representing fellowship with the holy God. In the final two-line strophe, we are told to be what God's presence in us exhibits—a brilliant light to the world:

---

4 Ibid., 698.

HANDEL'S *Messiah*

And *nations* shall come to your light,
and kings to the brightness of your rising.

(Isaiah 60:3 RSV)

The *King James Version* of the Bible uses the term "Gentiles" instead of "nations," thus saying, "The Gentiles shall come to your light." The *Scofield Reference Bible* tells us:

> The prophets connect the Gentiles with Christ in a threefold way: (1) As the Light, He brings salvation to the Gentiles, a distinctive feature of the church age; (2) as the Root of Jesse, He is to reign over the Gentiles in His kingdom; and (3) as believing Gentiles in the present age, together with believing Jews, they constitute "the church which is His body," in which the earthly distinction of Jew and Gentile disappears.[5]

The text chosen by Jennens and used by Handel prefers the use of this term "Gentiles." Observe the closing phrases below:

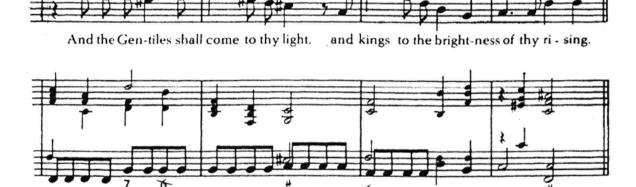

What started out as a song of lamentation has transcended to a brilliant climax in a strophe flooded with light. "And nations (or Gentiles) shall come to your light" means that "they should be greatly attracted to your light and joy." Then the bass soloist leaps an octave to a high C (in the above music score example) on the words, "And kings to the brightness of your rising," concluding the piece in the hopeful key of F-sharp major. Attracted by the resplendent radiance of the new Jerusalem, the nation—and even kings—stream into the Holy City. The darkness has found its answer in a word of hope: God will be glorified in the Israel and

---

5 Note taken from *The New Scofield Reference Bible*, Oxford, 1967, 747.

Gentile converts.[6] In the last chapter of Isaiah, the Lord says, "For I know their works and their thoughts, and I am coming to gather all nations and tongues, and they shall come and shall see my glory" (Isaiah 66:18 RSV).

The *Contemporary English Version* paraphrases the Scripture text for the *recitative* as follows:

> The earth and its people are covered with darkness,
> but the glory of the LORD is shining upon you.
> Nations and kings will come to the light of
> your dawning day.

For some people, the promise of God's mighty intervention could not only be a promise but may also appear to be a threat. Are they still living in darkness when the Light has been revealed, and yet they don't understand it, or are they afraid of it? John the Baptist, in his testimony, makes it clear that each of us is also called to testify to the light. Perhaps the church of today is still in that darkness and has not done its part in displaying the fullness of the Light. What are we waiting or hoping for in our future? What are our expectations?

Light and darkness are deep spiritual symbols. In the latter years of the twentieth century, our world observed the effects of the moral nihilism behind Fascist and Communist regimes; and in the twenty-first century we've seen the consequences of terrorism. In light of the natural disasters the world has recently experienced, one might feel that we are experiencing a time of pessimism and fear on this earth.

It is only through a strong faith in God that the Christian can face the tragic world of today. Yet the Christian's confidence also comes with a huge responsibility. The church is to be the bearer of God's self-revelation in Jesus Christ, and since that Light has been revealed, it is up to the church to arise and shine.

Faith has the potential to completely change the culture of a society. Is the church of Christ today ready to meet the challenge to be a light to the world? Do we know the reality of the great living truths of the faith that have the proven capacity to affect history and transform cultures as well as radically alter individual lives?[7] Os Guinness, in his book *The Call*, says that today's "followers of Jesus confront in the modern world the most powerful culture in human history so far, as well as the world's first truly global culture. This culture has unprecedented power to shape behavior."[8] So the responsibility is great. Arise . . . and shine!

---

6 Muilenburg, 698.
7 Os Guinness, *The Call* (Nashville, Tennessee: Thomas Nelson, Inc., 2003), 58.
8 Ibid., 56.

HANDEL'S *Messiah*

CHAPTER ELEVEN

"The people who walked in darkness"

(ARIA FOR BASS)

A journey from darkness into the light. This chapter delves into the use of the chromatic scale and modulation to explain Handel's movement from darkness into light.

The people who walked in darkness
have seen a great light;
Those who dwelt in a land of deep darkness,
on them has light shined.
(Isaiah 9:2 RSV)

Whenever Handel wishes to expand upon a theme, he composes an *aria* (Italian for "air") as he does in this *aria* for bass, expressing the dramatic contrast between darkness and light. The previous recitative ended on a beautiful F-sharp major chord, but it now dissipates into the gloomy B minor key in which "the people are walking in darkness," as if groping.

The music begins with a four-measure introduction by the orchestra. When the soloist begins to sing, the orchestra plays in octaves, with the *basso-continuo* imitating him. The main idea of the piece is not a melodic line, but a 4/4 meter rhythm that suggests people walking, with eight footsteps to each musical measure.

This piece illustrates Handel's brilliant sensitivity to key tonality as he moves from darkness to light in his modulation from the minor key to a major one with a progression of key changes. In measure 13, on the words, "have seen a great light," the music has modulated to a joyful D major. Another modulation to G major in measure 18 brightens our spirits even more. Finally, in measure 30, the listener feels the light shining, as the music has modulated even further to a gleaming A major.[1] Let's look at the beginning words, "The people that walked in darkness:"

The instrumental accompaniment is in unison with the bass soloist and both appear to be groping, as if hitting up against all obstacles. The bass continues singing, "And they that dwell in the land of the shadow of death." The soloist experiences a kind of vocal gymnastics, and the listener can almost feel the vibration of his low chest voice mirroring the depths of the people's darkness. Look at the groping notes in the following example:

---

1 Leonard Van Camp, *A Practical Guide for Performing, Teaching and Singing* Messiah (Dayton, Ohio: Lorenz Corporation, Roger Dean Publishing Co., 1993), 6.

The groping unison accompaniment changes to harmony, the concealment is arrested on the word "death," and the bass ends his *aria* by making a bold statement, "upon them hath the light shined," sung in harmony with the instruments.[2] Look at the ending:

In this *aria*, Handel exhibits many of his compositional skills. Regarding pure sound effect, his skill in word-painting to express darkness versus light could not be stronger. For mood effect, he wrote the music to press upward, steadily increasing in volume.

As Paul Henry Lang writes in his book, *George Frideric Handel,* "Melodic construction is the most difficult component of composition, the bold, broad, widely arching melody, the one with the 'long breath' being of particular difficulty . . . Handel the melodist is fascinatingly powerful."[3] Handel usually wrote his melodies in the diatonic scale, the scale with seven pitches commonly known to the Western world as "do-re-mi-fa-so-la-ti-(and repeating)do." In this piece, however, he uses the chromatic scale similar to that used by Johann Sebastian Bach in most of his compositions. This scale includes all of the twelve semitones, or the filling in of whole steps with half steps (as in playing both the black and the white keys on a piano). In this case, Handel uses this sinuously chromatic figure, the stepwise climbing and then falling, to enhance this feeling of searching.[4]

For a musical composition that was hastily written in just twenty-four days, this particular piece is intelligent in both its music and message.[5] The tone of the words matches the tone of the music, producing

2 Alfred Mann, ed., *Handel's* Messiah *in Full Score* (New York: Dover Publications, 1989), 217.
3 Paul Henry Lang, *George Frideric Handel* (New York: W. W. Norton, & Co., 1966), 328.
4 Joseph Machlis and Kristine Forney, eds., *The Enjoyment of Music,* 6th edition (New York: W. W. Norton & Co., 1990), 68.
5 Lang, 329.

great synergy. We definitely feel this movement from the minor to the major keys. We hear the words as they tell us that in God there is no darkness at all. When the nations finally come to Jerusalem's light, they should be illuminated with the knowledge of the Lord and His righteousness, and exhibit joy and hope.

The *Contemporary English Version* of the Bible paraphrases the text:

> Those who walked in the dark
> have seen a bright light.
> And it shines upon everyone
> who lives in the land of darkest shadows.

We have experienced a beginning of this dawning, and we welcome it to "break forth, O beauteous light." It does just that in the very next chorus, "For unto us a child is born," written in a bright major mood.

HANDEL'S

CHAPTER TWELVE

"For unto us a Child is born"

(CHORUS)

*What an incredible gift of a son!
An entire chorus devoted to
Isaiah's lofty names
for this anointed child!*

For unto us a child is born,
to us a son is given;
and the government will be
upon his shoulder,
and his name will be called
"Wonderful Counselor, Mighty God,
Everlasting Father, Prince of Peace."

(Isaiah 9:6 RSV)

George Frideric Handel

A re you one of the people for whom "For Unto Us" is your favorite *Messiah* chorus? Handel borrowed this bouncy theme from one of his own Italian opera duets, "No, di voi non vo fidarmi." Definitely one of the highlights of *Messiah,* this piece that begins and ends in G major in 4/4 meter is another major pillar in the construction of the oratorio. As we pass from *aria* to *recitative* and on to a chorus, the contrasts and careful placing of the large choral pillars serve as anchors of support for the drama, as this diagram shows:

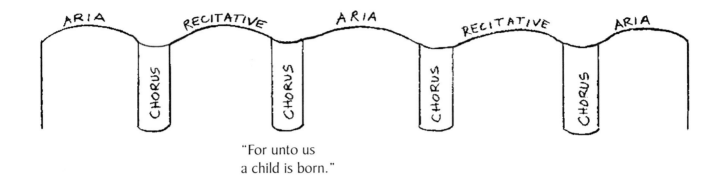

"For unto us
a child is born."

The orchestra begins with a six-measure introduction that brightens the atmosphere, especially after the preceding "darkness" *recitative* and *aria*. We can especially hear the joy in the violins as they are joined by the oboes, and this happiness is contagious as our own bodies begin to sway along with the sopranos when they enter singing, "For unto us a child is born."

Many times I have participated as one of the sopranos in the chorus. Years ago when I was a student at Westminster Choir College in Princeton, New Jersey, and singing under the conducting baton of Sir Colin Davis, he directed the choir members to "pretend you are some of the gossiping village people; you're so excited, and you can't keep a secret. Get your tickers going inside."

"For unto us a child is born" is a busy theme, for the melody line hops from note to note, requiring the singers to have buoyancy as well as verbal and vocal agility in order to be fluid on the runs. The florid melodies should be sung tenderly, with an effort to embrace the notes. The word "born" is first given importance in the soprano line, but later by each voice since it is sung as a *melisma*, or dramatic expansion of fifty-six notes (or fourteen groups of four sixteenth notes each). This requires a long breath or a "rationing" of one's breath supply. Observe the *melisma* that the basses sing below:

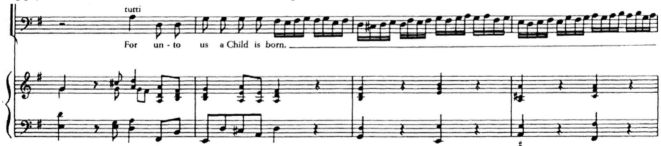

HANDEL'S *Messiah*

The altos, tenors, and basses each enter with precision on the attack of their particular phrases. This is a difficult chorus to sing, requiring that the singers be well rehearsed in the mechanics of vocal production and diction. The choir is instructed by the conductor to sing "For unto us" with a quiet "s" on "us"; then they are directed to omit the "r" on "born" in "a child is born" (pronounced "bohn").[1] All voices need to have flexibility and breath-support in order to maintain their pitch. This music is terrific! The melody just dances along, high and light, and is full of energy in all the voice parts.

The phrase, "And the government shall be upon his shoulder," begins as the tenors skip to a dotted rhythm, leading all the voices to pick up this rhythm. Handel has all four voices joining together in great harmony, with the *basso-continuo* ascending stepwise on an A major scale, causing all to explode on "Wonderful Counselor, the Mighty God, the Everlasting Father, the Prince of Peace" while the violins are dancing with glee on sixteenth notes. Look at the music below:

---

1 Leonard Van Camp, *A Practical Guide for Performing, Teaching, and Singing* Messiah (Dayton, Ohio: Lorenz Corporation, Roger Dean Publishing Co., 1993), 7.

When a composer wants a feeling of power, he or she turns from the *melismas* (expanding phrases), or polyphonic weaving, and draws the chorus up into tremendous vertical blocks of sound on such words as "Wonderful Counselor" and "Hallelujah." Handel is a genius in moving from polyphonic music to chordal texture in such a short space. He works with short, powerful motifs, often combining them in double counterpoint. In describing this piece in their book, *The Enjoyment of Music*, Machlis and Forney declare, "It is amazing how the elements of harmony, rhythm, and melody can all come together. These words peal forth in earth-shaking jubilation, yet with what economy of means the effect is achieved."[2]

> And his name will be called
> "Wonderful Counselor, Mighty God,
> Everlasting Father, Prince of Peace."
> (Isaiah 9:6b RSV)

This message demands big music and huge gestures. These are majestic names for God, and we get caught up in the pomp and glory as the choir punctuates the word, "Wonderful." Each name is followed by a rest in the music, which acts as an exclamation point. In the words of the text, we hear of a king whose lofty titles proclaim a new age of peace and justice. There are four titles for this king, not five. The comma between "Wonderful" and "Counselor" in the *King James Version* of the Bible is incorrect. The first two kingly names should read, "Wonderful Counselor" and "Almighty God," which indicate attributes of wisdom and might. The other two titles, "Everlasting Father" and "Prince of Peace," proclaim the nature of His rule.

These attributes of wisdom and might suggest a wonderful counselor who is far more wonderful than any sage or guru of today could be, for *He is Almighty God*. The other two attributes speak of the nature of His rule: "Everlasting Father" means a "father forever," who will constantly care for us with a love that neither time nor death can destroy. The title, "Prince of Peace," is especially attractive in that His type of kingdom is determined by the character of the King, and the glory of His reign will be justice and righteousness. God's plan was for us to be reconciled to Himself, and when we have this peace with God, we have peace in our hearts, and peace with each other. These four are only a few of the titles given to Christ that appear throughout the Scriptures. Other names for Christ that will turn up later include "Lord of Glory," "the Good Shepherd," "the Bread of Life," "Son of David," "King of Kings," and "the Lamb."

---

2 Joseph Machlis and Kristine Forney, eds., *The Enjoyment of Music*, 6th edition (New York: W. W. Norton & Co., 1990), 68.

HANDEL'S *Messiah*

The *Contemporary English Version* of the Bible offers us this paraphrase:

> A child has been born for us.
> We have been given a son who will be our ruler.
> His names will be Wonderful Advisor and Mighty God,
> Eternal Father, and Prince of Peace.
> His power will never end; peace will last forever.

Judaism, Christ's own faith tradition, did not recognize Jesus as the Messiah. To their credit, "They had such a high spiritual ideal of the divine monarch. If not, they might have hailed many a messiah for they had many great and good kings. But in the very purity of their ideal, they doomed themselves to disappointment."[3]

As Christians, we have a historical credo that views the Old Testament as the clue to the meaning of life, death, and resurrection of Jesus Christ. In Jesus, we have been given an impelling key to the meaning of the Old Testament. Thus, in Christ we see the Old Testament Scripture fulfilled, yet we know others don't see it that way. It is true that Jesus as the Christ was rejected and crucified. But this should come as no surprise to us, because the Scriptures are filled with stories of the people's sin and rebellion against God. The exegesis of the passage has been debated for a long time, and the question of kingship has even been posed: "Did Isaiah have a living monarch in mind when he cried, 'Unto us a son is born'"?[4]

As Christians, we look to God's redemptive action through history as the context in which His law is to be understood. Biblical theology must present the whole story. Today, we must approach biblical study with the attitude that this is God's intended revelation, along with the conviction that Israel's faith in its deeper dimensions is an integral part of our own faith through participation in the new Israel, of which we are members by faith in Jesus Christ.[5]

"For unto us a child is born" is a great piece to sing and a favorite of many, both for the listener and singer. Everyone feels the joy, the vibrancy, and the crisp tempo as exaltation seems to be bouncing off the walls. Unforgettable is the pomp and glory. These words, in their inspired use of music, truly express kingship—a kingship embodied in great hopes for the future.

---

3 R. B. Y. Scott, "The Book of Isaiah," *The Interpreter's Bible,* Vol. V (New York: Abingdon Press, 1956), 233.
4 Ibid., 234.
5 Ibid., 234.

Christianity has claimed these verses of Isaiah 9:1-7 for its own. This passage has become a hymn of faith, because to the Christian, phrase by phrase and line by line, all that Isaiah prophesied has been fulfilled in the birth of Jesus of Nazareth as the Son of God. And for two thousand years, the Christian church has taken these verses and sung this good news from God in thanksgiving to Him, "Unto us a child is born, unto us a son is given." Jesus Christ, the Prince of Peace, is the unspeakable gift.[6] The fact that God gave us His Son is truly incredible!

---

6 "Extreme Faith," *The Contemporary English Version of the Bible* (New York: American Bible Society, 1995), 703.

CHAPTER THIRTEEN

"Pastoral symphony"

(PIFA)

*Handel sets the pastoral scene....
as a tribute to the nameless,
common, everyday
people.*

George Frideric Handel

The "Pastoral symphony" is the only other totally orchestral piece of the oratorio besides the overture. It is generally thought that Handel copied this gentle melody he had heard thirty years earlier in Calabria and never forgotten.[1] Scholars think that Handel used the piece as a bridge to gracefully set the pastoral scene for the following three recitatives sung by the soprano, connecting words of promise of a child being born to words of fulfillment of that promise.

In this piece, Handel uses the muted strings to set the scene of the nativity. He definitely employs tone-painting and musical symbolism, since the purpose of his music is the expression of human feeling. Following this symphony, the soprano will tell us, the listeners, about the shepherds and the appearance of the angels to them. So with this piece, our minds can picture a peaceful, pastoral, bucolic setting.

---

1 Leonard Van Camp, *A Practical Guide for Performing, Teaching and Singing* Messiah (Dayton, Ohio: Lorenz, Roger Dean Publishing Co., 1993), 53.

The "Pastoral symphony" is marked *pifa* in the original score penned by Handel. This term refers to the Italian instrument known as the *piffaro*, a double-reed woodwind instrument like the shawm (or piva), which is a bagpipe of northern Italy.[2] The peaceful, gently flowing rhythm is marked as a dotted 12/8 meter, and its theme is taken from an Italian folk dance, played as a lilting *siciliana*.

Handel took his musical images from daily life around him, often using the simple folk songs of the country and the popular tunes of city life. The "Pastoral symphony" vividly recalls the music of the *pifferari*, the rural Italian peasants and shepherds from the Abruzzi region of Italy in the eighteenth century who would come down from the mountains to play their bagpipes in Rome every Christmas morning, imitating the arrival of the shepherds. They played on wind instruments, imitating a lullaby for the Christ child in a slow 6/8 meter.[3]

Was there more to the inclusion of this piece other than its simple function as a bridge between the Old Testament and the New Testament scriptures? Scholars question why Handel put this musical interlude into the oratorio. The Baroque era covered the years in European history from 1600-1750. As a time of conflicting currents of absolute monarchy and rising bourgeois power, it also included the sweeping religious movements called the Reformation and the Counter-Reformation. Excluded from the salons of the aristocracy, the middle class created a culture of their own by opening access to the arts to the general public. Perhaps the "Pastoral symphony" was included in *Messiah* as a tribute to the middle class.[4]

The performance of this *pifa* only lasts one minute. Handel himself was at the organ, playing the *basso-continuo*. Notice in the following score the inclusion of the phrase, *con fag.*, which means bassoons are added. Again, we see that the German name *Fagott* was used here to avoid using "B" for bassoon, which might be confused with the abbreviation for "the bass singers." The entire *Pifa* is shown here:

---

2 Ibid., 54.

3 Joseph Machlis and Kristine Forney, eds, *The Enjoyment of Music*, 6th edition (New York: W. W. Norton & Co., 1990), 133.

4 Milton Cross and David Ewen, *An Encyclopedia of the Great Composers, and Their Music*, Vol. 1 (New York: Doubleday & Co., 1953), 342.

Today, some performances of *Messiah* use larger orchestras that double the voices, and many concerts are enhanced by modern technology. Both of these methods enable the performances to be heard in the behemoth concert venues currently being constructed.

"There were shepherds abiding in the field"

(RECITATIVE FOR SOPRANO)

In three short sound bites, the soprano announces the birth of the Messiah, inaugurating a new era on the earth!

> There were shepherds . . .
> > And the angel said unto them, "Fear not'"
> > > . . . And suddenly there was with the angel . . ."
> > > > (Luke 2:8, 10, 13 KJV)

George Frideric Handel

These three *recitatives*, taken from the New Testament's gospel of Luke, are grouped as a trinity of chapters because they comprise the "infancy narrative" of *Messiah*. The evangelist Luke was chosen over the evangelist Matthew, even though both include the "Christmas" nativity in their gospels. Perhaps the reason Matthew's version wasn't chosen is that when he wrote his gospel, he worked from the Septuagint, a Greek mistranslation, written about AD 60 (a decade or two before Luke). In his gospel, Matthew stressed the genealogy, the arrival of the Wise Men, and the angelic annunciation made to Joseph, but he left out many of the specific details.[1]

In contrast, Luke placed emphasis on the shepherds and the angel's pronouncement to Mary. Perhaps Luke's gospel was chosen by the librettist due to the "common, everyday people" theme that was introduced in the "Pastoral symphony." (The other two gospels of Mark and John do not include the nativity story at all.) One might wish to ask Jennens why he chose one text over the other. It is notable that his magnificent compilation from the Bible manages to avoid the usual gospel Christmas narrative almost completely, except for the brief nativity section. He skips the stories of Mary (the mother of Jesus), her cousin Elizabeth (the

---

1 Walter Russell Bowie, "The Gospel According to St. Luke," *The Interpreter's Bible*, Vol. VIII (New York: Abingdon Press, 1956), 53.

mother of John the Baptist), and the three kings. He was only interested in the biblical verses having specific theological content. He even omits the verses that mention the manger.

The fact that the oratorio is called by the Old Testament word "Messiah" and not by the New Testament term "Christus" is the consequence of Jennens' particular theological preoccupation.[2] Ironically, an incidental advantage of the allusive and prophetic Old Testament text is that a non-believing performer and listener may find it easier to ignore the Christmas message than when listening to Bach's "Passions," for example.

Handel himself was a modestly religious man, but what counts here in *Messiah* is his understanding of how to express a vast range of instantly recognizable emotions in memorable music—an understanding refined in the course of writing forty operas. Handel was primarily a dramatic composer, and it shows from the oratorio's first chord to its final Amen. If "he did see the heavens open" (as he said at the end of his writing), perhaps it was because he was overwhelmed by the power of his own music.[3]

These three "sound-bite" *recitatives* should be studied together. Typical of *recitatives*, they cover a great deal of territory in just a few lines of music, taking us from point A to B rather quickly. They are pleasant sequences of the Christmas story. Even though the text omits Mary, Handel chose a female voice, representing the part of the angel, to sing the infancy narrative. This soprano solo is a very special moment in *Messiah*, for Handel has not yet had a soprano soloist sing. He typically used two or three different soprano soloists in a performance, one of whom (especially in this musical movement) might be a young boy.

In 1748, the famous impudent prima donna, soprano Francesca Cuzzoni, made an appearance in *Messiah* in England as one of the soloists. She had been a big star in Handel's operas in the 1720s.[4] Cuzzoni's strength was in the *cantabile* (meaning "singable, flowingly and clearly"), and she was known for her ability to express pathos and melancholy. She was prone to temper tantrums, and once refused to sing in the opera *Ottone,* so Handel threatened to drop her out of the window! Here, for our first sound-bite, the soprano sets the scene with these words taken from Luke's gospel:

> There were shepherds abiding in the field,
> keeping watch over their flock by night.
> And, lo, the angel of the Lord came upon them,
> and the glory of the Lord shone round about them:
> and they were sore afraid.
>
> (Luke 2:8-9 KJV)

2 Clifford Bartlett, ed., Messiah: *Full Score* (New York: Oxford University Press, 1998), v.
3 Ibid., vi.
4 David W. Barber, *Getting a Handle on Handel's* Messiah (Toronto, Canada: Sound & Vision Publishing Limited, 1994), 77.

CHAPTER 14 *There were shepherds abiding in the field* 103

Why did God choose lowly shepherds—of all people—to be surprised by His revelation, and not the scribes and Pharisees? And why did Jennens choose to include them in this magnificent libretto? In this first soprano *recitative*, Handel uses *stile rappresentativo* (representational style), which is the dramatic or theatrical style of *recitative* used in the earliest operas of the seventeenth century, based on the natural spoken inflections of the voice.

If we look at the following score, we'll notice that the first part of the *recitative* moves freely over a foundation of four simple chords. But immediately following them, the pace picks up in the accompanied *recitative* with rolling sixteenth notes on the words, "And lo, the angel." Handel invited the violoncello and bassoons to join him in playing the *basso-continuo* line to comprise the "senza rip." (doubling the bass line yet without the fuller orchestra). Handel was inventive with his change of pace—slow to fast, then surprising the listener with an immediate slower passage again.[5] Look at the first sound bite before we move on to the second:

5 Leonard Van Camp, *A Practical Guide for Performing, Teaching and Singing* Messiah (Dayton, Ohio: Lorenz, Roger Dean Publishing Co., 1993), 54.

"And the angel said unto them"

(RECITATIVE FOR SOPRANO)

George Frideric Handel

In these short *recitatives* the soprano soloist serves as narrator, driving the action forward, accompanied by rolling sixteenth notes. Professor Leonard Van Camp observes, "'And lo, the angel of the Lord came upon them' starts off slowly but then picks up. The exciting message should unfold with forward motion, energy, and expression. In the words 'the glory of the Lord,' we are reminded of the radiant light symbolizing divine revelation."[1] Later, he adds, "This is an example of a *recitative* where the text must propel the music ahead, rather than being a prisoner of a steady beat."[2] And moving ahead, it does just that as *Recitative* Fifteen continues with these words:

> And the angel said unto them, Fear not: for, behold,
> I bring you good tidings of great joy, which shall be to all people;
> for unto you is born this day in the city of David a savior, which is Christ the Lord.
>
> (Luke 2:10-11 KJV)

We hear these welcomed words of the angel's joyful announcement to the shepherds so often that the impact of them has worn off. What they were saying was this: A savior was actually born on earth. God was actually coming near to us, His creation, to be intimate with us. How could it be that the high, Almighty God would stoop so low? The phenomenon was so great that the world naturally

---

1 Leonard Van Camp, *A Practical Guide for Performing, Teaching and Singing* Messiah (Dayton, Ohio: Lorenz, Roger Dean Publishing Co., 1993), 55.
2 Ibid., 56.

would have expected to have it framed in some mighty extravaganza—some huge episode. Instead, there was a stripping away of all of the world's pride by the immense simplicity of God. This birth was of a little child unnoticed in the stable of a nondescript town. It was in simplicity and lowliness that the life of Jesus began. The simple, smelly, sleepy shepherds were told of it first, and they reacted immediately.[3]

The Reverend Jack Hayford says:

> We can imagine the shepherds saying to Mary and Joseph when they finally arrive at the manger, "We don't know how to tell you this, but we heard angels tell us that we would find you here. Please don't think we're crazy." Then the shepherds immediately return to their homeland glorifying and praising God, perhaps as the forerunners of the Christian missionary or evangelical movement.[4]

These three *recitatives* comprise the verses regarding the story of the birth of the incarnate Son of God. He who was larger than the entire universe became a tiny baby. The due time was now! How long the people had waited for the promised Messiah! The spiritual darkness, which had covered the earth for four thousand years, was about to be rolled away. The way to forgiveness and peace with God was about to be opened to all people. This was definitely good tidings, or good news, for all people, which implied that everyone in Israel would be affected. Luke intended for the angel's announcement to underscore this universalism of his gospel.[5] The news was so good that we could not keep it quiet or not tell others about it! God had actually done it! What an interesting way of saving our lives!

In one short sentence, the angel has pronounced three mighty claims. The angel speaks of a *Savior, which is Christ the Lord.* (God is called "savior" in Isaiah 43:3 and 5:15.) Not only is Jesus called "savior," but He is also called "the Christ" and "Lord." Observe the music of *Recitative* Fifteen below:

---

3 Walter Russell Bowie, "The Gospel According to St. Luke," *The Interpreter's Bible,* Vol. VIII (New York: Abingdon Press, 1956), 54.

2 The Rev. Jack Hayford, sermon delivered on the Trinity Broadcasting Network, n.d., 2006.

3 Bowie, 53.

"And suddenly there was with the angel"

(RECITATIVE FOR SOPRANO)

In the following *Recitative* Sixteen, with three long measures of sixteenth notes in the accompaniment, the soprano suddenly enters with these words:

> And suddenly, there was with the angel a multitude
> of the heavenly host, praising God and saying:
>
> (Luke 2:13 RSV)

Handel surprises the listener again with a tempo change, heightening the anticipation. The birth of the Messiah that had been announced a few verses earlier causes rejoicing among God's entire host of angels, just when the shepherds had thought they had seen it all. The soprano soloist, as the radiant and glorious angel, carries the listeners along with her as the tempo accelerates to the soaring high "A" as she floats her phrase on "praising God, and saying," bringing her *recitative* to a strong conclusion. Even the music is excited as it leaps from high to low. Handel wrote this music with a burst of *crescendo*, exhibited by the entire chorus responding with "Glory to God" in the next chorus.[1]

The Christmas narrative, or the birth of the Savior, is not just a story we read every year, but it is also a reality. And the Holy Spirit's role in conception is extremely important, so much that it began to be recited

---

4 Clifford Bartlett, ed., Messiah: *Full Score* (New York: Oxford University Press, 1998), vi.

in the creeds of the Christians by the second century. Observe the following score of *Recitative* Sixteen, which completes our three short sound bites, preparing us for the next choral response, "Glory to God:"

HANDEL'S *Messiah*

CHAPTER SEVENTEEN

"Glory to God"

(CHORUS)

*This chorus represents a multitude singing
in shimmering beauty and splendor
. . . resplendence!*

Glory to God in the highest, and on earth
peace among men with whom he is pleased!
(Luke 2:14 RSV)

George Frideric Handel

This lovely piece in D major, 4/4 time, begins rather abruptly, as the preceding soprano announcement declared, "There was with the angel a multitude of the heavenly host, praising God and saying . . . 'Glory to God.'" It is as if God's multitude of angels arrives, and this angelic chorus all responds with a resounding YES.[1]

The very first word, "glory," is sung as if by a thousand angels with round vowels and puffy cheeks. A vision of Christmas-card perfect round mouths actually helps choir members to pronounce the "glow" of "glory" with perfect articulation.[2]

---

5 Leonard Van Camp, *A Practical Guide for Performing, Teaching and Singing* Messiah (Dayton, Ohio: Lorenz, Roger Dean Publishing Co., 1993), 57.
6 Ibid., 58.

Quite naturally, most choirs would want to announce good tidings in a bright *fortissimo* (very loudly), yet Handel intended a rather quiet beginning for this piece. In the original score, he marked the trumpets, *da Lontano e un poco piano* (as from a distance, and rather softly.) He wanted an entrance as if from afar, or a gradual approach. The trumpet players, according to Handel's instructions, were meant to actually play offstage. Because of this, they must be tuned carefully and able to see the conductor's upbeat. It is the first time Handel calls for trumpets in *Messiah*.[3] Observe the trumpets indicated in the following score:

The entire text for this chorus is:

> "Glory to God in the highest, and on earth peace
> among men with whom he is pleased!"

(Luke 2:14 RSV)

---

7 Ibid., 57.

HANDEL'S *Messiah*

In the text taken from the gospel of Luke, notice the order of the two-fold proclamation. "Peace" is mentioned second, and "Glory to God" is first. This first message, the "Gloria in Excelsis," is a messianic acclamation that anticipates God's glory in heaven and inaugurates a new era on earth. The second message, "And peace on earth," can be understood in the light of its Hebrew counterpart of "shalom" and paraphrased, "salvation." Some translations interpret "peace" as "good will toward men," while others say "peace among men with whom He is pleased" (or with whom He favors).[4]

Why should peace come second? Isn't peace a prime goal in our hectic lives? There are tons of self-help books on the market for finding peace in one's life, peace of mind, peace in relationships, and peace in the world. Yet even though peace may be the climax or goal of one's great hope, it is certainly not the beginning. The beginning must be in the adoration of God Himself; from Him everything else flows. Our peace cannot come from our human efforts, but only from God through His grace.[5]

Today, we must open our minds and hearts in thankfulness for what God has given us in Christ before we can hope that the trials, hardships, and distractions within our lives will fall into place, thereby giving us a peace that cannot be destroyed—a peace that transcends all understanding. It is through the Christian gospel that people today grasp a need for a response and are able to exclaim, "Glory to God in the highest!" We can respond to God as a violin responds to the bow of the master. We can experience a new level of God's grace by opening our souls and entertaining the "glory of God."

As the chorus progresses, the sopranos and altos are singing, "Glory to God," while the tenors and basses graciously reassure us in reply, "Yes, and peace on earth." The conductor, Sir Colin Davis, requested that the men sing "not like policemen, but like archangels with a blessing!"[6] Peace is a joyous and promising message.

Look closely at the following score:

---

8 Walter Russell Bowie, "The Gospel According to St. Luke,"55. *The Interpreter's Bible,* Vol. VIII (New York: Abingdon Press, 1956), 55.
9 Bowie, 55.
10 Van Camp., 58.

Handel raised the subdominant (the G-sharp in the violins) in order to establish the dominant harmony. This occurs immediately before the tenors and basses leap down an octave on "And peace on earth." Then the joyful *fugue*-like entrances begin and "goodwill" is tossed from singer to singer.[7] This goodwill is intended for all people of the Christian community. The phrase, "among men with whom he is pleased," or "for men whom he favours," is addressing all people of God's good pleasure. The words are not restricting the peace to just the nation of Israel; Luke intends this blessing for all in the Christian community.[8] Let's look at the final measures of this piece:

1 Ibid., 58.

2 Bowie, 56.

HANDEL'S *Messiah*

The end of the piece highlights the sopranos' stepwise singing of "good will," with all the other voices and instruments nodding in agreement. Then, the angels and trumpeters disappear quietly together, leaving the violins, violas, and *basso-continuo* to end the piece on a *pianissimo* (very softly) as if they've left the scene in awe. (Remember, they had entered the piece "from afar.")

The year 1685 was an incredible one for musicians. Two of the greatest composers were born within months of each other: George Frideric Handel and Johann Sebastian Bach. Dominico Scarlatti was also born that year. All three were keyboard composers and giants in the late Baroque style. It is ironic that Bach and Handel never met; they missed overlapping with each other's schedule in London by one day. Handel and Scarlatti, however, became friends during Handel's Italian years.

In his book, *The Lives of the Great Composers,* Harold Schonberg concludes:

> Handel, a musical giant in his own right, did not have Bach's harmonic ingenuity or mastery of counterpoint, but his harmonies are still confident and secure. The incredible Bach *thought* contrapuntally as naturally and inevitably as he breathed. Handel used a freer, less textbookish kind of counterpoint only as a tool for certain effects.[9]

3 Harold Schonberg, ed., *The Lives of the Great Composers,* 3rd edition (New York: W. W. Norton & Co., 1970), 48.

HANDEL'S *Messiah*

CHAPTER EIGHTEEN

"Rejoice greatly, O daughter of Zion"

(ARIA FOR SOPRANO)

*The soprano's rejoicing is spontaneous, stressing that
"He surely is the righteous Savior."*

George Frideric Handel

Composers would frequently write *arias*, self-contained compositions within an opera, when they wanted to expound on a particular theme in their larger works. Such is the case here with the theme of rejoicing. An exalted joy is established at the very outset of this soprano *aria* by the leaping motif played by the violins, which are "rejoicing greatly" with their sixteenth notes and trills. The soprano herself seems to be as light and limber as a dancer leaping for joy, and the challenge demands a technical agility.[1]

The text for *Messiah* has taken us from the brief "nativity passages" back to the Old Testament with its prophecy from the priest Zechariah, a member of the tribe of Levi who began his prophetic ministry circa 520 BC, soon after the prophet Haggai and the time of the rebuilding of the temple.[2] The Scripture passage for this *aria* is:

---

4 Leonard Van Camp, *A Practical Guide for Performing, Teaching and Singing* Messiah (Dayton, Ohio: Lorenz, Roger Dean Publishing Co., 1993), 60.
5 Guthrie Note from *Nelson's NKJV Study Bible*, copyright ©1997 by Thomas Nelson, Inc. Used by permission.

Rejoice greatly, O daughter of Zion!
Shout aloud, O daughter of Jerusalem.
Lo, your king comes to you;
triumphant and victorious is he,
humble and riding on an ass,
on a colt, the foal of an ass.

I will cut off the chariot from Ephraim
and the war horse from Jerusalem;
and the battle bow shall be cut off,
and he shall command peace to the nations;
his dominion shall be from sea to sea,
and from the River to the ends of the earth.

(Zechariah 9:9, 10 RSV)

Robert Dentan, in his commentary in *The Interpreter's Bible*, tells us:

This oracle in Zechariah 9 was probably inspired by the Fall of Persia before the advancing armies of Alexander the Great (about 333 BC); and the prediction of, and the future universal reign of the messianic King. Alexander had administered a decisive defeat to Darius, the Persian emperor, at the Battle of the Issus in southeastern Asia Minor in October, 333 BC. Instead of immediately pursuing Darius toward the east, the conqueror moved south through Syria, with the aim of first seizing Egypt from the Persians. Within the year all Syria was in his hands and shortly afterward Egypt fell without a struggle.

These are among the most important events in world history, and the little Jewish community in Jerusalem, located in the hills a few miles east of Alexander's line of march, saw in them the working of the mighty hand of God. The prophet Zechariah sees in the triumphant advance of the Greek armies the beginnings of the Messianic Age, so these verses have a vital meaning for New Testament interpreters today."[3]

---

6 Robert C. Dentan, "The Book of Zechariah," *The Interpreter's Bible,* Vol. VI (New York: Abingdon Press, 1956), 1095.

In short, this was a vital Scripture passage for the librettist to have chosen. Up until this point in Handel's *Messiah*, we have experienced God's gift of a Son to us, then basked in all of His resplendent glory, and now we are celebrating the inauguration of the Messianic Age!

In these verses, we find a sobering reminder to Jerusalem, the ancient city filled with profound symbolism and history, as well as a connection with Jesus' triumphal entry into Jerusalem, where He arrives riding humbly on a colt of a donkey. (The donkey was the mount of princes and kings.) Yet He is victorious! Now, however, we must concentrate on this "messianic kingship" in its Old Testament context. The prophet Zechariah sees the army of Alexander the Great as only a tool in the hand of God. In his exegesis in *The Interpreter's Bible*, Robert C. Dentan tells us, "Riding invisibly with the colt is the God of Israel, and the long-expected Prince of Peace, who is about to enter Jerusalem and re-establish both the geographical borders and the spiritual glories of the ancient kingdom of David."[4] In this *aria*, the soprano soloist is summoning her sisters in the faith to:

> Rejoice greatly, O daughter of Zion
> Shout aloud, O daughter of Jerusalem.
> (Zechariah 9:9 RSV)

This happy *aria* for soprano begins in B flat major; but soon into the piece, Handel raises the subdominant to establish the dominant harmony. Notice the E flat raised to an E natural in the measures below:[5]

7 Ibid., 1096.
8 Alfred Mann, ed., *Handel's* Messiah *in Full Score* (New York: Dover Publications, 1989), 218.

The rejoicing is spontaneous as the soprano sings several spirited little runs. The original version of this *aria* was written in two different time signatures! This was obviously due to Handel's haste in composing. The violin and soprano parts contained triplet patterns throughout and were marked as 12/8 time, yet the *basso-continuo* part was written in 4/4. So, in 1749, Handel made corrections himself to our present version in 4/4, which is even reduced in length.[6]

The next words of the text, "Behold thy King cometh unto thee," are predicting the triumphal entry of Christ into Jerusalem, coming as a humble and peaceful monarch, linking humility and victory, as the descending yet reverent music indicates.

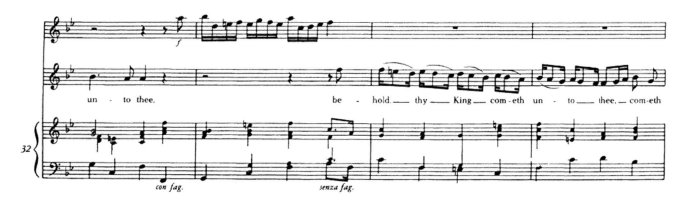

The following three lines from the biblical text were not included in Jennens' libretto, yet the profound theological dimension of these next few verses should not be overlooked. Today, differing religious worldviews do not comprehend the thorough profundity of the incarnate Jesus. The fact that He came into the world as a human and transformed the very nature of history, society, and culture is HUGE. He turned the world upside down![7]

> Triumphant and victorious is he,
> humble and riding on an ass,
> on a colt, the foal of an ass.
> (Zechariah 9:9 RSV)

---

1 Van Camp, 61.
2 Dentan, 1095.

HANDEL'S

The *Contemporary English Version* paraphrases the words as follows:

> Everyone in Jerusalem, celebrate and shout!
> Your king has won a victory, and he is coming to you.
> He is humble and rides on a donkey;
> He comes on the colt of a donkey.

Unfortunately, Charles Jennens omitted the reference to "humble and riding on a donkey." This definitely reminds Christians of Jesus' triumphal ride into Jerusalem on the first Palm Sunday. Their long-expected king is coming victoriously, even though He is not a warrior, or riding upon a war horse—but upon the very beast that symbolizes a nation at peace . . . a donkey. The use of the word "triumphant," which literally means "righteous," is a mark of the suffering servant of the Lord. He is "humble" in the sense of being oppressed, humiliated, poor, and lowly.[8] This concept of the donkey is particularly important to Christians—both Matthew 21:1-6 and John 12:14-15 mention this passage—because it clearly illustrates the fulfillment of the prophecies regarding Jesus' ministry. The suffering and rejection aspects of the Messiah's role are the very themes that set Jesus apart from the popular idea of a conquering and powerful political messiah expected during His lifetime.

The allusion to Genesis 49:10 and 11 is clear: "The scepter shall not depart from Judah . . . ." along with "Binding his foal to the vine and his donkey's colt to the choice vine . . ." and "Judah will produce a mysterious ruler, who is not a worldly conqueror but will maintain His right by peaceful means." The contrast is strongly marked between the ass and the war horse, the emblems of peace and war, respectively.[9]

These verses in Zechariah's prophecy include an important transition. The arrival of the saving King is followed by a description of the effects of His long-term reign. Viewed from the broader context of prophecy, Zechariah was combining two stages in God's plan together that are actually separate in time. The coming King would arrive twice. Jesus came first as a humble king of peace and salvation, manifested in His earthly ministry and death on the cross. Second, Jesus will come as a victorious ruler over all the world who will speak peace to the nations, thus fulfilling Zechariah's prophecy.[10] In the awesome "D" section of this *aria*, the mood changes and becomes slower.

---

3 Guthrie, Motyer, Stibbs, and Wiseman, eds., *The New Bible Commentary, Revised* (Grand Rapids, Michigan: Eerdmans Publishing Company, 1970), 795.

4 Ibid, 795.

5 Note from *Nelson's New King James Version Study Bible*, 1547.

In measure 58, we come to the key word "Savior." Indeed, Yahweh is unique in His saving power; there is none other who can save. This is why the title "Savior" is related to the other eschatological names that reveal God's compassion and intimate attitude toward Israel. When God comes to redeem His people from their bondage, He comes as their peaceful comforter.[11] These words suggest that in the messianic age, all "weapons of mass destruction," as the war horse represents, will be banished. This section of the *aria* contrasts sharply, and its chromatic passing-note tones slow down on the reverent words, "He is the righteous Savior, and He shall speak peace unto the heathen." Observe the passing-note tones in measure 57 of the score above on the word "righteous."

Soon the soprano returns to the tempo she sang at the beginning of the piece, making this a *da capo aria*, (as the form is ABA), which means that the singer performs all of the musical material and then returns to the first "A" section. Again, the soprano calls the women of Zion to rejoice, all the way to the end. This *coloratura* passage requires agility and flexibility in its execution. For the soprano, the *tessitura*, or the area of concentration of notes, can sometimes be in the stratospheric range. Thus, a lighter voice can glide effortlessly from note to note, floating easier than a heavier voice.[12] The flight of notes is highlighted by a fifty-note *melisma*. Look at the following score:

6 Dentan, 1096.
1 Van Camp, 61.

Later, after the soloist valiantly sings her adagio (slower) ending, the strings quickly dash off with the main theme to their gracious cadence. Beginning with chapter eighteen (and moving to the end of Part the First with chapter twenty-one), we hear four different biblical passages that relate to Christ's ministry on earth prior to Holy Week. Chapter eighteen speaks of the King who brings peace; chapter nineteen speaks of the healing of the sick; chapter twenty (A) tells us about the Shepherd who leads His flock; and chapters twenty (B) and twenty-one speak of the Savior who gives rest and offers an easy yoke, as well as a light burden.[13]

So we come to the conclusion of this soprano *aria,* "Rejoice greatly." We too have a lot to rejoice and be hopeful about. We rejoice that Jesus lived among us, that He is our healer, and that He is our redeemer. No piece celebrates more clearly the message of joy and praise over the birth of the King of Kings than this *aria* written by Handel, in which the music is marked with enthusiasm and joy throughout. We are reminded by St. Paul in Ephesians 5:18-19, "Be filled with the spirit, as you sing psalms and hymns and spiritual songs" and . . . oratorios.

---

2 Ibid., 62.

CHAPTER NINETEEN

"Then shall the eyes of the blind be opened"

(RECITATIVE FOR ALTO)

Miraculous healings!

With great emotional fervor, the alto sings of God's miraculous power as the deliverer and spiritual healer of His helpless people.

George Frideric Handel

This lovely *recitative* predicting healing miracles represents the variety and beauty of the *arias* and *recitatives* in *Messiah*. Again we hear the alto soloist, from whom we have heard only a similarly miraculous prediction of a virgin birth in chapter eight's, "Behold, a virgin shall conceive." This *recitative* was originally written for the soprano to sing, but Handel made revisions in the first few performances of *Messiah*, and now we have this lovely melody line sung by the alto voice. This change from soprano to alto shows Handel's kind concern for balance in his distribution of the vocal parts.[1] The text is as follows:

> Then shall the eyes of the blind be opened,
> and the ears of the deaf shall be unstopped;
> Then shall the lame man leap as an hart,
> and the tongue of the dumb sing.
>
> (Isaiah 35:5, 6 KJV)

---

3 Leonard Van Camp, *A Practical Guide for Performing, Teaching and Singing* Messiah (Dayton, Ohio: Lorenz, Roger Dean Publishing Co., 1990), 63.

Not only are the words of these verses powerful within themselves, but the music applied to the words also gives the text great emotional power. The listener will notice the vivid imagery of the physical disabilities of the blind, the deaf, the lame, and the dumb and their expected miracles—four parallel descriptions of God's miraculous healing power. The piece is a brief eight measures in length, with a simple *basso-continuo* accompaniment. The *recitative* is written in the dramatic *stile rappresentativo*, which is characterized by freedom of rhythm and irregularity of phrasing.[2] The B flat chord of the previous piece would ordinarily indicate moving to G major, but we end up in A major for this recitative. This, in turn, gives way to the unexpected key of F major[3] in the next *aria*, "He shall feed His flock." Observe the *basso-continuo* in the entire *recitative* below:

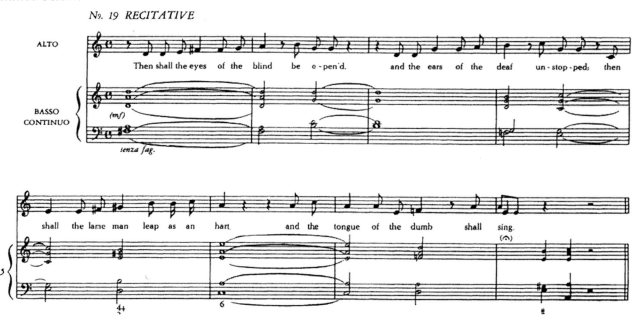

It is interesting to note again that this is an oratorio, a musical presentation that does not have any embellishments of scenery or costumes. But sometimes without these embellishments, we ignore the dramatic situation as if there is no plot. This is not the case here because a major story is being told. In this oratorio, none of the singers is given a title or character name, so we do not get into personalities or particular characters. In *Messiah*, Handel, along with help from his librettist, Charles Jennens, brilliantly presents the concept of the complete picture by telling the whole story of salvation.

---

4 Don Michael Randel, ed. *The Harvard Dictionary of Music,* 4th edition (Cambridge, Massachusetts: Harvard University Press, 2003), 840.

5 Van Camp, 63.

The *Contemporary English Version* of the Bible joyfully declares:

> The blind will see, and the ears of the deaf will be healed.
> Those who were lame will leap around like deer;
> tongues once silent will begin to shout.
>
> (Isaiah 35:5, 6)

Biblical scholar R. B. Y. Scott observes:

> The message, addressed to the blind and dumb, encourages the weak and the fearful. It gives them the hope of God working miracles of physical healing in their bodies, and spiritual healings in their souls. God is manifesting His power and glory as the deliverer of His helpless people, and is looking forward to a joyful return of His people to Zion.
>
> We, who at times are weak and fearful, can identify with those to whom this passage is addressed. God has prepared an open highway, through what has been an arid and trackless desert. We, today's pilgrims, are to take the highroad, where there is no common traffic and no threat of death. It is the ransomed people of the Lord who crowd that highway, singing with great joy as they draw near to Zion. Surely it is the most helpless of the exiles who will have the greatest cause to praise God. Those of us who are in need of spiritual healings can be comforted with these words.
>
> This is a theme of great joy; the sun has risen, and sorrow and sighing shall flee away. And as Isaiah 35:10 says, "The redeemed of the Lord shall return with singing." There shall be an upsurge of hope, and spiritual healings shall take place which shall enable all to see God's truth, hear His voice, and walk in His ways.[4]

This *recitative* is a grand climax to the sorrows that come just before the people are restored and the Lord is gloriously manifested. It is the darkness before the dawn. It describes the second of the four consecutive passages, chosen by the Handel's librettist, Charles Jennens, which speak of Christ's ministry on earth prior to Holy Week. As prayerful Christians, we can encourage and comfort people who are truly hurting by reassuring them that their deliverance is coming soon. After all, didn't our Lord tell the paralyzed to get up and walk!

6 R. B. Y. Scott, "The Book of Isaiah," *The Interpreter's Bible*, Vol. V (New York: Abingdon Press, 1956), 359.

Handel's *Messiah*

CHAPTER TWENTY (A & B)

"He shall feed His flock like a shepherd"

(ARIA FOR ALTO)

"Come unto Him, all ye that labour, and are heavy laden"

(ARIA FOR SOPRANO)

This much-loved aria, shared by the alto and soprano, is a gentle invitation to be comforted by God as our shepherd.

George Frideric Handel

S ome people consider this *aria*, shared by the alto and soprano, to be the most beautiful one in *Messiah*. It is similar to the "Pastoral symphony" in its quiet spirit and tone, and is marked *largetto e piano* (slow and quiet). The pastoral rhythm of 12/8 meter is most comforting with its gentle, swaying lilt.

Along with the preceding *recitative*, "Then shall the eyes of the blind," this *aria* was also intended to be entirely sung by the soprano, but Handel changed it to give the alto more to sing. Handel actually wrote the alto part on a page and inserted it in front of the original version. The insert ends with measure 25, and copyist John Christopher Smith drew a large arrow to measure 26, marking the name of the soprano soloist "Frasi" on the score (referring to the soprano Giulia Frasi, who lived from 1740-1772).[1]

---

1 Alfred Mann, ed., *Handel's* Messiah *in Full Score* (New York: Dover Publications, 1989), 219.

This *aria* is sung first in F major by the alto, then raised up a fourth to B flat major for the soprano. The librettist Jennens has cleverly combined the Old Testament in Isaiah 40:11 with the New Testament verse in Matthew 11:28 in this one movement.

The alto enters, singing her tender, carefree melody with these consoling words:

> He shall feed His flock like a shepherd,
> and he shall gather the lambs with His arm
> and carry them in His bosom,
> and gently lead those that are with young.
>
> (Isaiah 40:11 KJV)

These words welcome us into God's mighty arm, which before was figuratively raised in triumph, but is now lowered in compassion. Yahweh, as the Shepherd, leads His exiles home just as the shepherd leads his sheep, and He especially gathers the young lambs who are vulnerable and unable to follow where He leads. He guides us, as His sheep, to quiet waters.[2] This Good Shepherd image exhibits God's tenderness, His protection and nourishment of His sheep, and how He leads us in His right paths beside still waters, restoring our souls. These words are similar in tone to the words the tenor soloist sang at the very beginning of *Messiah* when he pleaded, "Comfort ye, My people." God continues to nurture and gather His lambs, as the soprano takes over singing this great invitation from the New Testament:

> Come unto Him all ye who labor and are heavy laden,
> And He will give you rest. Take His yoke upon you, and
> learn from Him; for He is meek and lowly in heart,
> and ye shall find rest unto your souls.
>
> (Matthew 11:28-29 KJV)

When first spoken, these words were addressed to those who labored and were heavy laden because of the works of the Law—burdens placed upon them by the scribes. Yet Psalm 119:24 tells us that following the law should not be a burden, but "should be a delight and a protection against evil."[3]

---

2 James Muilenburg, "The Book of Isaiah," *The Interpreter's Bible*, Vol. V (New York: Abingdon Press, 1956), 433.
3 Ibid., 434.

HANDEL'S *Messiah*

But at this time in biblical history, the rules of priestly purity within the Pharisaic religion were being placed upon all people, not just the priests. The rabbis often spoke of the "yoke of the law," and the people to whom Jesus spoke were already figuratively wearing a yoke.[4] (Even today, some people might feel the burden of the Ten Commandments upon them as a yoke in their twenty-first century lives.) Noted biblical scholar William Hendricksen observes, "In Jewish literature, a 'yoke' represents the sum total of obligations which, according to the teachings of the rabbis, a person must take upon himself . . . because of their misinterpretation, alteration and augmentation of God's holy law, the yoke which the rabbis placed upon the shoulders of the people was that of a totally unwarranted legalism."[5]

The symbol of the yoke was familiar in their day, for the beasts wore yokes in order to carry out their work of bearing loads. And perhaps Jesus, as a carpenter, even made yokes for the oxen owned by the villagers. Hendricksen goes on to say:

> When Jesus spoke of the yoke, he meant to put off the yoke of earthly things. Jesus contrasted the heavy yoke, or the weight of the Law, with the genuine joy of being a disciple. When Jesus says, "Take my yoke upon you and learn from me,"….he means to "Accept my teaching, namely that a person is saved by means of simple trust in me…" Symbolically speaking, Jesus here assures the oppressed people whom he addresses that his yoke is kindly and his burden is light. Jesus' yoke was a simple following of the Old Testament law as interpreted by him in a prophetic new spirit. What Jesus is really saying is that a simple trust in him and obedience to his commands, out of gratitude for the salvation already imparted by him, is delightful. His yoke emphasized justice, mercy, and the love of God. The words uttered by Jesus are a great *invitation* to accept the commandments, not as a demand, but as an act of voluntary obedience.[6]

Following Jesus' law required an attitude of faith for which the benefits were grace and freedom, with a yoke of love. His way becomes easy and light, and in it, we find rest.

The actual yoke was a crossbar with two U-shaped pieces that encircle the necks of a pair of oxen, trained to work together, and sharing equal loads, as in a bond. The soprano soloist has invited us to "take on

4 Samuel Johnson, "The Gospel According to St. Matthew," *The Interpreter's Bible*, Vol. VII (New York: Abingdon Press, 1956), 389.
5 William Hendricksen, *The Gospel of Matthew* (Grand Rapids, Michigan: Baker Book House, 1973), 504.
6 Ibid., 505.

the yoke." Yes, His yoke does demand something, as it is a symbol of subjugation, bondage, or servitude. Yet, strangely, when we give our life to Christ, this becomes a positive thing; those burdens are shared with Him on the other side of the double yoke, so they become easy and light. Thank God that these words can also be a message of reassurance that He will intervene, promising "rest to the heavy-laden." What good news!

What gives with this reference to "sheep"? And who among us wants to be compared to a sheep? There's more to come in chapter twenty-six, "All we like sheep." How does it feel to be called a sheep? Well, it's not very flattering for humans to be compared with these smelly animals. What could we possibly do that would resemble the behavior patterns of sheep? We don't wish to think of ourselves as stubborn, wayward followers, or even turning "every one to his or her own way." But the parallel use of this figurative language is accepted and even reassuring because we can trust our Shepherd. Christ brings quietness, serenity, strength, and calm in the face of our frustrations and futility. He has a tremendous compassion for the contrary sheep-like creatures that He has made.

The *Contemporary English Version* of the Bible paraphrases these two texts:

> The LORD cares for his nation, just as shepherds care
> for their flocks. He carries the lambs in his arms,
> while gently leading the mother sheep.
>
> (Isaiah 40:11)

> "If you are tired from carrying heavy burdens, come to me and
> I will give you rest. Take the yoke I give you. Put it on your
> shoulders and learn from me. I am gentle and humble, and you
> will find rest."
>
> (Matthew 11:28-29)

Musically, "Take His yoke upon you" is a sequence of slowly changing rich harmonies; spiritually, "Take His yoke upon you" is an invitation to discipleship, as well as an acceptance of His commandments. It is surrendering, or accepting a quietness of spirit in submitting to the Father's will, which promises rest to the heavy-laden. We don't have to do it on our own . . . for, by doing so, "what needless pain we bear!" Accept the rest that is offered. Accept with humility the burden that is lighter and easier than anything we could ever do on our own.

HANDEL'S *Messiah*

This piece, which lasts almost six minutes, is the longest musical piece in Part the First of *Messiah*. This movement in chapter twenty and the following in chapter twenty-one (the last musical piece in Part the First) should be connected with no pause as Handel indicated (in his original score) with *segue il coro*. Observe the final stanza below:

"His yoke is easy"

(CHORUS)

The tossing of the melody from voice to voice in this chorus suggests the lightness of Christ's yoke of faith, love, and freedom.

Through the music of *Messiah*, we are able to participate—in a new way—in the life of the Savior and at the outset we can identify with the prophets, the lowly shepherds, and even, sheep! Indeed, through Handel's music in a unique way, the Messiah of the world is made "flesh and walks among us."[1]

In the preceding chapter, the soprano has just told us to "Take His yoke upon [us]," and now the chorus sings, "His yoke is easy." George Frideric Handel was a genius in using continuity of spirit and musical ideas. Not only does he expand on the concept of "the yoke," but he also allows the soprano to prepare the key change for the chorus' entrance by moving to a B flat major key, the exact key of this chorus.

In the preceding chapter, the soprano's "Come unto Him" had a gentle rocking 12/8 meter. Now the rhythm becomes a strict 4/4 tempo, marked *allegro* (lively) as the sopranos enter on the phrase, "His yoke is easy, His burthen is light," the text taken from Matthew 11:30.

---

1 Jay Welch, jacket cover to Columbia Recording album, Handel's *Messiah*, The Philadelphia Orchestra, Mormon Tabernacle Choir, Eugene Ormandy, Conductor, n.d.n.p.

The accompaniment begins simply with the *basso-continuo* played by the organ and string bass, which provides a light accompaniment for the chorus. Then the strings join with them. The entire piece is composed of long phrases of quickly moving notes and repetitive words.

Handel begins the piece with the lightest voices, presenting the concept of lightness and ease. This is typical, since the Baroque composers had a fondness for text-painting. The sopranos skip along lightly, singing their joyful *melisma* on the word "easy." The tenors enter the *fugue*, followed by the altos and basses, respectively.

Each voice part appears to be tossing the melody back and forth, with all joining together chordally to finish the piece. It is a delightful *fugue* with its lively interplay of voices. Yet, the music breathes "a certain heaven-defying recklessness which a less dramatically-minded composer than Handel would hardly have read into the English words."[2]

Again these words, referring to yoke and implying oxen, remind us that Jesus, as a carpenter, probably made yokes for the oxen of His village. Oxen work as beasts of burden in many parts of the world. Figuratively, the people were already wearing a yoke—the yoke of the Law. Rabbis taught about the "yoke of the Law," suggesting that the people act like monks by putting off the yoke of earthly and worldly concerns and putting on Christ. We are reminded that Christ's yoke is one of faith, love, and freedom.[3]

This is another piece that Handel copies from his own Italian love duets, which were set to secular Italian words. Sedley Taylor, in his book *The Indebtedness of Handel to Other Composers,* tells us that, "Some

2 Sedley Taylor, *The Indebtedness of Handel to Other Composers* (New York: Cambridge University Press, 1906, reprinted by Johnson Corporation, 1971), 43.
3 Samuel Johnson, "The Gospel According to St. Matthew," *The Interpreter's Bible,* Vol. VII (New York: Abingdon Press, 1956), 390.

critics feel that 'His yoke is easy' is set to an almost grotesquely inappropriate passage. Here are the original words: 'The Flower which laughs at dawn is killed by the sun, and finds a grave in the evening.' The word in this text which is comparable to the word 'easy' is 'laughs'; and is therefore evidently a piece of word-painting, quite appropriate in its original position, but grievously out of place where it now stands."[4]

The ending comes as a surprise: "And the Lord hath laid on Him the iniquity of us all." It abruptly changes the tempo to *adagio* (slowly) and moves into minor harmony. Taylor continues, "Handel bids the voices enter in solemn canonic sequence, and his chorus ends with a combination of grandeur and depth of feeling such as is at the command of the consummate genius only."[5]

Due to his haste in composing *Messiah* in just twenty-four days, Handel often didn't mark all of his rhythmic patterns consistently. Therefore, his copyist attempted to distinguish the consistency of the melodic and rhythmic patterns for Handel.[6]

As a soprano, I could not help but notice that the melody line of this piece soars, so the sopranos have a few challenging high B flats to sing. When I sang *Messiah* under the baton of conductor, Sir Colin Davis, he told the sopranos when singing the high notes, to "make them easy; lighten up, just like the song says." He instructed the tenors and basses to sing "like cellos."

This oratorio turned out to be a financial masterstroke. By abandoning elaborate staging and using local soloists and choristers instead of temperamental, expensive Italian singers, Handel was able to produce these popular new works known as oratorios at a moderate cost, compared to his operas. His oratorios secured his place in music history and culture because they were able to be performed again and again.

For the first performance of *Messiah* in London, Handel's chorus was all male, probably not more than twenty singers, including six boys who sang the treble (soprano) part. They were professionals from the Chapel Road Choir and Westminster Abbey. The soloists were expected to sing along with the choristers.[7] It is interesting that, in Handel's day, the soloists were only given a single sheet of music—their part only. Today's scores have choral parts showing all the voice parts and even a piano reduction of the entire score.

Each time Handel conducted *Messiah,* he made slight changes. No version of this oratorio was intended to be more definitive than any other. The performers constantly changed, as well as the orchestra members, depending upon the availability of certain instruments. Even though it was divinely inspired, the music did

4 Taylor, 41.
5 Ibid., 43.
6 Alfred Mann, ed., *Handel's* Messiah *in Full Score* (New York: Dover Publications, 1989), 219.
7 *The New Grove Dictionary of Music,* Vol. 8 (New York: W. W. Norton & Company, 1980), 111.

HANDEL'S *Messiah*

not "come down from on high in finished form."[8] While the general public refers to Handel's piece as *The Messiah*, Handel and his librettist always called it *Messiah*—without the article.

At the end of this piece, "His yoke is easy," there is a dramatic pause, a half rest equaling two beats. This interrupts the expansive mood while uniting the voices in grand chords. As a member of the chorus, the singer must watch the conductor AND COUNT.

Look at the ending phrase of this chorus:

Friday, August 28, 1741

The voices unite on the last phrase, "And His burthen is light," which brings Part the First of *Messiah* to an end. This section of the masterpiece lasts a total of fifty-one minutes when performed. The date for

8 Leonard Van Camp, *A Practical Guide for Performing, Teaching and Singing* Messiah (Dayton, Ohio: Lorenz, Roger Dean Publishing Co., 1993), 6.

CHAPTER 21 *His yoke is easy*   *133*

completion of Part the First is entered in Handel's original score as Friday, August 28, 1741.[9] (Observe this in the score on the previous page.)

The Christmas season would hardly be complete without the annual production of Handel's *Messiah*. Every year it is performed in hundreds of cities throughout the world. Performances of *Messiah* have been going on for over 269 years, and the inspiration of the work continues to this day. Despite the fact that Handel wrote many operas, keyboard compositions, and orchestral works, his main contribution to music is the development of the oratorio (a form of sacred musical drama sung by soloists and choir with orchestral accompaniment). Although *Messiah* is performed mainly during the Christmas holidays, it is also appropriate for Easter since Part the Second and Part the Third tell of Christ's death and resurrection. Handel originally intended it to be performed during Lent. Let us move on to "Part the Second," as Handel liked to call it.

---

9 Mann, 219.

HANDEL'S *Messiah*

PART THE SECOND

CHAPTER TWENTY-TWO

"Behold the Lamb of God"

(CHORUS)

A powerful metaphor! John the Baptist recognizes with deep poignancy the significance of Jesus as the "Paschal Lamb." This begins "Part the Second," the entire movement which is a lamentation about Christ's suffering.

George Frideric Handel

This is the first chorus of "Part the Second," as Handel referred to this section of *Messiah*; and perhaps, the most sublime pages in the score. This second section tells the Passion story of Jesus' suffering, His sacrifice on the cross, humankind's rejection of God's offer of redemption, and man's utter defeat when trying to oppose God's power. It ends with the "Hallelujah Chorus." This first chorus is fittingly written in G minor and a 4/4 *largo* (slow) tempo with many plodding dotted-eighth notes. The violins begin the piece with their wistful trills. Observe the following opening phrase, and notice the octave leap in the voices:

Part the Second

The text is as follows:

"Behold the Lamb of God that taketh away the sins of the world."

(John 1:29 KJV)

This Scripture text introduces the representation of Christ as the "Lamb of God," an image found in the gospel of John as well as in John's Revelation, chapter 7. There has been much discussion about the proper interpretation of this title, "Lamb of God." Biblical commentator Massey H. Shepherd Jr. remarks, "It is but one of the many examples of an amazing subtlety in the Johannine writings, using terms and expressions that combine many themes and evoke many images and symbols."[1]

---

1 Massey H. Shepherd Jr., "The Gospel According to John," *The Interpreter's One-Volume Commentary on the Bible*, Charles Laymon, ed. (New York: Abingdon Press, 1971), 710.

HANDEL'S *Messiah*

This term, referring to the "Paschal Lamb" from the Jewish Passover meal, has become an elaborate metaphor. The lamb is the dominant sacrificial victim; and on the eve of every Passover supper, a lamb was chosen for the meal. For the Israelites, the lamb symbolized innocence, gentleness, and purity. Even though Christ was called the "Passover Lamb" or the "Passover which is sacrificed for us," the connection to the observance as being one "that takes away sin" had not quite been made. In the Jewish Passover, the lamb was commemorating the deliverance from bondage, not sin.[2]

But both John the evangelist and Isaiah the prophet had perceptions of the lamb that were of the "Suffering Servant," through whose victorious suffering for the sins of many restores all people to God. John saw the reference to Isaiah's suffering servant in Isaiah 53:7-12, with Jesus being the fulfillment of the Old Testament prophecy regarding God's ultimate redemption of humankind in and through His chosen people. In this Scripture passage, John sees the deep poignancy of the lamb as that suffering servant:[3]

> He was oppressed, and he was afflicted,
> yet he opened not his mouth;
> Like a lamb that is led to the slaughter,
> and like a sheep that before its shearers is dumb,
> so he opened not his mouth.
>
> (Isaiah 53:7 RSV)

In the John 1:29 text of this sorrowful chorus, John the Baptist declares, "Behold the Lamb of God, that taketh away the sins of the world." The setting in which these words were uttered is the day after John the Baptist had been questioned by the Pharisees as they observed the large crowds he was drawing who wanted to be baptized. He told the people, "Repent, for the Kingdom of Heaven is at hand." The Pharisees questioned his authority to baptize, and John responded, "I baptize with water, but one is coming who will baptize with the Holy Spirit."

Then Jesus walks onto the scene. Bible scholar Wilbert F. Howard states:

> Content with affirming to the Pharisees the greatness of Christ, John now gets specific about the person and work of Christ. He knows of Jesus' significance and uses "sacrificial" language by announcing that Christ will be the sin-bearing Lamb of God as he points to him and cries: "Behold, the Lamb of God, who takes away the sin of the

---

2 Wilbert F. Howard, "The Gospel According to St. John," *The Interpreter's Bible*, Vol. VIII (New York: Abingdon Press, 1956), 483.
3 Ibid., 484.

world." In the Bible there are many other references to the taking away of sins, and in John's first letter (l John 3:5), we are told, "He will forgive our sins, and cleanse us from all unrighteousness." The very next day John declares again of Jesus, "Behold, the Lamb of God."[4]

The librettist has cleverly combined the Old Testament and New Testament in this one movement. The phrase, "Behold the Lamb of God," is much bigger than the mere words seem to express, for many concepts have been joined together in just this one phrase. In it we have the picture of the suffering servant, as a sheep led to the slaughter. Also, in this phrase we are given the image of the Paschal Lamb, commemorating the deliverance of Israel from its slavery. These two concepts have been incorporated in the language of the Holy Eucharist Mass we celebrate around Communion tables in our churches. Regardless of the depth of the concept of the "Lamb of God," the main point was the removal of the infection of sin. Instead of emphasizing Christ's suffering itself, Handel focuses on the redemptive power "that taketh away the sin of the world."[5] In Adam all people have been made to die; but in Christ, all may live forever.

The "Agnus Dei" in the Holy Eucharist Mass contains three couplets. The first is "O, Lamb of God, who takes away the sin of the world, have mercy upon us." This couplet is repeated. The third couplet is changed slightly and ends with the words, "Grant us thy peace." The phrase "Lamb of God" has become a powerful metaphor for today's Christian community. The main concept is God's accomplishment of the redemption of the world by the sacrifice of Jesus; and through that we come to know His peace, which passes all understanding.

When the chorus sings this emotional piece with drooping reflection, the words "Behold the Lamb" are passed from one voice part to another as if they are whispering, "Look, there He is" to each other in the crowd. As each voice part enters on "Behold," we picture that particular group of singers falling on their knees in reverence when encountering the Divine.[6] The voices all come together on the words, "that taketh away the sin of the world." The sopranos appear awestruck as they sing the phrase on only one note, while the other voices sadly whisper underneath. Follow the soprano line of the score:

---

4 Ibid., 485.
5 Leonard Van Camp, *A Practical Guide for Performing, Teaching and Singing* Messiah (Dayton, Ohio: Lorenz, Roger Dean Publishing Co.), 71.
6 Joseph Machlis and Kristine Forney, eds., *The Enjoyment of Music*, 6th edition (New York: W. W. Norton & Co., 1990), 456.

HANDEL'S *Messiah*

The orchestra continues playing a few measures after the voices have ended, as the listeners are left with their own thoughts. The piece is solemn, yet joyous, which is the essence of reverence; and is "Baroque" in its richness. We have come to realize that salvation is embodied in this one man as we say, "Behold, the Lamb of God." Now that we have encountered the Savior and know the peace that He brings, we are free to earnestly worship Him. Surely one cannot simply listen to this music and feel nothing![7]

The original copy of this chorus shows that the beginning was apparently first composed as follows:[8] (Compare this to the music in the beginning of this chapter.) Today's version has several rhythmic changes that include dotted eighth notes followed by sixteenths.

7 Van Camp, 71.
8 Alfred Mann, ed., *Handel's* Messiah *in Full Score* (New York: Dover Publications, 1989), 219.

"Part the Second" definitely follows a gradual development; when we perceive the dominant theme of suffering, the progression of thought becomes clearer. The beginning of this entire movement is a lamentation about Christ's suffering, which moves gradually toward a joyous acclamation of His resurrection that reaches its peak in the "Hallelujah Chorus." The unity of the entire oratorio is implicit in the Christian purpose of the work from the very outset.[9]

---

9 Stanley Godman, *Goethe and Handel* (Oxford, England: Goethe Society, 1954), 81.

CHAPTER TWENTY-THREE

"He was despised"

(ARIA FOR ALTO)

*This chapter quotes the
entire "Suffering Servant" poem
found in Isaiah 52:13-53:12,
a confessional lament of the nations,
which is dominated by the contrast between
Jesus' humiliation and suffering on the one hand,
with the exaltation and triumph on the other.*

George Frideric Handel

The pensive G minor mood of the preceding chorus, "Behold the Lamb of God," now changes to the key of E flat major for this *aria*, a calculated move by Handel to enhance the reflective mood. The alto vocalist sings these words in rich tones:

> He was despised and rejected of men;
> a man of sorrows,
> and acquainted with grief.
>
> (Isaiah 53:3 RSV)

Hearing these words of such naked pain brought about by loneliness and solitude makes us aware of the effects of a lonely existence and the tragedies of life. Jesus was taunted by the bystanders as they cried, "Come down from the cross *if* You are the Son of God," "He saved others, but He can't save Himself," and "If You are the king of the Jews, save Yourself." These were words meant to wound—and words that despise.

The first half of the strophe from Isaiah 53:3a is referred to as the "Suffering Servant" passage, written by the prophet Isaiah. The idea of suffering is magnified in chapters 40-55 of Isaiah, as well as in the life of Job. We are reminded of Job's piercing lament in Job 19:7-20, and we will hear his acclamation of faith ("I know that my redeemer liveth")[1] later in *Messiah* (chapter forty-five).

Isaiah is both a poet and a prophet; he writes with a lyrical intensity matched by none. He lifts his voice in exulting triumph as he sees the approach of Israel's conquering Lord. He also knows the depths of grief and alienation, and his words are supported by his profound faith. In his exegesis of this passage from Isaiah, James Muilenburg writes, "The elevation and urgency of his prophetic mood are matched by forms of expression commensurate with the thoughts which surged through his soul."[2]

Jennens used these words from the poem of Isaiah's suffering servant of the Lord for four of the musical settings by Handel (chapters twenty-three, twenty-four, twenty-five, and thirty). The entire poem from Isaiah 52:13-53:12 is dominated by the contrast between humiliation and suffering on the one hand, and exaltation and triumph on the other. The form of the poem is a dramatic dialogue in which God is speaking at the beginning and end of the poem, with kings of the nations speaking in between. Henry Sloane Coffin claims, "This is the most influential poem in any literature. It gives insight as to why the righteous suffer. It interprets the reason for the death of the Son of God, and it apparently caught the imagination of Jesus himself and confirmed his conviction of his Father's will for him. Could any other poem do more?"[3] Here it is in its entirety:

> Behold, my servant shall prosper, he shall be exalted and lifted up,
> and shall be very high.
> As many were astonished at him—his appearance was so marred,
> beyond human semblance,
> and his form beyond that of the sons of men—
> so shall he startle many nations;
> kings shall shut their mouths because of him;
> for that which has not been told them they shall see,
> and that which they have not heard they shall understand.

---

1 James Muilenburg, "The Book of Isaiah," *The Interpreter's Bible,* Vol. V (New York: Abingdon Press, 1956), 386.
2 Ibid., 386.
3 Henry Sloane Coffin, "The Book of Isaiah," *The Interpreter's Bible,* Vol. V (New York: Abingdon Press, 1956), 614.

Who has believed what we have heard?
And to whom has the arm of the LORD been revealed?
For he grew up before him like a young plant,
and like a root out of dry ground;
he had no form or comeliness that we should look at him,
and no beauty that we should desire him.
He was despised and rejected by men;
a man of sorrows, and acquainted with grief,
and as one from whom men hide their faces
He was despised, and we esteemed him not.

Surely he has borne our griefs and carried our sorrows;
yet we esteemed him stricken, smitten by God, and afflicted.
But he was wounded for our transgressions,
he was bruised for our iniquities;
upon him was the chastisement that made us whole,
and with his stripes we are healed.

All we like sheep have gone astray;
We have turned every one to his own way;
And the LORD has laid on him the iniquity of us all.
He was oppressed, and he was afflicted,
yet he opened not his mouth;
Like a lamb that is led to the slaughter,
and like a sheep that before its shearers is dumb,
so he opened not his mouth.

By oppression and judgment he was taken away;
And as for his generation, who considered
that he was cut off out of the land of the living,
stricken for the transgression of my people?
And they made his grave with the wicked
and with a rich man in his death,
although he had done no violence,
and there was no deceit in his mouth.

Yet it was the will of the LORD to bruise him;

He has put him to grief;

When he makes himself an offering for sin,

He shall see his offspring, he shall prolong his days;

The will of the LORD shall prosper in his hand;

He shall see the fruit of the travail of his soul and be satisfied;

By his knowledge shall the righteous one, my servant,

make many to be accounted righteous;

He shall bear their iniquities,

therefore I will divide him a portion with the great,

and he shall divide the spoil with the strong;

Because he poured out his soul to death,

and was numbered with the transgressors;

Yet he bore the sin of many,

and made intercession for the transgressors.

(Isaiah 52:13–53:12 RSV)

What makes this poem so profound is that its interpretation of the God-appointed role of Israel (His servant) gave the Christian church the explanation for the death of the Son of God.

Why was this poem so important? History is understood in light of the epochal events associated with the rise of Cyrus. The dominant motif in the poem is God's purpose, which causes tension regarding its imminent fulfillment. Cyrus, the Persian king, plays a role of great importance: not only are his conquests portrayed in very dramatic forms, but God's choice of Cyrus as His instrument becomes a dramatic issue in which Israel finds her uniqueness imperiled. The Hebrew refugees in Babylon were an apprehensive people. After more than a generation of being exiled there, they watched as Cyrus' new military power rose suddenly upon the scene and was moving westward, sweeping everything away before it.[4]

When Babylon fell to Cyrus' army, the Jews experienced a time of relief and eager anticipation, for the opportunity to return to their homeland had arrived. But after some of the people reached Jerusalem and began the arduous task of rebuilding their destroyed land, the difficulties loomed overwhelmingly, which

---

4 Muilenburg, 419.

HANDEL'S *Messiah*

depressed them. They were comforted by the prophet's messages about God's judgment on His enemies, along with glowing hope for the faithful.

"He was despised" is written in a slow 4/4 tempo, accompanied by the violins wailing with many trills. After each short phrase sung by the alto, the instruments seem to imitate the voice. Then dramatically the alto sings unaccompanied, "He was despised" and "rejected." These two phrases are followed by a tragic-sounding diminished seventh chord on the word, "man," which presents a very unstable feeling. Look at the following score:

These are the specific words taken from the text:

> He was despised,
> rejected of men;
> a man of sorrows,
> and acquainted with grief.
>
> (Isaiah 53:3a RSV)

It is noteworthy that the use of "men" and "man" is most likely used for the purpose of alliteration, continuing the thread of imagery throughout the *aria*. Not only is the musical symbolism stressed with its use of flats or lowered tones, but the falling line of the melody expresses darkness, which is particularly effective in conveying the tragic mood.

To the composer, these patterns of verbal inflection suggest melodic inflections, or alterations in pitch or tone. The melodic imagery can enhance the effect of words expressing human emotions, such as a cry of loneliness. The repetition of the words, "He was despised," is profoundly moving. "Sorrows" and "grief" modulate into dark keys of B flat minor and F minor. The phrase, "acquainted with grief," is probably translated "humbled" or "disciplined."

We now move on to the second part of this *aria*, the "B" section, which increases the dramatic intensity. The words are taken from Isaiah 50:6, and are as follows:

> He gave his back to the smiters,
> and his cheeks to them who plucked out the hair.
> He hid not his face from shame and spitting.
>
> (Isaiah 50:6 RSV)

During this second movement, the tragic mood continues in the relative minor key of C, and the words and tempo pick up immediately on "He gave his back" with its agitated orchestral accompaniment. Observe the music below:

HANDEL'S

The strophe is rich in the vocabulary of pain and affliction as Jesus is subjected to the harshest physical persecution and insult. The disfigurement caused by plucking out the hairs on his face (destroying the beard) was the deepest insult for a Jewish man at this time.[5] Add to this the humiliation of being spit upon in public and the shunning for being categorized as "unclean".

The second movement ends on a G minor chord and then returns to the beginning, or the "A" section, in the E flat again with "He was despised." The form of this piece is *da capo*, or ABA (the sandwich form). The "B" section, the middle part, is a different motif entirely, followed by a repeat of the first section. After the repeat, the accompaniment carries the listeners to the end with reprises of the motifs of the opening "despised and rejected" themes.

This alto solo is rather long and lasts for nine minutes and forty-five seconds. During Handel's day the celebrated contralto soloist, Susanna Cibber, performed this *aria*. It is thought that Handel composed the piece with "her voice in mind."[6] Professor Leonard Van Camp comments, "At the end of her solo, the alto reduces her sound to a mere whisper, inviting the audience to join her in her world of profound sadness, the very essence of Handelian intensity."[7] It is said that Mrs. Cibber's singing of "He was despised" deeply moved the audience and caused the Chancellor, the Reverend Dr. Patrick Delany of St. Patrick's Cathedral in Dublin, to say (mindful of the singer's notorious reputation for immorality), "Woman, for this thy sins be forgiven thee!"[8]

The *Contemporary English Version* of the Bible paraphrases these two passages as follows:

> He was hated and rejected;
> His life was filled with sorrow and terrible suffering.
>
> (Isaiah 53:3a)

> He let them beat his back and pull out his beard.
> He didn't turn aside when they insulted him and spit in his face.
>
> (Isaiah 50:6)

5 Ibid., 585.
6 David W. Barber, *Getting a Handle on Handel's* Messiah (Toronto, Canada: Sound & Vision Publishing Limited, 1994), 48.
7 Leonard Van Camp, *A Practical Guide for Performing, Teaching and Singing* Messiah (Dayton, Ohio: Lorenz, Roger Dean Publishing Co., 1993), 74.
5 Winton Dean, ed., *New Grove Dictionary of Music*, Vol. 8 (New York: W. W. Norton & Co., 1980), 388.

CHAPTER 23  *He was despised and rejected*

One cannot help but feel a terrible pathos, for these words arouse great feelings of pity and sympathy for Jesus' emotional sufferings. In researching the Scriptures for a better understanding of these verses, I was saddened to read the following verses that the librettist chose to leave out of his text from Isaiah 53:3. Jennens only used the first half of the verse that said, "Jesus was a man of sorrows and acquainted with grief." The comma is followed by these words, "as one from whom men hide their faces. He was despised, and *we esteemed Him not* [emphasis added]."[9]

The *Contemporary English Version* suggests, "No one wanted to look at him. We despised him and said, 'He is a nobody!'" (Isaiah 53:3b). What really is convicting is that WE ESTEEMED HIM NOT. The people in the story didn't even know who Jesus was or what He was doing for them! Perhaps Jennens did not include the second half of the phrase because the reality of the words was too painful to think about. "We esteemed him not" would have given a heart-wrenching climax to the strophe and been a powerful link to the following chorus, taken from the very next line in Isaiah 53:4, "Surely He hath borne our griefs."

---

1 Muilenburg, 618.

HANDEL'S *Messiah*

"Surely He hath borne our griefs"

(CHORUS)

In this chorus, the kings of the nations are professing a collective confession of sin in the words, "Surely He has borne our griefs." The music implies heavy strokes of the whip upon Jesus' back.

This is the first of three consecutive choruses performed as a triptych. Two of the three choruses are in the key of F minor; the third chorus, "All we like sheep," begins in F major and then returns to the original F minor for the *adagio* (slow) coda.

The text of this chorus is a continuation of Isaiah 53, the poem from which "He was despised" was taken. The form of the poem is a dramatic dialogue in which God is speaking at the beginning and end of the poem; while the other speakers, who are the kings of the nations, are speaking in the middle. It is in this middle section that we find these passionate words:

> Surely He has borne our griefs, and carried our sorrows.
> Yet we esteemed him stricken, smitten by God, and afflicted.
> But he was wounded for our transgressions,
> He was bruised for our iniquities;
> Upon him was the chastisement that made us whole,
> and with his stripes we are healed.
>
> (Isaiah 53:4, 5 RSV)

The piece begins with the marking *largo e staccato*, meaning to play "slowly, with detached notes."[1] The meter is 4/4 with dotted sixteenth notes on the word "surely," giving the word three syllables and repeating it for emphasis, followed by a broad expanse on the words, "borne our griefs and carried our sorrows." The alliteration is notable with the use of the words "surely" and "sorrows."

For Isaiah, the author, the presence of sin in the situation was indisputable. But the sinner here is not the sufferer. The sufferer is the one bearing the consequences of the sins of others, rather than Himself. Our sins, as the kings confess in this section, have been transferred to Him. He bears *our* grief and carries *our* sorrows. The Suffering Servant emphasis is upon "our" and "He."[2] Handel stresses the enlightenment of the people in regard to the realization of their guilt, and now in their suffering by feeling guilty. It is the confession of the kings of the nations that is significant in itself: they are indicating their acknowledgment of the importance and mission of the Servant.

Israel's harsh treatment came about through historical circumstances. The exiled community was involved with its forebears. Their humiliation was not of their own choosing. But, believing in God's sovereignty, the Servant takes it as God's assignment. It is punishment for national sin, education for a mission, and now the redemptive sin offering.[3] The second half of verse four has been omitted from the libretto: "Yet we esteemed him stricken, smitten by God, and afflicted."

The *Contemporary English Version* paraphrases this verse:

> He suffered and endured great pain for us,
> but we thought his suffering was punishment from God.
>
> (Isaiah 53:4)

In Old Testament days, the Israelites interpreted suffering as a divine punishment for sin. They were convinced that a moral order guided the destinies of humankind: even though the wicked might prosper for a long while, they were sure that God's righteous judgment would eventually reach them. They took their own calamities as indications of God's wrath. The prophet Isaiah is attempting to inspire his people, the Israelites,

---

2 Don Michael Randel, ed. *The Harvard Dictionary of Music,* 4th edition (Cambridge, Massachusetts: Harvard University Press, 2003), 452.
3 Henry Sloane Coffin, "The Book of Isaiah," *The Interpreter's Bible,* Vol. V (New York: Abingdon Press, 1956), 621.
4 Ibid., 622.

HANDEL'S *Messiah*

with his words. His belief had lifted him, and would also lift the people to heartening fellowship with God in His redemptive purpose for humankind.[4]

Henry Sloane Coffin remarks:

> The intensity of the prophet's theocentricity continues from beginning to end. This is the same author of the very first words in *Messiah* sung by the tenor, "Comfort, my people, says your God." Israel, God's chosen and called servant, has been blind to her purpose. Yet Yahweh is gracious and promises her his imminent redemption. The servant of the Lord enters the scene, calling upon the nations to hear. The promise of redemption is renewed.
>
> The poignant confession of the servant follows, and then the next poem joyfully cries out, "Yahweh has become king!" Yahweh then promises the exaltation of the servant, in Isaiah 52; and in response to this, we have this confessional lament of the nations, in Isaiah 53.[5]

(Read the entire poem in chapter twenty-three.)

The second strophe in this grandly pathetic chorus is rich in the vocabulary of pain and affliction. It even broadens into a collective confession of sin, speaking for all humankind. As Leonard Van Camp reminds us, "It is our grief, our sorrows, our transgressions, our iniquities, our peace."[6]

> He was wounded for our transgressions
> and He was bruised for our iniquities.
> (Isaiah 53:5a RSV)

The *Contemporary English Version* uses the words, "He was wounded and crushed because of our sins." Notice the figured bass in the musical excerpt that follows. "Wounded" could be interpreted "pierced through" for our transgressions, and "bruised" could be translated "crushed" for our iniquities. The music Handel composed for these two words, "bruised" and "wounded," is extremely dramatic and comprises mournful chords. Observe the following music score:

---

5 Coffin, 621.

6 Ibid.

7 Leonard Van Camp, *A Practical Guide for Performing, Teaching and Singing* Messiah (Dayton, Ohio: Lorenz., Roger Dean Publishing Co., 1993), 75.

CHAPTER 24 *Surely He hath borne our griefs*  151

The suffering of the Servant is due to the sin of the people, and now they are confessing. These sufferings of Jesus had a twofold effect: 1) they were the penalty for sins; and 2) they were the means for reconciliation and restoration with God. The last strophe is:

> The chastisement for our peace was upon him.
> (Isaiah 53:5a NKJV)

The words tell us that "upon him was the chastisement that made us whole." The chastisement of the Servant was necessary for the well-being of all the nations. Chastisement implies disciplinary pain. When the chorus sings these words, the listener can almost hear the heavy strokes of the whip upon Jesus' back as the words are accented. Leonard Van Camp suggests that the chorus "sing the word 'chastisement' with noisy and intense consonants in order to make this motif sound like a whip in the scourging of Christ."[7] Handel's scoring of this phrase looks like this:

---

1 Van Camp, 78.

HANDEL'S *Messiah*

When we view the consequences of our wrongdoing in the light of other people's suffering, our senses are heightened. Isaiah's intent was to inspire the people, lifting them up to be in fellowship with God as part of His redemptive plan. The primitive church of the New Testament adopted all the Old Testament views of suffering but modified them in the light of Jesus' passion and the cross. Jesus Himself had taught that His suffering was a divine necessity. The atoning effect of His suffering rested upon His willingness as "the sinless one" to give His life for sinners. By His vicarious suffering as the Servant, He restores all people to God.[8] Christ didn't just take our sins upon Himself. He became those sins for us. This piece mournfully closes on an open A flat chord; but without delay, the next chorus, "And With His Stripes," begins.

2 James Muilenburg, "Suffering and Evil," *The Interpreter's Dictionary of the Bible in Four Volumes,* Vol. 4 (New York: Abingdon Press, 1962), 452.

CHAPTER TWENTY-FIVE

"And with His stripes we are healed"

(CHORUS)

Continuing the theme of anguish, this chorus uses the fugue motif to develop the piece contrapuntally.

George Frideric Handel

We have just finished hearing the chorus, "Surely, he hath borne our griefs . . . and upon him was the chastisement that made us whole." The last half of that verse in Isaiah 53:5b provides the few words of this chorus:

> And with his stripes, we are healed.
>
> (Isaiah 53:5b RSV)

The *Contemporary English Version* of the Bible says:
> By taking our punishment,
> He made us completely well.

What convicting words! The stripes and wounds that were inflicted upon Christ were necessary for the healing of the people. James Muilenburg observes, "The punishment was borne vicariously, and the vicarious suffering was efficacious in the eyes of God. The chastisement which broke Jesus' body, made us whole. The blows and stripes which prostrated him, healed us. These words, 'And with his stripes, we are healed,' are a continuation of the fantastic poem by Isaiah describing the suffering servant of the Lord [Isaiah 52:13-53:12 is found in its entirety in chapter twenty-three of this book]. The entire poem is dominated by the contrast between humiliation and suffering on the one hand, and exaltation and triumph on the other."[1]

---

3 James Muilenburg, "The Book of Isaiah," *The Interpreter's Bible,* Vol. V (New York: Abingdon Press, 1956), 615.

This chorus, written in F minor, is the second of a triptych of three choruses, continuing the tone of anguish. The piece is marked *alla breve moderato* (which means "cut time" or moderately fast tempo);[2] and *senza rip.* (which indicates to double the instruments, yet without the entire orchestra).[3] The oboes are instructed to play along with the soprano line. The chorus is based on a *fugue* motif that was developed during the Baroque era (also used by Bach in his "Well-tempered Clavier," and by Mozart in his "Requiem").[4]

The subject of this spacious *fugue* is marked by the downward leap of a diminished seventh—an emotionally charged interval—on the words, "His stripes."[5] The diminished seventh is formed by contracting a minor, or perfect interval, by a semitone, or half step.[6] This usage provides a dramatic and fitting surprise in this sorrowful chorus. In *fugues*, the conflicts and tensions of the earlier movements are resolved. The subject of the *fugue* is presented by the sopranos, then imitated, or answered, by the altos in the tonic. Likewise, the basses echo the tenors. All voices are singing together in counterpoint until they move toward a harmonic ending, or cadence. Observe the music in the following score:

No. 25

---

4 Don Michael Randel, ed., *The Harvard Dictionary of Music,* 4th edition (Cambridge, Massachusetts: Harvard University Press, 2003), 33.

5 Ibid., 732.

6 Leonard Van Camp, *A Practical Guide for Performing, Teaching and Singing* Messiah (Dayton, Ohio: Lorenz, Roger Dean Publishing Co., 1993), 78.

7 Joseph Machlis and Kristine Forney, eds., *The Enjoyment of Music,* 6th edition (New York: W. W. Norton & Co., 1990), 457.

8 Randel, 414.

This piece is one of the strictly contrapuntal choral pieces in the oratorio. Handel, like Bach, was a counterpoint master. Author Phil Goulding says that "Handel is a magnificent improviser, and works with sweeping brush strokes. When comparing Johann Sebastian Bach and George Frideric Handel, both men were inspired by an ethical ideal; but Bach was a Lutheran, while Handel was a man of the Enlightenment whose moral sense was bound to no creed or dogma."[7] In spite of this, his music can speak to listeners of any or even non-existent faith on a very personal level.

There are a few minor differences in Handel's original score of this chorus and the score that we use today. In the original version, the two words "we are" (spelled "wee are" by Handel) appear in this order, not in the reversed order "are we" as some other versions might indicate.[8]

In measure 71, the alto is given two notes to be sung (an octave of C's). The two notes written for the second quarter beat appear in equal size in the original version. As the violin part shows, the upper tone is to be preferred.[9] (The lower tone was meant for the men's voices in the alto section who sang along with younger male choristers.) See the score below:

1 Phil G. Goulding, *Classical Musicians: The 50 Greatest Composers and Their 1,000 Greatest Works* (New York: Fawcett Columbine, 1992), 326.
2 Alfred Mann, ed., *Handel's* Messiah *in Full Score* (New York: Dover Publications, Inc., 1989), 220.
3 Ibid., 220.

Handel's *Messiah*

These three choruses (chapters twenty-four, twenty-five, and twenty-six) are connected in Handel's original score. At the end of this particular chapter, we find that Handel has altered the key signature with naturals as if the next chorus, "All we like sheep" were a continuation, or the third in the triptych of choruses. His use of naturals in the key signature is not used anywhere else in his original version.[10]

This chorus modulates to a C major chord, which is the dominant fifth of the key of F major, the key in which the next chorus, "All we like sheep" immediately begins. There is no thick black double bar line after "healed," another indication that it is not a definitive end but that the next chorus should be connected to this chorus. So, on we go!

4 Ibid., 221.

"All we like sheep have gone astray"

(CHORUS)

How humiliating to be compared to sheep!
Handel uses all four voice parts to represent a herd of sheep,
literally going every-which-way, wandering aimlessly.

George Frideric Handel

This chorus is the third part of the triptych that began with chapter twenty-four, "Surely, He hath borne our griefs"; chapter twenty-five, "And with His stripes"; and now, chapter twenty-six, "All we like sheep." This chorus in F major shows a striking contrast to the two choruses preceding it. In his book, *A Practical Guide for Performing, Teaching and Singing* Messiah, Leonard Van Camp suggests, "This chorus is too frivolous and inappropriate for the words"[1] of Isaiah 53:6:

> All we like sheep have gone astray;
> we have turned every one to his own way;
> and the Lord has laid on him, the iniquity of us all.
> (Isaiah 53:6 RSV)

---

1 Leonard Van Camp, *A Practical Guide for Performing, Teaching and Singing* Messiah (Dayton, Ohio: Lorenz, Roger Dean Publishing Co., 1993), 81.

The transition to this chorus is even a bit of a surprise to the listener. The very first phrase "All we like sheep," is a confession and part of the same poem from Isaiah 52:13-53:12, which Henry Sloane Coffin rightly claims is "the most influential poem in any literature."[2] As listeners or participants, we are all involved in the Servant's suffering. We are compared to sheep that have turned away from God—each on his or her own self-centered course. The image of the sheep prepares the way for the next strophe that was not chosen as part of the libretto by Charles Jennens for Handel to put to music. The words of this omitted verse lament:

> He was oppressed, and he was afflicted,
> yet he opened not his mouth;
> Like a lamb that is led to the slaughter,
> and like a sheep that before its shearers is dumb,
> so he opened not his mouth.
>
> (Isaiah 53:7 RSV)

This is the very verse that led to the designation of Jesus Christ as "Lamb of God."[3] (See also John 1, verses 29 and 36, and pages 135-140 of this book.)

Let us look at the beginning of the chorus, which commences with all four voices (SATB) singing together as a "herd of sheep," polyphonically—but not for long:

---

2 Henry Sloane Coffin, "The Book of Isaiah," *The Interpreter's Bible*, Vol. V (New York: Abingdon Press, 1956), 614.
3 Coffin, 625.

Notice some special instructions in the score on the previous page. *Con fag* in the *basso-continuo* indicates that the bassoons should play along,[4] and the oboes are asked to mimic the soprano melody. (The German name for bassoon [*con Fagott*] was used by Handel instead of the abbreviation "bass," which might have been confused with the vocal bass part.)

The music begins with an unusual *fugue*, as the voices turn off in many different directions; the notes literally go astray (as going astray is the very point!). In his book, *The* Messiah *Book: The Life and Times of G. F. Handel's Greatest Hit,* Peter Jacobi teases his choir, "It's a good thing we didn't go astray as the sheep we were singing about!"[5] The sopranos reach up to a high G, while the tenors fall down the scale to an E. The altos and basses also run off in different directions.

Van Camp says, "Here Handel vividly paints the waywardness of humankind and our tendency to wander aimlessly like sheep. This waywardness was intended to portray the undisciplined, foolish, and aimless way we deal with life."[6] Joseph Machlis and Kristine Forney claim, "This is one of the spots where Handel's ear for his adopted language (English) goes astray, and suggests 'All we like sheep' could not possibly sound right, no matter who set it to music."[7] The choral conductor may propose that the phrase is easier to sing if the vocalists observe the comma between "all we" and "like sheep."

Again, that is the very point! The melody of a piece, usually what we can hum or sing, most likely has a very pleasing shape. This chorus is tricky in that it goes astray and contains difficult runs. The 4/4 meter is a rhythm of relentless contrapuntal energy and briskly moving harmonic masses that finally come to a halt in its moving finale.[8] Handel marked *adagio* (slowly) on the following tragic words:

> And the Lord hath laid on him
> the iniquity of us all.
> (Isaiah 53:6 RSV)

After the nations realized that Israel's woes were also destined to happen to them, they were moved to make a confession of sin. The effects of sin are social, so their consciences were awakened. This poem presents the insight of a universal guilt in nations who have "turned every one to his own way." The end of the text is poignant, as if the people singing have finally realized the consequences of their sins.

---

4 Don Michael Randel, ed., *The Harvard Dictionary of Music,* 4th edition (Cambridge, Massachusetts: Harvard University Press, 2003), 304.
5 Peter Jacobi, *The* Messiah *Book: The Life & Times of George F. Handel's Greatest Hit* (New York: St. Martin's Press, 1982), 31.
6 Van Camp, 83.
7 Joseph Machlis and Kristine Forney, eds., *The Enjoyment of Music,* 6th edition (New York: W. W. Norton & Co., 1990), 457.
8 Van Camp, 82.

HANDEL'S

This collective acknowledgment ends the stirring confession. We are all involved in the Servant's suffering, and this passage gives us much to contemplate today. What are our current transgressions and iniquities? How do we turn away from God, each of us in his or her own self-centered way? Ironically, some of us may find comfort in not following the flock too closely. Like the prodigal son in Jesus' parable, we find ourselves far from our Father God's home—with our lives in a mess. Many of us today are like sheep, for we are too helpless to protect ourselves or escape from danger when attacked; we are acting like we're lost, without a shepherd.[9] Thank goodness, we can appeal to the Good Shepherd to save us from the self-destructive course we've chosen for ourselves.

This particular chorus was adapted from Handel's set of Italian duets that he had written in July, 1741. Although the original draft of the oratorio was written in such a short time, it is said that Handel spent more time on revising this masterpiece, *Messiah*, than any of his previous oratorios.[10] Every time he performed it, he changed or added something new.

Observe the following music score, and notice how Handel emphasizes significant voices by dissonances. The leading tone (seventh note of the key) and the tonic (first note of the key) are struck together immediately before the final cadence chord. The alto note is the E, while the soprano comes down to an F on "us." The *fugue* in "All we like sheep" ended originally with a full F minor cadence, which Handel shortened to the present half close:[11]

1 Coffin, 623.
2 Jacobi, 31.
3 Alfred Mann, ed., *Handel's* Messiah *in Full Score* (New York: Dover Publications, 1989), 220.

CHAPTER TWENTY-SEVEN

"All they that see Him, laugh Him to scorn"

(RECITATIVE FOR TENOR)

George Frideric Handel

A radical recitative, the words of which are taken from the passionate Psalm 22, also from which come Jesus' words on the cross, "My God, My God, why hast thou forsaken me?"

We turn now to the Davidic collection of songs with Psalm 22, the first of those often called the "Passion Psalms,"[1] as the tenor sings his *recitative*:

> All they that see Him laugh Him to scorn,
> They shoot out their lips and shake their heads saying . . .
> (Psalm 22:7 KJV)

Again, this short accompanied *recitative* takes the listener from point A to point B in the drama and prepares the scene for the following mocking chorus, "He trusted in God."

The words of this radical *recitative* and the chorus that follows are taken from this psalm that is often used in the "Seven last words of Christ," when Jesus quotes in Aramaic while hanging on the cross, "My God,

---

4 William R. Taylor, "The Book of Psalms," *The Interpreter's Bible*, Vol. IV (New York: Abingdon Press, 1956), 116.

why hast thou forsaken me?"—an appeal stated in only four words, "Eli, Eli, lama sabachthani." The psalmist David, in a sense of alienation, is also asking God, "Why are You so far from helping me? Can't You hear my cry?"[2] It seems as if the psalmist is at his lowest point.

The words preceding this verse remind us of Job's lament, which basically said, "I am a worm, and no man; a reproach of men, and despised of people" (Job 30:9-11). Job feels that he is despised and hated by the people; nevertheless, he is hopeful and trusting that God will deliver him, as He had repeatedly delivered his forefathers.

Likewise, here the psalmist David was truly suffering. Jennens chose to use these words, "All they that see me laugh me to scorn," and the following verse for the next chorus, "He trusted on the LORD that he would deliver him," to show the depth of the mocking and verbal abuse. We all know how it feels to be hated, made fun of, or not liked by our peers, and how painful it is to be despised, to be a victim, or to be discredited.

These words were written by David the songwriter, who sensed his helplessness in the face of surrounding foes. He had an utter dependence upon God, and in the end, rejoiced in the confident assurance of God's aid and deliverance.

The *recitative* begins in B flat minor and then moves to E flat major; it is written in a 4/4 *larghetto* (slow) tempo. Leonard Van Camp describes it "as if the whipping of Christ is mimicked by the wagging heads and derisive laughter of the crowd assembled to watch the crucifixion. The tenor soloist must be powerful and convincing, or the next chorus, 'He trusted in God to deliver him' will seem very much out of place and ineffective."[3]

The *Contemporary English Version* of the Bible passage simply says, "They poke fun at me." The people are smearing his name and laughing in ridicule. Likewise, the strings appear to be laughing in the rhythmic pattern of dotted sixteenth notes in their accompaniment. The piece lasts all of thirty seconds. Look at the musical excerpt on the following page:

---

5 Charles Pfeiffer, *Wycliffe Bible Commentary* (Nashville, Tennessee: Moody Bible Institute, 1962), 503.
6 Leonard Van Camp, *A Practical Guide for Performing, Teaching and Singing* Messiah (Dayton, Ohio: Lorenz, Roger Dean Publishing Co., 1993), 85.

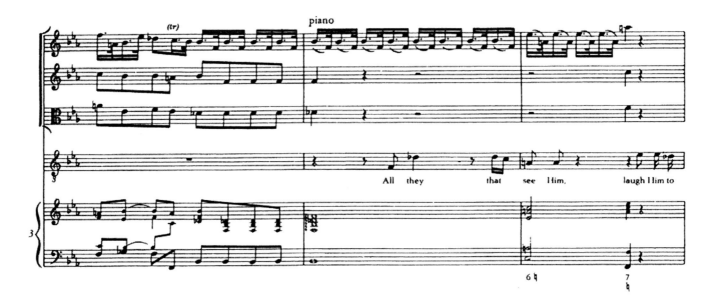

In Handel's original version, the vocal part was written in the tenor clef. Yet according to the names of the soloists whom Handel added in the original score, the part was assigned to a soprano rather than a tenor in some of his performances.[4] Now, on to the mocking chorus, "He trusted in God."

1 Alfred Mann, ed., *Handel's* Messiah *in Full Score* (New York: Dover Publications, 1989), 220.

HANDEL'S *Messiah*

CHAPTER TWENTY-EIGHT

"He trusted in God that He would deliver Him"

(CHORUS)

An angry crowd scene!

This chorus flows into the very next insult of Psalm 22, verse 8, as if the tenor, who just spoke of "laughing at Jesus," was joined by a crowd of hecklers, or tormentors. This verse was quoted by the religious leaders (the chief priests, along with the scribes and elders) who jeered at Jesus on the cross. This passage truly reveals the libretto's darker side. See the bass entrance in the music below.

George Frideric Handel

The basses begin the taunting in *tutti* (all together), supported by the *basso-continuo* and bassoons. Notice also the direction *tasto solo*, which instructs the thoroughbass to play the bass note only, without chords.[1]

In a *fugue*-like manner, each voice part enters: the tenors, supported by the violas; the altos with the second violins; and finally, the sopranos with the first violins doubling their melodic line. This taunting is continuous for *sixty* measures, only stopping to pause before all four voices come together in chordal harmony.

This is a very dramatic chorus, which resembles an angry operatic crowd scene. The chorus continues with the mocking and arrogant tone of the preceding *recitative* by its relentless delivery of the words:[2]

> He trusted in God that He would
> deliver him; let Him deliver him,
> if He delight in him.
>
> (Psalm 22:8)

The effect of the music is almost savage, and it is difficult to sing with its multitude "of chromatics and challenges at every turn."[3] The psalmist's enemies are truly mocking his confidence, and in effect saying, "If God likes him so much, let Him help him." Their cruel taunts are confirming his belief that God has abandoned Him: they strip Him of His humanity and reduce Him to the lowest form of animal existence—a worm.[4]

Handel's original score shows two versions of the text, "that He *might* deliver Him" and "that He *would* deliver Him." Subsequent editions have changed "might" to "would" in each instance.[5]

The *King James Version* of the Bible says:

> All who see me mock at me,
> they make mouths at me,
> they wag their heads;

2 Don Michael Randel, ed., *The Harvard Dictionary of Music,* 4th edition (Cambridge, Massachusetts: Harvard University Press, 2003), 871.

3 Leonard Van Camp, *A Practical Guide for Performing, Teaching and Singing* Messiah (Dayton, Ohio: Lorenz, Roger Dean Publishing Co., 1993), 86.

4 Joseph Machlis and Kristine Forney, eds., *The Enjoyment of Music,* 6th edition (New York: W. W. Norton & Co., 1990), 482.

5 Charles M. Laymon, ed., *The Interpreter's One-Volume Commentary on the Bible* (New York: Abingdon Press, 1971), 268.

6 Alfred Mann, ed., *Handel's* Messiah *in Full Score* (New York: Dover Publications, 1989), 221.

HANDEL'S *Messiah*

He committed his cause,
trusted in God that He would
deliver him; let Him deliver him,
seeing He delighted in him.

The mockings of humankind seem to imply that God is now indifferent to the plea of the psalmist David. Indeed, he begins this very psalm with the painful, questioning words, "My God, my God, why has thou forsaken me?" (This is the fourth saying of Jesus while He was hanging on the cross, quoted in Matthew 27:46.)[6]

Sin is defined as "separation from God," yet nothing could be further from the truth in this case. This is all part of God's plan, and His will cannot be thwarted. As part of that plan, Jesus must be mocked, rejected, scorned by men, and despised by the people. He also must descend into hell for our sakes. This is the doctrine of the "atonement," a plan that God Himself has prepared as a way for humans to be reconciled to Him.[7]

The Message Bible paraphrases Psalm 22:8:

"Let's see how God handles this one,
since He likes him so much."

The details of Calvary seem to be so clear in the mockery and the shame reflected in this psalm. We can participate in this chorus in two ways. First, we can be one of the crowd waiting to see if His God will deliver Him; and second, we can recall history and remember how God had not failed to help those who "trusted in Him" in previous generations. We know, as the Israelites did, that our forefathers had trusted in God and He had delivered them. We also must hold on in faith, anticipating God's saving help. God's plan will prevail, so we can stand firm in this "blessed assurance."[8]

Historically, let us remember that when Handel moved to England permanently in 1717, it was to compose and produce the highly stylized Italian operas that were popular at the time. However, by the late 1730s, English concert-goers were tired of Italian opera with all of its elaborate dramatic conventions. So, Handel increasingly turned to the new form of the English oratorio. His oratorios from this period were

---

6 Note taken from the *Harper Study Bible* (Grand Rapids, Michigan: Zondervan Bible Publishers, 1962), 788.
7 William R. Taylor, "The Book of Psalms," *The Interpreter's Bible*, Vol. IV (New York: Abingdon Press, 1956), 118.
8 Ibid., 119.

dramatic settings of the Old Testament stories that were most familiar to his English audiences. Although Handel retained many of the outward forms of opera in these oratorios, he placed a much greater importance on the chorus. This is one of those choruses that is considered a column which supports the drama by advancing the story, connected together by the *recitatives* and *arias*. This turbulent chorus is a good example of the importance of the chorus in an oratorio playing the role of the protagonist.

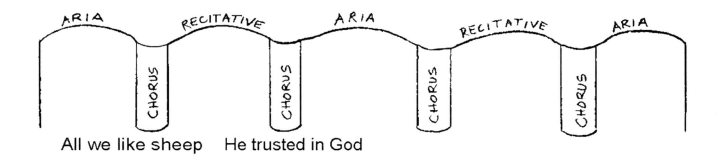

All we like sheep   He trusted in God

HANDEL'S *Messiah*

CHAPTER TWENTY-NINE

"Thy rebuke hath broken His heart"

(RECITATIVE FOR TENOR)

Upon hearing the tenor sing, one cannot help but feel the agony of rejection and the emotional pain of being cut off from God.

George Frideric Handel

The setting for this *recitative* is on the hillside at the cross during the moments when the taunting crowd has begun to leave (with only a few stragglers remaining), after having jeered and thrown heartbreaking insults at Jesus. Mr. Jennens, the librettist, has chosen these words from Psalm 69 for the tenor to sing due to their overwhelming reference to Jesus:

> Thy rebuke hath broken His heart,
> His is full of heaviness. He looked for some
> to have pity on Him. But there was no man,
> neither found He any to comfort Him.
> (Psalm 69:20 KJV)

This weary Psalm 69 is a companion to Psalm 22, which we just read in the last two musical pieces. Both psalms have messianic implications and deal with "undeserved suffering of the psalmist, which has been due in large part to a steadfast loyalty to God."[1] This particular verse 20 accentuates the plight of his piety being mocked; the psalmist has prayed for deliverance, but as yet, has been unanswered. One feels the utter abandonment of the psalmist and the lonely Christ.[2] The tenor soloist sings this "accompanied" *recitative* as if he were a bystander at the cross, catching the mood of the psalmist's plaintive cry for help and deliverance as he is looking for pity and comfort, but there is none.[3]

As David's psalm has shown, the one who is crying for help is definitely a pious and devout follower of God. He has earnestly asked God for help—that in His own time, He would rescue him. He says to God, "You know my shame and dishonor."[4]

The *recitative* begins four mini-movements sung by the tenor. The piece has no key signature, but begins in A flat major and immediately moves through many chord changes (F minor, then G minor, and finally E minor).[5] This is the opening music:

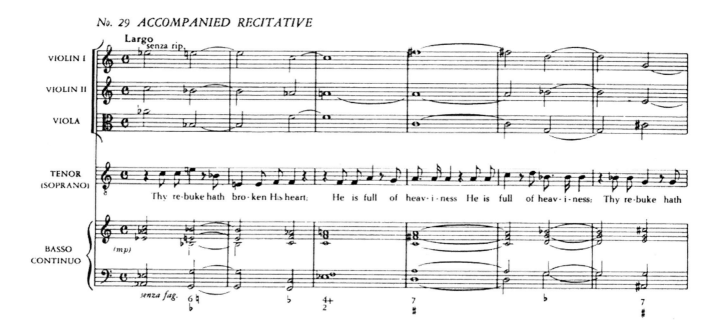

---

1 *Eerdman's One-Volume Commentary on the Holy Bible*, 493.

2 William R. Taylor, "The Book of Psalms," *The Interpreter's Bible*, Vol. IV (New York: Abingdon Press, 1956), 365.

3 Leonard Van Camp, *A Practical Guide for Performing, Teaching and Singing* Messiah (Dayton, Ohio: Lorenz, Roger Dean Publishing Co., 1993), 89.

4 Taylor, 365.

5 John Tobin, *Handel's* Messiah: *A Critical Account of the Manuscript Sources and Printed Editions* (London: Cassell and Company, LTD., 1969), 151.

Take note of measure 3 in the score on the previous page, which Handel has changed from his original version shown below. His changes give particular emphasis to the halting effect in the declamation of the words, "He is full of heaviness." He changed the second note to an "F," and the third note to an "A."[6]

The *Revised Standard Version* of the Bible translates these words of David's psalm:

> Insults have broken my heart
> so that I am in despair.
> I looked for pity, but there was none;
> and for comforters, but I found none.
>
> *(RSV)*

The *Contemporary English Version* paraphrases the same words:

> I am crushed by insults,
> and I feel sick.
> I had hoped for mercy and pity,
> but there was none.
>
> *(CEV)*

The worst part of this rejection and emotional pain is actually the spiritual agony of being cut off from God. The agony seems to become intensified: there is a mood of utter desolation, despair, and heart-brokenness, as well as a sense of human injustice, cruelty, and dishonor.[7] Leonard Van Camp describes the

---

6 Mann, *Handel's* Messiah *in Full Score,* 221.
7 Taylor, 365.

harmonies in Handel's music as "excruciating."[8] The Lord Jesus Christ knew of the injustices placed against Him.

Jennens changed the words from the first person point of view to the third. By this simple change, he makes the listener part of the action and an integral part of the drama. The suggestion of *testo* (meaning "narrator") and *turbe* (representing the Jewish or heathen population who spoke passionate words) heightens a sense of resemblance at this moment to passionate music itself. The listener to this tenor *recitative* hears the pain in the sobbing descending notes within the eighteen bars of music, a progression of chromatic notes.[9] The piece is intended to proceed immediately to the next *aria* for tenor.

Verse 20 is just one verse chosen out of a long lament in which the poet turns back to God with a strong hymn of praise in verse 30 when he declares, "I will praise the name of the Lord." The psalm ends with a joyous assurance. It is amazing that the librettist could find this one verse, from so many psalms, that fully expresses the absolute heartbrokenness of the afflicted!

8 Van Camp, 90.
9 Tobin, 151.

CHAPTER THIRTY

"Behold, and see if there be any sorrow"

(ARIA FOR TENOR)

Have you ever seen such pain?
The tenor, representing the daughter of Zion,
continues lamenting as he describes
the destroyed city of Jerusalem.
The words, associated with Jesus,
are an agonizing appeal to the world's
indifference toward Him.

George Frideric Handel

This pathetic *aria* for tenor is a lament by the daughter of Zion, taken appropriately from the Old Testament book of Lamentations. Its musical color comes from a palette of sadness and grief, written in the tonality of E minor. The meter is a 4/4 *largo a piano* (slow and soft), and it resembles a political funeral dirge as an expression of national grief for the loss of a loved one. The daughter of Zion figuratively represents the destroyed city of Jerusalem.

The authorship of this classic, timeless poem has been questioned. Some scholars attribute the Book of Lamentations to Jeremiah, who had experienced the siege and fall of Jerusalem and the troubles that followed. They defend this authorship by stating the fact that it was written in an acrostic form with the letters of the Hebrew alphabet. However, other scholars feel that there are too many differences evident between the Book of Lamentations and the Book of Jeremiah to make this reasoning plausible. In fact, the five chapters of Lamentations seem to have been written by five different authors after the first Babylonian siege of 597 BC. Regardless, there are many linguistic similarities between Jeremiah and Lamentations, the book that follows in the canon of the Scriptures.[1]

The speaker in this *aria* is the daughter of Zion. This verse, taken from Lamentations 1:12, begins with a powerful expression of human emotion—a cry that the librettist chose to omit in his script for Handel, but is included here. Verse 12 calls the world outside Israel to look upon this as a manifestation of Yahweh's righteous sovereignty:

> *Is it nothing to you, all ye that pass by?*
> Behold and see if there be any sorrow like my sorrow,
> which was brought unto me, which the Lord inflicted
> on the day of his fierce anger.
>
> (Lamentations 1:12 KJV, emphasis added)

That first question could be asked rhetorically: "Hey, all of you who walk along this road, is it nothing to you? Have you ever seen pain like my pain? Did you see what God did to me in His rage? Don't you even care?" Jerusalem's, or the daughter of Zion's, focus is on the immediacy of her pain; she is addressing a third party, telling them to pay attention to her. (She is asking for a witness to recognize the immensity of her sorrow.) She is both suffering and reporting how it feels to suffer: "See if there be any sorrow like my sorrow." The daughter of Zion is in a mess and feels that she has no one to comfort her because she attributes the primary source of her terrible plight to Yahweh. Her grief is palpable. Even if she has provoked divine anger, she feels that her suffering is without comparison.[2]

The words in this verse have been associated with Jesus in His passion, since He identified Himself so closely with human sin and its consequences. It is a tragic condition of a people. The words are an agonizing appeal to us, as the travelers on the road, about our indifference and even neglect of Christ. These words remind us to learn from the lessons of the past and retain our faith in God's compassion, even in the face of overwhelming obstacles.[3]

---

1 Theophile J. Meek, "The Book of Lamentations," *The Interpreter's Bible*, Vol. VI (New York: Abingdon Press, 1956), 12.
2 Kathleen O'Connor, "The Book of Lamentations," *The New Interpreter's Bible*, Vol. VI (Nashville, Tennessee: Abingdon Press, 2001), 1032.
3 Meek, 13.

The melody of this hauntingly beautiful piece exhibits an intense yet controlled grief against the dismal backdrop of Lamentations, with the conflicting emotion of a glimmer of hope. Truly, the sound communicates what the words express. Look at the score below:

The *Contemporary English Version* paraphrases these words:

> Jerusalem shouts to the Lord:
> "Please look and see how miserable I am!
> No passerby even cares.
> Why doesn't someone notice my terrible sufferings?
> You were fiercely angry, LORD,
> and you punished me worst of all."
>
> (Lamentations 1:12)

These verses almost boast of the certainty of a "hearing by God." It is a direct calling to the Lord God, who must exhibit the Old Testament concept of the Hebrew word *hesed* (steadfast love, loyalty, and faithfulness), as His covenant obligation.[4] (This concept defines God's consuming concern for His people that leads Him to come to their rescue and His unshakable loyalty to the relationship between the people and

---

4 Meek, 14.

Himself which His saving act had created.) These three pieces, chapters twenty-nine, thirty, and thirty-one, seem to go to the very depths of despair as if going to the very bottom of the ocean floor, only to begin to rise, just as chapter thirty-two says, "But Thou didst not leave His soul in hell."

As we remember, an *aria*, taken from the word "air," is a lyrical piece usually expressing one thought or emotion and may be removed from context and performed alone. This *aria*, "Behold and See," is frequently taken out of context and performed as a solo piece in church services, especially during Holy Week. This haunting *aria* surprisingly ends on a B major chord, setting the scene for the third tenor solo in this group of four short pieces, "He was cut off out of the land of the living," which begins in B minor.

CHAPTER THIRTY-ONE

"He was cut off out of the land of the living"

(ACCOMPANIED RECITATIVE FOR TENOR)

George Frideric Handel

This tenor recitative is the lowest point in this epic story. The text from Isaiah speaks of the Suffering Servant being led to His execution as an offering for sin, reconciling many unto God.

This movement lasts all of fifteen seconds. The text is a continuation of the famous poem by Isaiah about the "suffering servant of the Lord," as found in its entirety in Isaiah 52:13-53:12. This is the same poem from which "He was despised," "Surely He has borne our griefs," and "All we like sheep" have already come, and been discussed.

Isaiah's Scripture was chosen for its dramatic effect. In his exegesis on Isaiah in *The Interpreter's Bible,* James Muilenburg says, "Three major areas of eschatological thought which occupy the prophet's mind are creation, history, and redemption. His soul was sharpened by his people's griefs to penetrate the secrets of God and body them forth in moving speech."[1]

At this time in history, Isaiah's writings have a depth that is marked by the way in which nature responds to the movement of events. His primary matrix is eschatological—yes, he mentions a great divine event that marks the decisive end of the age.[2] When we realize what was happening in biblical history at the time this Scripture passage was written, we add another rich layer to our understanding of Handel's music.

---

1 James Muilenburg, "The Book of Isaiah," *The Interpreter's Bible,* Vol. V (New York: Abingdon Press, 1956), 623.
2 Ibid., 399.

In this particular sequence in the drama of the oratorio, Jennens has chosen to include these two lines:

> He was cut off out of the land of the living,
> For the transgressions of Thy people was He stricken.

(Isaiah 53:8 KJV)

This metaphorical language clearly indicates death. The servant is portrayed as being led to execution, similar to a lamb being led to the slaughter. The emphasis is on the "silence of the lamb," in the context of suffering and humiliation. James Muilenburg notes, "By oppression and judgment, He was taken away. This represents Israel, which no longer existed as an independent nation, but as a people who are now a corpse cut off out of the land of the living."[3] Leonard van Camp suggests, "The key word is 'stricken' which indicates 'death by crucifixion.'"[4]

In oratorios, we sometimes ignore the dramatic situation as if there is no plot. None of the singers is given a title or character name, and in *Messiah* there is no narrator telling the story or connecting the events. There are no costumes or scenery. But the listener is cautioned not to forget the concept of the whole picture.

Handel frequently used a soprano to sing this *recitative* instead of a tenor. The previous two pieces were sung by a tenor, and perhaps this change of voice is just what the listener needs to heighten his interest. The *recitative* is only five measures long, as we see in the score below:

---

3 Muilenburg, 625.

4 Leonard Van Camp, *A Practical Guide for Performing, Teaching and Singing* Messiah (Dayton, Ohio: Lorenz, Roger Dean Publishing Co., 1993), 90.

HANDEL'S

The *basso-continuo* accompaniment begins in the key of B minor, quickly becomes moored, and resolves in E major for the next tenor *aria*. (Observe the chord changes in the score on the previous page.)

In the final strophe of the poem, we find that the movements of events are all under God's control and His purpose is revealed. God is the speaker, and He tells us that He planned it all. The goal of His purpose is that "Judah should become in truth, as well as in name, 'His people,' and should survive as His witness in the world. The Lord is both her judge and her defender. Both through Israel and through Christ, God was reconciling the world unto Himself."[5]

In verse 11, the Servant makes Himself an offering for sin, allowing many to be accounted righteous.

> He shall see of the travail of his soul, and shall be satisfied:
> By his knowledge shall my righteous servant justify many;
> for he shall bear their iniquities.
>
> (Isaiah 53:11 KJV)

The Servant pours out His soul to death, is numbered with the transgressors, bears the sins of many, and makes intercession for the transgressors. When Christ makes Himself an offering for sin, this does not imply that Israel placates a hostile God. The *King James Version* here rightly stresses God's prompting of this sacrifice. God the Father, with His love, precedes our reconciliation in Christ. God initiated this; He didn't delegate it. God loved us so much that He entered into our earthly existence. John Calvin, in his *Institutes,* states, "Because He first loved us, therefore He afterwards reconciles us unto Himself." The Servant was imprisoned, subjected to an unjust trial, and condemned to death. He was "cut off from the land of the living, stricken for the transgressions of the people, and to the very last, He was persecuted and rejected."[6]

We hear in the "Suffering Servant" passage many aspects of His suffering: how He suffered for us, His silent suffering in life and death, and finally, the Lord's purpose and the future destiny of the Servant, which becomes manifested in His exaltation.

---

5 Muilenburg, 628.
6 Ibid., 626.

Some people might ask, "Where was God during this time?" He was right there with Jesus, suffering along with Him, and for us. This short *recitative* is often omitted in many performances of *Messiah*. But I feel that the entire story must be told. This piece signifies the lowest point in the drama. It is as if you dove into a swimming pool to the very bottom; then you push off from the bottom and begin to ascend to the top. This piece represents the "bottom of the pool," or the utter abandonment of the lonely Christ, a position He had to take in order to bring about perfect salvation for us.

CHAPTER THIRTY-TWO

"But Thou didst not leave His soul in hell"

(ARIA FOR TENOR [OR SOPRANO])

A push off from the bottom of the pool . . . for this aria begins to lighten the mood of death and abandonment, thus representing the resurrection of our Lord Jesus Christ.

George Frideric Handel

The E major of the preceding *recitative* for tenor is the dominant V to A major in this *aria* for tenor. In the text from Psalm 16:10, the psalmist David expresses his contentment based on his trust in God. He is thankful to the Lord for his many blessings. He says, "I have set the Lord always before me: because he is at my right hand, I shall not be moved. Therefore my heart is glad, and my soul rejoices. My body also dwells secure." Here is the Scripture for this *aria*:

> For thou will not leave my
> soul in hell, neither wilt thou
> suffer thine Holy One to see corruption.
> (Psalm 16:10 KJV)

This is a turning point in the tone of the music of *Messiah*. We've already hit rock bottom in chapter thirty-one, literally "to hell and back," so we begin our ascent with "Thou didst not leave his soul in hell." The music now begins to lose its heaviness; it is becoming lighter, thus representing the resurrection. The violins begin the celebratory, happy tune in A major in 4/4 meter marked *andante larghetto* (walking slowly). It is almost a laughing tune with trills (tr.) in the violins, along with the *basso-continuo* accompaniment.[1] Look at the following score:

Again we are reminded that an *aria* has a formal musical structure. (The term *aria* is Italian for "song," as in "air," signifying that when a piece is sung, it releases the tension.)[2] An *aria* is reflective and expresses feelings, rather than presenting information or forwarding the action. This is a perfect time for the tenor to break the tension in the drama as he expands and redeems the theme presented in chapter thirty-one: "He was cut off out of the land of the living."

1 Leonard Van Camp, *A Practical Guide for Performing, Teaching and Singing* Messiah (Dayton, Ohio: Lorenz, Roger Dean Publishing Co., 1993), 92.
2 Willi Apel, *Harvard Dictionary of Music,* 2nd edition (Cambridge, Massachusetts: Harvard University Press, 1964), 49.

HANDEL'S *Messiah*

The *Revised Standard Version* of Psalm 16:10 says:

> For thou dost not give me up to
> Sheol, or let thy godly one see the Pit.

With the use of the phrase "the godly one," or "the holy one," the psalmist David is referring to himself. However, the pivotal key to the interpretation of this psalm is found in the preceding verse 8 with the reference to "right hand":

> I keep the LORD always before me;
> Because he is at my right hand,
> I shall not be moved.
>
> (Psalm 16:8 RSV)

We now interpret this verse as referring to Jesus Christ as "sitting at the right hand of the Father God." Thus, we begin to understand that "God did not leave his soul in hell, nor allow His Holy One to see corruption."

In Acts 2:25-28, Peter made reference to this passage in his address on the day of Pentecost. He quotes from these very verses of Psalm 16, suggesting that David, as the prophet, was foretelling the resurrection of Christ, "that his soul was not left in hell."[3]

The *Contemporary English Version* helps us understand the text in user-friendly terms:

> I am your chosen one. You won't leave me in
> the grave or let my body decay.
> (Psalm 16:10)

It is interesting to see what the librettist did *not* choose as the text for *Messiah*. Jennens did not choose verse 9b (immediately before the chosen text), which says, "My flesh also shall rest in hope," or "my body also dwells secure." Surely this is a hint about immortality. But technically, there is no reference to—or a hint—of

---

3 William R. Taylor, "The Book of Psalms," *The Interpreter's Bible*, Vol. IV (New York: Abingdon Press, 1956), 85.

the doctrine of resurrection after death. The Hebrew means only that he is not abandoned by God to Sheol (hell).[4]

Handel ends this *aria* by modulating to the dominant key of the succeeding piece. Again, he prepares our ear for what is to come. We breathe a little lighter, as the violins lightly trill to the end and bring us to a favorite chorus that follows: "Lift Up Ye Heads, O Ye Gates."

---

4 Ibid., 86.

HANDEL'S *Messiah*

CHAPTER THIRTY-THREE

"Lift up ye heads, O ye gates"

(CHORUS)

This favorite antiphonal chorus is part of a victory procession in which the Lord's throne moves up the hill toward the great gates of the temple. The King of Glory wants in!

George Frideric Handel

A favorite chorus in "Part the Second" is this chorus, "Lift Up Ye Heads," taken from Psalm 24:7-10 (KJV). (These verses are dated probably late in the pre-exilic period):

> Lift up your heads, O ye gates;
> And be ye lift up, ye everlasting doors:
> And the King of Glory may come in.
> Who is this King of Glory?
> The Lord, strong and mighty,
> The Lord, mighty in battle!
>
> Lift up your heads, O ye gates:
> even lift them up, ye everlasting doors;
> And the King of glory shall come in.
> Who is this King of Glory?
> The Lord of hosts,
> He is the King of Glory!

Figuratively, these verses represent the scene in which God, the King of Glory, is seeking admission to His temple. Picture this: God, with His true worshipers, is standing at the entrance to His church, challenging the evildoers inside the church to open the gates to Himself, the victorious God. William Taylor, in his exegesis on Psalms in *The Interpreter's Bible*, suggests, "The gates of the church may represent a hostile entity that must be purified by the Lord."[1]

Renowned Bible commentator Charles Laymon says:

> The entire Psalm 24 is a hymn to the King of Glory, and is referred to as an "entrance liturgy for the Lord's coming to His temple as King." During the festival of the enthronement (a cultic procession bearing the ark), the Lord's throne moves up the hill of the Lord toward the great gates of the temple and sings in praise of the world—embracing sovereignty and the creative power of God. The procession asks the priests for the conditions of entrance to the temple. The procession calls on the temple gates to open and admit the Lord, symbolized by the ark.
>
> The God who seeks entrance is the King of Glory. From within the temple the priests demand further identification of the deity. The procession answers that he is the God of the old holy tradition, the mighty warrior and commander of Israel's hosts.[2]

These verses, chosen by Jennens for the *Messiah* libretto, are an antiphonal song in which the voices of a company in front of the gates of the temple alternate with the voices from behind the gates. Handel appropriately expresses this with an antiphonal choir answering responsively.

The scene is a victory procession that comes to, and stops right in front of the gates of the temple. But the gates are too low to receive the high and exalted One who is about to pass through them. (Among the Romans, the greater the victor, the higher was the triumphal arch that the king of glory may walk through. It is to be noted that the Lord is here described as a king.) The Egyptians believed that when the doors of the earthly temple opened, the portals of heaven swung wide as well. The God who seeks entrance is the King of Glory, the ruler whose power and authority are unlimited.[3] Doesn't this scene have all the elements of a good action DVD?

---

1 William R. Taylor, "The Book of Psalms," *The Interpreter's Bible*, Vol. IV (New York: Abingdon Press, 1956), 134.

2 Charles M. Laymon, *The Interpreter's One-volume Commentary* (New York: Abingdon Press, 1971), 269.

3 Ibid., 270.

Handel begins this chorus in F major, with dotted eighth notes beating out this jubilant rhythm. A three-part treble choir sounds like heralding trumpets as they sing, "Lift up your heads, O ye gates, and be ye lift up, ye everlasting doors, and the King of glory shall come in." Look at the music score:

The tenors and basses ask, "*Who* is this King of Glory?" The treble voices answer, "The Lord strong and mighty." This is followed by an alternating form with the lower voices singing, "Lift up your heads," and the upper voices asking, "Who is this King of Glory?" which is finally answered by the lower voices who respond with "The Lord of Hosts."[4] Look at the music score below:

---

4 Leonard Van Camp, *A Practical Guide for Performing, Teaching and Singing* Messiah (Dayton, Ohio: Lorenz, Roger Dean Publishing Co., 1993), 94.

Notice the three treble voice parts. The sopranos are divided into first and second sopranos and are joined by the altos. It is interesting to note that in later copies of the musical score of *Messiah*, "Boys" was marked in pencil for the second soprano part. Thus, the "Soprano I" part was allotted to the women soloists, not the youngest boys of Handel's choir.[5]

This piece continues antiphonally, with the voices of the group in front of the gates alternating with the voices of those behind the gates. As Machlis and Forney comment in their book, *The Enjoyment of Music*, "The question, 'Who is the King of Glory?' elicits a reply of Handelian grandeur. The text originally asks, 'Who is this King, not *the* King.' Then it went to "the King." However, it is easier to drop the 's' sound vocally, and sing 'this,' which is accepted today. Yet, the distinction should be noted. The music *crescendos*, as the repeated question seems to build in anxiety."[6]

Many measures later, we hear the question asked again by the treble voice, "Who is the King of Glory?" William Taylor remarks, "This time we hear the confident reply; and with the answer, 'the Lord of Hosts,' the gates swing open. This is the magic answer, the 'open sesame' they've been waiting for."[7]

In the following score, Handel raises the melody line each time the sopranos repeat "the Lord of Hosts," as if they are climbing:

5 Alfred Mann, ed., *Handel's* Messiah *in Full Score* (New York: Dover Publications, 1989), 221.
6 Joseph Machlis and Kristine Forney, eds., *The Enjoyment of Music*, 6th edition (New York: W. W. Norton & Co., 1990), 168.
7 Taylor, 135.

The *basso-continuo* part, primarily written for the harpsichord or organ, continues to carry the chorus along to a dramatic rest before the final words, "of Glory." This rest of three long beats is very effective. It has been said that silence is as much a part of communication as is speaking (or in this case, singing).

In some churches these verses in Psalm 24:7-10 are used as the "Call to Worship." The minister will announce, "Lift up your heads," as if prompting the listeners to draw near to worship the Lord. Interestingly enough, in this text, the gates have also been interpreted to mean "the gates of death yielding to their master," as in death and resurrection. Additionally, the "gates" have been used to represent "the gates of the human heart barred against God." In many Scottish churches, the metrical version of these verses is found in the Scottish Psalter. The phrase, "Ye gates, lift up your heads on high," is used to open the evening service on Communion Sundays.[8]

---

8 Ibid., 136.

CHAPTER THIRTY-FOUR

"Unto which of the angels said He"

(RECITATIVE FOR TENOR)

George Frideric Handel

The words of this piece, posed in the form of a sarcastic question, are a stirring defense of the divine superiority of Jesus as the Messiah over the angels. So . . . did he ever tell an angel this?

This brief *recitative* is usually performed without a conductor. Ironically, the piece was omitted at the premiere performance, but purists believe that it should not be omitted in performances today.[1] This *recitative* and the following chorus both point toward proving the divinity of Christ, explaining His supreme role in our redemption, and securing His rightful place alongside the Father.

"Unto which of the angels said He" is a very short *secco*, or "dry" *recitative*, which means it has very few chords in the accompaniment. Even though there are only a few chords in this piece, the sound that one hears is gorgeous. Look at the music on the following page:

---

1 Leonard Van Camp, *A Practical Guide for Performing, Teaching and Singing* Messiah (Dayton, Ohio: Lorenz, Roger Dean Publishing Co., 1993), 93.

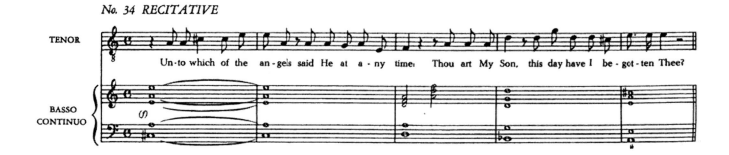

TENOR

Un-to which of the an-gels said He at a - ny time: Thou art My Son, this day have I be-got-ten Thee?

BASSO CONTINUO

The text comes from a stirring defense of the divinity of the Messiah, as found in the letter to the Hebrews. Scholars believe that the letter was written prior to the fall of Jerusalem and the destruction of the temple in AD 70. The entire letter to the Hebrews stresses the superiority of Jesus Christ over all that is held to be important to the Jewish religion—the prophets, angels, Moses, the Levitical priesthood, the covenant, and the sacrifices. The words of the text appear in the form of a question, and they are delivered perhaps with a bit of sarcasm:

> Unto which of the angels said He at any time:
> "Thou art My son, this day have I begotten Thee?"
> > (Hebrews 1:5 KJV)

The words, which are meant to be Messianically interpreted, are extremely significant in the working out of the purpose of God. The theological question being discussed is, "Who is this Jesus the Christ?" The unknown author of the text sees Jesus Christ as the fulfillment of the sacrificial plan of God.[2] The Revised Standard Version of the text uses these words:

> To what angel did God ever say: "Thou art my Son,
> today I have begotten thee?"

At this point in the oratorio, it is interesting that the librettist would introduce the contrast between Jesus Christ and the angels. In Jewish thought, angels held a very important role as the mediators of God's revelation to His people. Yet it had to be proven that Jesus was divine, that He was higher than the angels so He could have divine authority.

---

2 Alexander Purdy, "The Epistle to the Hebrews," *The Interpreter's Bible*, Vol. XI (New York: Abingdon Press, 1955), 604.

This verse begins a series of eloquent statements that are quotes from the Old Testament. Hebrews 1:5 is also found in Psalm 2:7 and 2 Samuel 7:14. Jesus is first being compared to the angels, and His superiority is shown by seven quotations: five of them assert the pre-eminence of the Son in His unique relationship to the Father; the other two quotations stress the servant function of the angels and their obligation to worship the Son.[3]

Eerdman's New Bible Commentary says:

> The whole method of explanation is very significant. It implies firstly that the Old Testament possesses a direct relevance and a decisive authority for Christian believers. Secondly, the words quoted are ascribed not to the human psalmist and prophets, but directly to God as their author. Thirdly, it is now possible for those who are acquainted with the final revelation in Christ to see in the words of the Old Testament a meaning and significance with reference to Christ, which could not possibly have been seen in the same way, either by those who wrote them, or by any before Christ came.[4]

The second half of the verse is followed by:

> Or to whom do I say:
> "I will be to him a father,
> and he shall be to me a son?"
>   (Hebrews 1:5b RSV)

Even though this verse is omitted by Jennens in his libretto, it seems to substantiate the superiority factor. The phrase, "Thou art my son," was a legal formula used in the ceremony of adoption in ancient Semitic countries. The father pronounced this ritualistic statement over the child whom he was adopting, with witnesses present to certify the act. The child thus became the son and heir of his father.[5]

---

3 Warren Quanbeck, "The Letter to the Hebrews," *The Interpreter's One-Volume Commentary on the Bible* (New York: Abingdon Press, 1971), 900.

4 Guthrie, Motyer, Stibbs and Wiseman, *Eerdman's New Bible Commentary,* Revised (Grand Rapids, Michigan: InterVarsity Press, 1970), 1195.

5 Quanbeck, 900.

HANDEL'S *Messiah*

Eerdman's New Bible Commentary continues:

> "Son" is the more excellent name by which Christ's superiority to angels is measured. The Son is superior to the angels: first, because of what He is eternally as God; second, because of what He has now become as the exalted God-man. The first quote from Psalm 2:7 introduces both thoughts. There never was a time when the Father could *not* say to Him, "Thou art my Son." But there came a day in time due to His resurrection in glorified humanity that He was begotten to a new status as the exalted Man. Consequently, He is not only the Son by virtue of His deity, but He is also now exalted to be the Son due to His humanity (the first-born among many brethren).[6]

Noted biblical scholar Warren Quanbeck says, "The use of the formula (expressing the relationship between father and son) in the enthronement ceremony stressed such a relationship between the covenant God and the king. Here the author sees the ceremony of enthronement as a prophetic event pointing forward to the coming of the true King and the words of the hymn as supremely fitting in the enthronement of the Messiah."[7]

So, if any of us doubts that Jesus is held in very high esteem, this text in Hebrews clinches the superiority of the Son Jesus Christ to any of the angels. For God says to Jesus, "You are My Son, this day have I begotten Thee." Well, He certainly didn't tell any angel *that*.

In his commentary on Hebrews, Alexander Purdy says, "Jesus is seen as the culmination of a historic process of God's purpose. Why is this so important? Because proof is expected! There is no room for mere intimations of Jesus' divinity. He must be fully divine and fully human. Nothing less will do. Only God could initiate so daring a ministry that we can be saved through our belief in His Son, Jesus the Christ."[8]

The final A major chord is the dominant of the D major chorus following in the next chapter. This short *recitative* serves as a hyphen between two choruses: the previous chorus, "Lift up ye heads" shows Jesus as the King of Glory entering His temple; and the following chorus, "Let all the angels of God worship Him," in which His superior status is shown. Jesus the Christ truly is the fulfillment of the sacrificial plan of God.

---

6 Eerdman's, *Guthrie, Motyer, Stibbs and Wiseman*, 196.
7 Quanbeck, 900.
8 Purdy, 599.

CHAPTER THIRTY-FIVE

"Let all the angels of God worship Him"

(CHORUS)

George Frideric Handel

How glorious! This polyphonic four-part "Angel Chorus" surrounds the scene with worship of the Son as He is enthroned as King.

As we've noticed, Handel revised *Messiah* for almost every new performance just to suit a new singer, or himself. He may have been sitting across the room while his assistant, John Christopher Smith, was making the first copy of the oratorio, which was kept up to date with later versions, changes, or clarifications. Even today conductors choose which pieces of *Messiah* they wish to perform, either according to a preference or perhaps due to the vocal talent available for the performance.

This chorus is not widely known because it is one of those frequently omitted. In his book, *Handel's* Messiah: *A Critical Account of Manuscript Sources*, John Tobin argues, "Nothing in *Messiah* can be omitted without damaging the work as a whole. For example, the chorus 'Lift Up Ye Heads' is incomplete and lacking in purpose unless it is followed by the joyful adoration 'Let all the angels of God worship Him.' Likewise, 'The trumpet shall sound' is less meaningful if we are denied the promise of immortality expressed in the air's middle section."[1]

---

1 John Tobin, *Handel's* Messiah: *A Critical Account of the Manuscript Sources and Printed Editions*, (London: Cassel & Co., 1969), 155.

This chorus, "Let all the angels of God worship Him," is a lively *allegro* in 4/4 time written in D major. Look at the following music score:

Following the beginning of this chorus, the voices break into a *fugue* that is continuous all the way to the end, repeating only these eight words: "Let all the angels of God worship Him." The text resumes in the first chapter in Hebrews, following with the very next verse:

> And again, when he brings the first-born into the world, he says,
> "Let all God's angels worship him."
>
> (Hebrews 1:6 RSV)

Eerdman's New Bible Commentary explains:

> The use of the words "first-born which He brings into the world" emphasizes the incarnate Son in the historic Jesus. Jesus is the "first-born" in a double sense: first, as the only-begotten of the Father, existing before the created universe and lord over it; and secondly, as the first-born from the dead, who has, as the great path-maker of salvation, opened the way for many to enter as sons and daughters into glory. These verses indicate that at His Second Coming, Jesus embodies the prophetic vision of God coming to judge as fulfilled in the Person of His Son. It is at this time that His deity will be openly manifested.[2]

Thomas Nelson's *New King James Version Study Bible* further clarifies this chorus: "The angels worship the Son when He is enthroned as the King over the entire earth after taking revenge on His enemies and restoring His people."[3] Perhaps this chorus is not as dynamic a composition as the words imply, but it is a worthy, solid chorus that rightly should be performed. It confirms that "all the angels of God worship Him," since the four-part "Angel Chorus" surrounds the scene with polyphonic music. The chorus tells us that the Son has divine authority, in contrast to the subservient role of the angels, who are simply moving the oratorio along in its storyline.

The *Contemporary English Version* of the Bible interprets Hebrews 1:6:

> When God brings his first-born Son into the world,
> He commands all of his angels to worship Him.

This text from the late pre-exilic era (800-600 BC), which comes from the Septuagint, is an expansion of the conclusion to the "Song of Moses" found in the Book of Deuteronomy, which was recited at renewal ceremonies[4] :

---

2 Guthrie, Motyer, Stibbs and Wiseman, *Eerdman's New Bible Commentary,* Revised (Grand Rapids, Michigan: InterVarsity Press, 1970), 1196.

3 Note taken from *The New King James Version Study Bible,* copyright, 1997, by Thomas Nelson, Inc. Used by permission, 2077.

4 Warren Quanbeck, "The Letter to the Hebrews," *The Interpreter's One-Volume Commentary on the Bible* (New York: Abingdon Press, 1971), 900.

HANDEL'S *Messiah*

Praise his people, O you nations;
For he avenges the blood of his servants,
and takes vengeance on his adversaries,
and makes expiation for the land of his people.
(Deuteronomy 32:43 RSV)

Deuteronomy 32:44 continues, "Moses came and recited all the words of this song in the hearing of the people, he and Joshua the son of Nun. And when Moses had finished speaking all these words to all Israel, he said to them: 'Lay to heart all the words which I enjoin upon you this day, that you may command them to your children, that they may be careful to do all the words of this law.'"

CHAPTER THIRTY-SIX

"Thou art gone up on high"

(ARIA FOR BASS)

George Frideric Handel

Ah, Jerusalem!
After His victory over the Canaanite kings,
the Lord transferred His residence from Sinai
to the holy mountain in Jerusalem.

This *aria*, originally written for bass in D minor, was revised for a favorite male alto (or castrato), Gaetano Guadagni, to show off his voice.[1] In fact, it was rewritten several times, and there is even a soprano version.[2] Handel's manuscript of the present version was written on a separate sheet of paper and inserted, probably in 1750.

Many listeners are not familiar with this *aria* because, unfortunately, chapters thirty-four through thirty-seven are frequently omitted from performances. But I would remind conductors that since *Messiah* was conceived and composed as a whole, it should be performed as such.

---

1 David W. Barber, *Getting a Handle on Handel's* Messiah (Toronto, Canada: Sound & Vision Publishers, Limited, 1994), 72.

2 Leonard Van Camp, *A Practical Guide for Performing, Teaching and Singing* Messiah (Dayton, Ohio: Lorenz, Roger Dean Publishing Co., 1993), 98.

Jennens' libretto presents the words of this *aria* as follows:

> Thou art gone up on high,
> Thou hast led captivity captive
> and received gifts for men,
> yea, even for thine enemies,
> that the Lord might dwell among them.
>
> (Psalm 68:18 KJV)

The *Revised Standard Version* of the Bible clarifies the text for us:

> With mighty chariotry, twice ten thousand,
> thousands upon thousands,
> the Lord came from Sinai into the holy place.
> He did ascend the high mount, leading captives in thy train,
> and receiving gifts among men, even among the rebellious,
> that the Lord God may dwell there.

The *Contemporary English Version* of the Bible says simply:

> When you climbed the high mountain,
> you took prisoners with you and were given gifts.
> Your enemies didn't want you to live there,
> but they gave you gifts."

This hymn is another reminder of the conquest of Canaan. This obscure verse tells how, after His victory over the Canaanite kings, the Lord transferred His residence from Sinai to the holy mount in Jerusalem, leading His captives and receiving the homage of His subjects.[3] Like an earthly king, the Lord enters His capital at the head of His troops, with the captives and the spoils of His battles in His train. He is receiving gifts—the loot—even from the rebellious. Those who have offered stubborn resistance to the conqueror must yield to Him. (This could mean the Jebusites, who held out against the Hebrews.)[4]

---

3 Lawrence Toombs, "The Psalms," *The Interpreter's One-Volume Commentary on the Bible* (New York: Abingdon Press, 1971), 281.
4 William Taylor, "The Book of Psalms," *The Interpreter's Bible*, Vol. IV (New York: Abingdon Press, 1955), 357.

Joyce Meyer's *Everyday Life Bible* explains that "David, the author of the Psalms, sang of the ark of the covenant which, after a great victory, was transferred or brought back to Zion. This earthly celebration of victory in battle, with the processional bearing the ark into the temple, is a type of method and course of the Messiah's kingdom, i.e., the certain triumph of God's kingdom and Christ's ascension to His place of enthronement."[5]

Renowned biblical scholar Lawrence Toombs notes, "God is ascending upon His holy mountain. Jewish rabbis associated this text with Moses who ascended Mt. Sinai, received the law from God and then gave it as a gift to Israel."[6] In his commentary on Ephesians, Francis Beare declares, "The psalm was even quoted by Paul in Ephesians 4:8, and the Christian interpretation clearly associates these words with Christ, rather than Moses. The psalm, since it affirms that 'he ascended,' assumes that he also had first descended from heaven as the Son of Man, Christ's earthly incarnation, and his further descent into Hades. The ascent therefore represents Christ's triumphant return to the heavenly sphere."[7]

In the very opening section of the music, the change from the preceding chorus in D major marked *tutti* (full orchestra) to this D minor key of the small ensemble, "suggests the typically reflective situation of the *aria*. The mood expressed is more thoughtful in its triumph than militant, and Handel reflects that with the tempo marking of *allegro larghetto* (moving in a broad sense) and with his use of the minor key. The piece is rather long for being relatively unknown and infrequently performed, with only the violins accompanying the bass, along with the *basso-continuo*."[8] The opening two lines of the score are shown on the following page.

Handel's original score clearly shows the *larghetto* marking; but the *allegro* indication is unclear, appearing faded and blotted rather than crossed out. Perhaps this is a minor point to make, but it may suggest a sequence of alterations made by the composer that will prove to be important. Handel seems to have evidently decided on a ¾ marking for the tempo, or "mood," of the *aria* that blended the original "lively" direction with the later "somewhat broad" notation:

5 Joyce Meyer, *The Everyday Life Bible*, Amplified Version (New York: Warner Faith, 2006), 879.
6 Toombs, 841.
7 Francis Beare, "The Epistle to the Ephesians," *The Interpreter's Bible*, Vol. X (New York: Abingdon Press, 1953), 688.
8 Alfred Mann, ed., *Handel's* Messiah *in Full Score* (New York: Dover Publications, 1989), 222.

HANDEL'S *Messiah*

Van Camp remarks, "With its big effects, its slow pace, and its massive repetitions, Handel's *Messiah* has the architecture of a monumental temple. The piece has the feeling of joy and triumph, not sorrow. Satan, sin and death are now under Christ's power."[9]

---

9 Van Camp, 99.

"The Lord gave the word"

(CHORUS)

A larger ensemble, representing the "company," now celebrates the grand procession of God into His sanctuary . . . God's word shatters the enemy, and a host of angels is quick to report the victory!

The Lord gave the word;
great was the company of preachers.

(Psalm 68:11 NKJV)

George Frideric Handel

This chorus in B flat major takes its text from the same Psalm 68 as the preceding chapter thirty-six, but this eleventh verse comes a bit earlier. The leading motif of the entire psalm is the Lord's assumption of His kingship in Zion. This post-exilic psalm is celebratory in nature and is related to Psalms 24 and 47, in which the kingship of the Lord is acclaimed and commemorated. The occasion in which the psalms were used as choral responses was the grand procession of God into His sanctuary.[1]

In the following score, notice the indication to use *con ripieno*, meaning to be played by a larger ensemble, or *tutti* (all instruments). Perhaps the instruments are representing the "company." Also, the

---

1 William Taylor, "The Book of Psalms," *The Interpreter's Bible*, Vol. IV (New York: Abingdon Press, 1955), 354.

rhythmic pattern suggests an accent on every dotted eighth note, especially on the word "company."[2] Look at the opening of this chorus:

The tenors and basses proclaim, "The Lord gave the word." Then all voices, like a great company of cheerleaders, sing, "Great was the company of the preachers."[3] The central idea is the spreading of the gospel by telling the salvation story. The *Revised Standard Version* of the Bible says:

> The Lord gives the command;
> Great is the host of those who bore the tidings.

---

2 Leonard Van Camp, *A Practical Guide for Performing, Teaching and Singing* Messiah (Dayton, Ohio: Lorenz, Roger Dean Publishing Co., 1993), 100.

3 Van Camp, 100.

Old Testament writers frequently used the oracular formula, with words such as "Behold" or "Thus saith the Lord" (as in this case) for literary emphasis and careful attention to the structural pattern. Here we are given an idea of an experience of worship or pageantry that was set on a very high level.[4] This Psalm 68 became a liturgy, as a recitation of Hebrew history, and was quoted by Moses when he gave the signal for lifting up the Ark of the Covenant when the Israelites broke camp and moved on. The actual prelude to the psalm says, "Let God arise, let his enemies be scattered" (Psalm 68:1).[5]

The Lord gave the word, and thousands called out the good news. God's command shatters His enemy, and His host of angels hastens to report the victory. "The word" was that God had chosen this mountain of Zion to live on and He would rule from this mountain forever.[6]

Just like in the manner of a victorious earthly king, the Lord enters His capital at the head of His troops with the captives and the spoils of His battles in His train. The intention of the poet is clear: he wants to present God as an invincible leader in battle.[7]

In his book, *A Practical Guide for Performing, Teaching, and Singing* Messiah, Leonard Van Camp says, "Those conductors, who have always omitted this chorus are in for a treat when they first rehearse it. It is a gem!"[8]

---

4 Taylor, 360.
5 Ibid, 355.
6 Ibid., 358.
7 Ibid., 357.
8 Van Camp, 100.

HANDEL'S *Messiah*

CHAPTER THIRTY-EIGHT

"How beautiful are the feet of them"

(ARIA FOR SOPRANO)

One of Handel's most lyrical "da capo" soprano arias,
announcing the swift approach of the messenger of salvation.

George Frideric Handel

In chapter thirty-seven, we studied the chorus containing the words, "Great is the company of the preachers," and now we turn our attention to the *aria* declaring, "How beautiful are the feet of them that *preach* the gospel of peace." In these biblical words set to music, God is weaving a tapestry of His ultimate plan that we don't always see. Likewise, Handel is composing a masterpiece for which the whole impact is not always fully grasped, and that is why it is very important to perform all the *arias* and *recitatives* in sequence. Machlis and Forney explain, "*Messiah* is not typical of the oratorios of Handel as a whole, as many are loaded with dramatic conflict, while *Messiah* is cast in a mood of lyric contemplation."[1]

This beautiful *aria* is often simply sung as a solo in church services, for it is deemed one of Handel's most lyrical creations. Its swaying *siciliano* rhythm is typical of the late Baroque instrumental movements or *arias* that evoke a gentle, pastoral mood. In this case, Handel wrote a slow 12/8 meter, with simple phrases

---

1 Joseph Machlis and Kristine Forney, eds., *The Enjoyment of Music,* 6th edition (New York: W. W. Norton & Co., 1990), 167.

and repeated dotted rhythms. The lilting *siciliano* rhythm was also used in the "Pastoral symphony" and "He shall feed His flock."[2]

The texts for this *aria* and the following chorus, "Their sound is gone out into all lands," should be connected as one unit. The scene involves watchmen standing on the walls, announcing the coming of the messenger of salvation whose theme is of good news. Jerusalem is redeemed, her devastated city restored, and all the nations see the power of God's saving act. Now God is proclaimed as King in Zion, the place where He has chosen to reveal Himself in His royal power. His kingship is supreme, only awaiting acknowledgement by the world.[3]

The present form of this *aria* appears in Handel's original score as the "A" section of a *da capo aria* (having an ABA form), with section "A" repeated at the end. In between is the "B" section, "Their sound is gone out" (found in the next chapter thirty-nine). However, now this *aria* stands on its own. Handel continued to revise these pieces and wrote several new settings for the entire text of the oratorio. Each time he conducted the *aria*, he revised it as different soloists became available.

Mr. Jennens adapted his text from the *King James Version* of the similar Scriptures:

> And how shall they preach unless they are sent?
> As it is written:
> "How beautiful are the feet of them that preach the
> gospel of peace and bring glad tidings
> of good things."
>
> (Romans 10:15; Isaiah 52:7)

We don't usually think of feet as being "beautiful," do we? And for those of you who jog or run marathons, just how beautiful *are* your feet? The vision of the feet in this Scripture is of "the feet of the one who runs from the scene of battle across the mountains to the city waiting for news. The prophet Isaiah is concentrating on the swift approach of the messenger and watches his feet as they bring him nearer to the

---

2 Leonard Van Camp, *A Practical Guide for Performing, Teaching and Singing* Messiah (Dayton, Ohio: Lorenz, Roger Dean Publishing Co., 1993), 103.
3 Charles Laymon, ed. *The Interpreter's One-Volume Commentary on the Bible,* (New York: Abingdon Press, 1971), 363.

city."[4] The commentary in the *New King James Version Study Bible* says, "The glorious message of this runner is salvation, meaning 'victorious deliverance.' This is the 'good news,' or glad tidings."[5]

The *Contemporary English Version* of the Bible is very clear:

> How can people have faith in the Lord and ask
> Him to save them if they have never heard about Him?
> And how can they hear, unless someone tells them? And how can
> anyone tell them without being sent by the Lord? The Scriptures
> say it is a beautiful sight to see even the feet of someone coming
> to preach the good news.
>
> (Romans 10:14-15)

The violins were the only instruments chosen to play along with the *basso-continuo* accompaniment, which Handel himself played on the organ or harpsichord. The soprano must surely feel the lilting rhythm of the *aria* as she is in concert with, and imitates, the tender, ethereal tone of the violins. The rhythm instinctively makes the listener sway in time as well. In the last line of the music, Handel marked the violin part *forte* (loud) as the violins repeat the soprano's theme to bring the contemplative piece to an end.

---

4 James Muilenburg, "The Book of Isaiah," *The Interpreter's Bible*, Vol. V (New York: Abingdon Press, 1956), 615.

5 Note taken from *The New King James Version Study Bible*, copyright, 1997, by Thomas Nelson, Inc. Used by permission, 1196.

If people today are to hear the gospel, there must be someone who will tell them the Good News. We assume that this is the job of those who have the gift of preaching and have been sent by God Himself. Yet, we cannot just wait for those who have been "called by God" to the ordained ministry to be the only people proclaiming the truth. We, too, can be sharing this universal grace and salvation for all.

Charles Laymon tells us, "There is an urgent need for worldwide proclamation of this free mercy of God that suggests the universality of salvation through Christ. Messianic expectations have been fulfilled in Christ; the salvation that He brings is the true satisfaction of the hopes aroused by prophecy.[6] This Scripture passage asks the question, "How are they to believe in Him of whom they have never heard?" But I ask, "Have you not heard?" I should hope that surely America has heard of Jesus Christ, yet there are still so many who need to hear of His saving grace.

---

6 Laymon, 787.

HANDEL'S *Messiah*

CHAPTER THIRTY-NINE

"Their sound is gone out into all lands"

(CHORUS)

In this "added" chorus (written in 1749),
Handel uses vocal entrances as waves of sound,
suggesting reverberation into all the lands.

George Frideric Handel

The Baroque period reached its peak with the music of Bach and Handel and roughly ended at the time of their deaths around the middle of the eighteenth century. It was a time of great composers and the development of many new forms of musical expression. In the Baroque era, the opera, oratorio, and cantata were developed for the voice; sonatas, suites, concerti, and *fugues* were new forms of instrumental music. Baroque means "irregular," or "extreme," and comes from the Portuguese term for the irregularly shaped pearl. Likewise, Baroque music is marked by musical irregularity, sweeping lines of melody, and exuberant decoration. It possesses a great amount of energy and emphasizes contrasts in moods, volume, and texture (especially the number of voices or instruments). The Baroque era was a time of longing, as compared to the air of self-assurance of the previous period called the Renaissance.[1]

---

1 Dale Cunningham, *Music and Its Makers* (New York: Sterling Publishing Company, Inc., 1963), 27.

We come to this unfamiliar chorus written in 1749 that was later added to Handel's original version of the score.[2] Perhaps Handel felt he needed to add a "chorus" to fill out the architectural structure of the oratorio, as well as expand on the theme of the words:

> Their voice is gone out to all the earth,
> and their words to the ends of the world.
>
> (Romans 10:18 RSV)

The words convey an urgency to preach the Christian gospel to a hurting world. The oratorio needed this full chorus, so the piece was added immediately following "How beautiful are the feet of them." Let's closely examine the opening music:

2 Alfred Mann, ed., *Handel's* Messiah *in Full Score* (New York: Dover Publications, 1989), 223.

HANDEL'S *Messiah*

The score calls for the first and second oboe parts to begin in *fugue*-like imitation of each other, and then to complement one another in harmony. The first four measures of the violin parts (shown on the previous page) demonstrate a rhythmic pattern that Handel favored in his orchestral writing throughout his life. (He used this technique also in chapter seven, "And He shall purify.") It suggests a specially pointed use of the French "down bow" technique, stressing the first and third beats of the measure.[3] The SATB chorus enters the *fugue* with each voice singing the exact same notes and words, only tiered as a *fugue*. The words are adapted from Romans 10:18:

> But I say, have they not heard? Yes indeed:
> "Their sound is gone out into all lands,
> and their words unto the ends of the world."
> (Romans 10:18 KJV adapted)

The chorus goes on and on, to high G's and low A flats, as if to "the ends of the world," all coming together in their final cadence as the following score shows:

3 Mann, 223.

In his exegesis of "The Epistle to the Romans" in *The Interpreter's Bible,* Gerald Cragg tells us:

> The apostle Paul, the author of Romans, had always preached the paramount importance of faith in response to what is heard. "Faith," he says, "comes from what is heard." A certain kind of religious belief may be *intuitively* grasped, but the distinctive kind of faith, which is characteristic of Christianity, is far too sharply defined to be reached by so vague a method.
>
> It is the objective quality which makes the role of the witness so important. Those who have seen and understood the mighty acts of God are charged with the responsibility of telling others: unless they do so, those within their reach may never come to the truth . . . . What sets preaching apart from all other kinds of speech (a talk, or public address, or lecture) is that it proclaims Christ and sets forth His abiding significance. "We preach Christ always," declared Martin Luther . . . . The purpose of preaching is to set forth Christ that He will win people's allegiance and lead them to that act of self-commitment which is our right response to what we see of God's love in Christ. [4]

Christians today have a great responsibility. We need to impact the world, telling people about the love and message of Jesus Christ. Many people have heard the gospel and may even believe that there is a loving God, but they have not personalized His love for themselves. Are we persuasively presenting this mighty message today? We, as a community of believers, understand our purpose in life is to share this good news. May the first words out of our mouths be about what God is doing in our lives and how grateful we are. Let's show the world that we are just everyday people, desiring to connect with each other, to encounter God in a real way. Let's be intentional! Let's engage in spirited conversations with a family member or a Facebook friend, sharing the Good News and the joy of knowing the Lord.

Again we are reminded of Handel's use of tone-painting; he used the voice entrances as waves of sound, expressing an echoing effect of reverberation into all the lands. He had a special psychological feeling for pictorial effects in music. Toward the end of the chorus, (in bar 31), the dynamic crescendo begins and must

---

4 Gerald Cragg, "The Epistle to the Romans," *The Interpreter's Bible,* Vol. IX (New York: Abingdon Press, 1956), 562.

be sustained up until the brilliant finish.[5] This particular chorus was needed to provide another "pillar" in the structure of this masterwork.

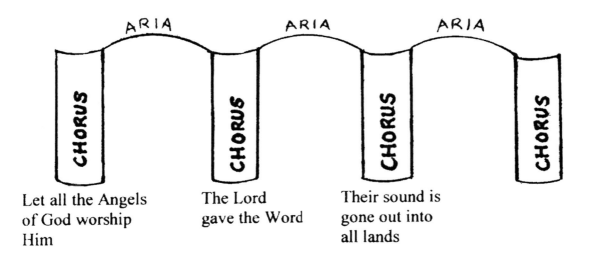

Let all the Angels of God worship Him

The Lord gave the Word

Their sound is gone out into all lands

5 G. H. Erich Schmid, *George Frideric Handel* (New York: C. F. Peters Corporation, 1979, originally Henry Litolff's *Verlag*, 1977), 45.

CHAPTER FORTY

"Why do the nations so furiously rage?"

(ARIA FOR BASS)

George Frideric Handel

How presumptuous of the people to plot against God Himself!

The text for this *aria* is taken from Psalm 2:1-2, which dates from a time after the reign of Solomon before the fall of Jerusalem, circa 931-586 BC. Lawrence Toombs observes, "The psalm was composed for use at a coronation of a king or at the annual enthronement festival. In the ancient world the accession of a king was the opportunity for his vassal states to assert their independence. In accents of shocked wonder, the Israelite king pictures this happening on a world-wide scale. This scripture could be entitled 'world rebellion,' and is very prevalent in today's world."[1]

The *aria* begins with a long introduction of fourteen measures of agitated strings. Then the bold bass soloist sings, "Why do the nations rage so furiously?" The tempo marking is *allegro* (a cheerful, quick tempo), "but the emotion is angry and restless, as if we are being 'rushed forward to our final judgment.' The hurried pace just doesn't let up. There is a florid expansion on the word 'rage,' demanding some virtuoso singing on the part of the soloist with its particularly challenging rhythmic pattern of difficult triplets, a feeling of three beats against the four beats of a steady accompaniment."[2] Notice the triplets in the following score:

---

1 Lawrence Toombs, "The Psalms," *The Interpreter's One-Volume Commentary on the Bible* (New York: Abingdon Press, 1971), 261.

2 Leonard Van Camp, *A Practical Guide for Performing, Teaching and Singing* Messiah (Dayton, Ohio: Lorenz, Roger Dean Publishing Co., 1993), 114.

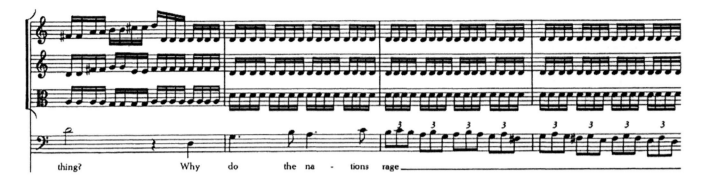

thing?   Why   do   the na - tions rage_____

The psalm opens with a question, as if posed by a king:

> Why do the nations so furiously rage together,
> and why do the people imagine a vain thing?
> (Psalm 2:1 RSV)

We can only laugh at the absurdity of the question. Who in his right mind would question God? Who would rebel against God? The music grows louder and the orchestra plays more furiously. The second question asks, "Why do the people plot in vain?"

The following verse in the psalm says:

> The kings of the earth take their places; the
> rulers take counsel together against the Lord and
> His Anointed [the Messiah, the Christ.] They say,
> "Let us break their bands [of restraint] asunder,
> and cast Their cords [of control] from us."
> (Psalm 2:2-3 AB)

These are the words in the very next chorus in chapter forty-one. The *Contemporary English Version* of the text helps us understand its meaning:

> Why do the nations plot, and why do their people make useless plans?
> The kings of this earth have all joined together to turn
> against the LORD and his chosen one.
> They say, "Let's cut the ropes and set ourselves free!"

Why would Jennens use this text in his libretto? It is a lively scene of commotion among the rulers and nations of the earth. William Taylor, in his exegesis of this psalm in *The Interpreter's Bible,* explains, "The opening of the reign of this new 'King of Glory, the Lord of Hosts' was troubled by reports of an impending revolt of his subject states. It was extremely important that the status of this King of Glory should be stressed, and that victory over his foes and world-wide dominion should be assured him, as a manifestation of the Lord's mastery in history and in the affairs of the nations."[3]

The Message Bible invites us into the absurdity of the situation, interpreting these verses as: "Why the big noise, nations? Why the mean plots, peoples? . . . At first God is amused at their presumption" (Psalm 2:1, 3).[4]

Why are the people plotting a widespread revolt against the king's dominion? William Taylor remarks, "Kings and princes are agitating and coming together to devise plans for war. Their aim is to devise an empty scheme, freeing themselves from the yoke of the King of Glory, the Lord of Hosts."[5] *The New Oxford Annotated Bible* commentary says, "The word 'anointed' in Hebrew is literally 'Messiah,' one of the titles of an Israelite king. After the extinction of the Hebrew monarchy, this became a name for the ideal king of a future, hoped-for restoration, and the psalm was reinterpreted accordingly."[6]

Taylor continues, "But the plot has a deeper significance; it is against the Lord and His Anointed. It is a conspiracy of heathen peoples against the Lord's orderings in world society."[7] Certainly this will prove itself futile, and God's will and purpose will prevail! Doesn't this still go on today?

Musicologist Dr. Alfred Mann, of the Eastman School of Music, gives us his interpretation of the score:

> Handel's original version of this bass *aria* was considerably longer. After measure 38, a pencil line was drawn in the original score vertically through the staves and the following measures were crossed out. The new ending is based on thematic material from the original remainder of the *aria,* presenting the harmonic scheme in strikingly condensed form but elaborating upon the original vocal and instrumental setting of the E minor cadence. The very last measure concluded with a single bar line and is followed by Handel's notation:

---

3 William Taylor, "The Book of Psalms," *The Interpreter's Bible,* Volume IV (New York: Abingdon Press, 1955), 23.
4 Scripture taken from *The Message.* Copyright, 1993, 1994, 1995, 2002. Used by permission of NavPress Publishing Group.
5 Taylor, 24.
6 Note taken from *The New Oxford Annotated Bible,* Revised Standard Version of the Bible. Copyright 1962, 1973 by Oxford University Press, Inc., 657.
7 Taylor, 24.

HANDEL'S *Messiah*

"Coro, let us break their Bonds asunder," suggesting an *attacca* or immediate connection to the following chorus.[8]

Observe the music below:

It was thought that the shortened form was most closely linked to Handel's performance routine. The *aria* should be followed by the next chorus without a repeat of *da capo* (repeating the first section) because it ends with an E minor cadence, and "Let us break" begins on the G in the key of C major (the third in E minor). This *aria* begins a quartet of musical pieces, which are all derived from Psalm 2:1-4, 9.

---

8 Alfred Mann, ed., *Handel's* Messiah *in Full Score* (New York: Dover Publications, Inc., 1989), 223.

Chapter Forty-One

"Let us break their bonds asunder"

(Chorus)

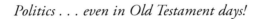

Politics . . . even in Old Testament days!

This chorus continues the cry of a rebellious people in a ¾ tempo driven hard and relentlessly. In the ancient world, the death of a strong king was commonly followed by revolts of states that had once been subject to him, asserting their independence. The first duty of the new king was to subdue the revolting states and re-establish authority over them. This scene is a planned revolt by the subject states that would now be under the yoke or political bondage of the new "King of Glory." So, the rulers of Israel and Judah were no strangers to such political problems. The words, "Break their bonds . . . and cords" are references to the harness of a work animal, providing a metaphor for this political bondage.[1] They plot together, as an angry crowd, to sing:

> Let us break their bonds asunder
> and cast away their yokes from us.
> (Psalm 2:3 KJV)

This is a rather long chorus in a confident, and rather joyous, C major. Look at the opening four measures of the score on the following page. Notice the bowing of the strings and the high G entrances of the sopranos and tenors. Also observe the descending fourths on the various entrances.

---

1 William Taylor, "The Book of Psalms," *The Interpreter's Bible,* Vol. IV (New York: Abingdon Press, 1955), 23.

No. 41 CHORUS

The rhythm of the chorus is a "one-and, two-and, three-and"—a rhythm which sounds as if it is "breaking" or snapping in half. The melody consists of descending perfect fourths (an interval of four notes apart), indicative of a falling weapon.[2] This time, the *fugue*-like melody is sung by a defiant, godless gathering of "humanity representing the rebellious human will. It is a struggle between worldly pride and ambition on the one hand, and the will of God and the Kingdom of His Christ on the other."[3] One can even hear the hissing sound in the recurring sibilants of the words "break their bonds," "us," and "asunder."

---

2 Leonard Van Camp, *A Practical Guide for Performing, Teaching and Singing* Messiah (Dayton, Ohio: Lorenz, Roger Dean Publishing Co., 1993), 115.

3 Taylor, 23.

The text is a continuation of Psalm 2:3, which belongs to the pre-exilic period. Psalm 2 was a poem written to express the confidence of, or to give confidence to, one of the royal line at the time of his accession and on an anniversary of his enthronement.[4] This text is followed immediately by the words, "He who sits in the heavens laughs; the Lord has them in derision."

It must have been a lively scene indeed, as the conspirators are later admonished in verses 10 and 11. They have been rebellious and can only expect complete destruction. In the face of this rebellion, the King is assured complete confidence of being ordained by God. In verse 7, the Lord says: "You are my Son, this day I have begotten thee." This is the formula of adoption, of being chosen by God, and is similar to what we will hear in chapter forty-six with the chorus, "Since by man came death."[5]

This chorus, "Let us break their bonds asunder," was necessary at this time in the musical construction of the masterwork to give weight to the framework of the oratorio. Again we are reminded by Joseph Machlis and Kristine Forney, in their book, *The Enjoyment of Music*, that, "The great chorus becomes the pillar of an architectonic structure in which the *recitatives* and *arias* serve as areas of lesser tension. The *recitatives* and *arias* are placed between the larger pillars of choruses, acting as the melodic arches."[6] The musical structure could be shown this way:

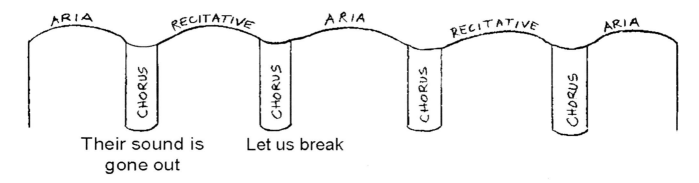

---

4 Ibid., 24.
5 Ibid., 25.
6 Joseph Machlis and Kristine Forney, eds., *The Enjoyment of Music,* 6th edition (New York: W. W. Norton and Company, 1990), 293.

HANDEL'S *Messiah*

CHAPTER FORTY-TWO

"He that dwelleth in heaven"

(RECITATIVE FOR TENOR)

George Frideric Handel

And now, God's reaction to the people's insurgency!

A *recitative* gives us information about the action in the story, and it approximates the rhythm and inflections of ordinary speech. In a style known as *recitative secco* (or dry recitative), the voice is accompanied only by a harpsichord and string bass that provide just a few infrequent chords, as if supporting the singer. The accompaniment is so infrequent that it allows the singer to have discretion in execution.[1] Such is the case in this little-known *recitative:*

> He that dwelleth in heaven shall laugh them to scorn:
> The Lord shall have them in derision.
>
> (Psalm 2:4 KJV)

---

1 Don Michael Randel, ed. *The Harvard Dictionary of Music*, 4th edition (Cambridge, Massachusetts: Harvard University Press, 2003), 707.

The entire *recitative secco* is as follows:

No. 42 *RECITATIVE*

TENOR: He that dwell·eth in heav·en shall laugh them to scorn, the Lord shall have them in de·ri·sion.

BASSO CONTINUO: senza fag.

This *recitative* is the third part of the quartet of verses dealing with the uproar and confusion of the people against the Lord of Hosts' enthronement. The conspirators have been rebellious; they've been "dashing their enemy into pieces," so it is only natural that they can expect complete destruction now.[2]

In his commentary on the Psalms, William Taylor remarks:

> In this text, we are "boldly transported from the earthly scene of the rebellious crowd to the heavenly" to hear God's reaction to the report of insurgency of the people. The abrupt change of scenery is startlingly dramatic as we are now in the courts of heaven. The Lord laughs and holds their vain conceits in derision. Then in terrifying anger, He sets about to show that the king whom He has set upon Zion is inviolable: "I have installed my king on Zion."[3]

The *Contemporary English Version* of the Bible says:

> In heaven the LORD laughs as he sits on his throne,
> making fun of the nations.
> The LORD becomes furious and threatens them.
> His anger terrifies them as he says,
> "I've put my king on Zion, my sacred hill."
> (Psalm 2:4-6)

---

2 William Taylor, Exegesis, "The Book of Psalms," *The Interpreter's Bible*, Vol. IV (New York: Abingdon Press, 1955), 24.
3 Ibid., 25.

The Message Bible is even clearer in its translation:

> Heaven-throned God breaks out laughing.
> At first he's amused at their presumption;
> Then he gets good and angry.

Surely God is sorely displeased with such human arrogance. J. R. Sclater, in his exposition on this psalm in *The Interpreter's Bible* says, "People may have to wait a long time for the enthronement of Christ over the world as seen from the earth's perspective; but it is already a fact in God's purpose. In the realm of the real there is no other King but Jesus."[4]

---

4 J. R. Sclater, Exposition, "The Book of Psalms," *The Interpreter's Bible*, Vol. IV (New York: Abingdon Press, 1955), 24.

Chapter Forty-Three

"Thou shalt break them"

(Aria for Tenor)

God speaks to the king . . . as His Son . . . giving him ultimate power in disciplining the people.

In this tenor solo, the mournful violins play against the tenor's rising line:

Thou shalt break them with a rod of iron,
Thou shalt dash them in pieces like a potter's vessel.

(Psalm 2:9 KJV)

It is interesting that the librettist found another text that uses the word "break," but this time it is used against the *people*. (Remember that in chapter forty-one the insurgent crowd was singing, "Let us break their bonds," as if defying and breaking out from under political bondage.) The masterful cohesiveness of the relationship of the texts of the oratorio is attributed to the librettist's knowledge of the Bible. Milton Cross and David Ewen, in their book, *An Encyclopedia of Great Composers and Their Music,* say, "All the *recitatives, arias,* and choruses of *Messiah* concern themselves with the emotion rather than the dramatic implications of the words, providing such a variety of feeling—from compassion and pathos to serenity, spirituality, and ecstatic joy—that there is never a faltering of pace or lack of contrast."[1]

---

1 Milton Cross and David Ewen, *An Encyclopedia of the Great Composers and Their Music,* Vol. I (New York: Doubleday, & Co., 1953), 341.

This is the last of the four musical pieces comprising a quartet of chapters taken from this short psalm. Notice the descending chromatic scale in the accompaniment of the musical score that follows:

God promised the King, as his Son, a share in the divine prerogatives, a world-wide dominion with free exercise of authority.[2] In the preceding verses 8 and 9, the Lord says to His Son:

> Ask of me, and I will make the nations your heritage . . .
> and the ends of the earth your possession.
> You shall break them with a rod of iron,
> and dash them in pieces like a potter's vessel.
>
> (Psalm 2:8-9 RSV)

The words are few, but mighty. In them we see God's fury as He says, "You shall break them." What must it take for God to want to break us, as one would "break" a wild horse, (meaning to "train to obey," or "to tame")? It definitely is a breaking of one's will. The development of the psalm as a whole is a striking

---

2 William Taylor, "The Book of Psalms," *The Interpreter's Bible*, Vol. IV (New York: Abingdon Press, 1955), 25.

reminder, along with relevant passages in the New Testament, as to the question of who has the ultimate power. Observe the ending of this *aria:*

William Taylor boldly reminds us who has that ultimate power:

> The plottings of the conspirators suggest scenes before and at the trial of Jesus by Annas and Caiaphas (found in John 18:13, 19-24). We are reminded of Jesus' own words, "I have overcome the world" (found in John 16:33). It connects with the scene when Pilate questions Jesus, "Don't you know that I have power to release you and power to crucify you?" Then Jesus answered him with marked emphasis, "You would have no power over me unless it had been given you from above"[3] (John 19:10-11 *Oxford Annotated Bible*).

The music of this entire "Part the Second" of the oratorio has swept onward until the final impending chorus—that incomparable song of joy in the next chapter, the famous "Hallelujah Chorus."

---

3 Ibid., 26.

 "Hallelujah!"

The towering chorus in the oratorio!
Good triumphs over Evil.
And the question . . .
To stand or not to stand?

George Frideric Handel

How do we love the Hallelujah Chorus? Let us count the ways. Very few words grab us as this one word "Hallelujah," the principal word of the entire *Messiah*, as it pounds in our heads. According to Machlis and Forney in their book, *The Enjoyment of Music*, "The musical investiture of the key word 'Hallelujah' is one of those strokes of genius that resound through the ages."[1] (Hallelujah is Hebrew for "Praise ye the Lord.")

Some listeners mistakenly feel this Hallelujah Chorus is the climax of the entire oratorio; but actually it appears 152 pages into the score, with fifty-eight pages still to go! Indeed, it is a supernatural and monumental chorus. Perhaps it is *the* towering piece within the entire oratorio; yet what makes the masterwork so compelling far exceeds the Hallelujah Chorus, for its ultimate message is the salvation that the Messiah brings to all humankind.

After the last "furious" scene that occurs from chapters forty through forty-three, in which we find the "raging nations" trying to "break out of their yokes of bondage" (to which the Lord "held them in derision"

---

1 Joseph Machlis and Kristine Forney, eds., *The Enjoyment of Music*, 6th edition (New York: W. W. Norton & Company, 1990), 434.

and then "dashed them to pieces"), we now feel a clearing in the air of the preceding tension, as if the good guy has arrived, riding victoriously on his white horse with all God's people shouting HALLELUJAH![2]

The SATB (soprano, alto, tenor, bass) chorus begins with its immortal opening on the word, "Hallelujah," sung ten times consecutively as if pounding wave upon wave, forcefully and urgently. These words have cumulative power, and the theme of rejoicing governs the mood, tonality, and rhythm, giving unity to the entire movement.[3]

Let's look at the score below:

2 Leonard Van Camp, *A Practical Guide for Performing, Teaching and Singing* Messiah (Dayton, Ohio: Lorenz, Roger Dean Publishing Co., 1993), 123.
3 Van Camp, 124.

HANDEL'S *Messiah*

The rhythm of the Hallelujah Chorus immediately catches our attention: we have great expectations as we feel the drumbeat and hear the joyous trumpet. We are part of the vast flag-waving crowd in the scene portraying our victorious Lord as we are caught up in the energy of the moment. The 4/4 rhythm pattern suggests that all four voice parts are united in agreement. Not only is the rhythm of the word "Hallelujah" interesting, but Handel also combined vital melodic intervals with this rhythm, as the throng exclaims "Hallelujah."

The violins and viola introduce the musical theme in D major with an energetic *allegro* (lively), followed by the chorus jumping in together on the first "Hallelujah." The first phrase of the text is taken from the last book of the Bible, in which we are told:

> And I heard as it were the voice of a great multitude,
> and as the voice of many waters, and as the voice of mighty thunderings
> saying, "Alleluia, for the Lord God omnipotent reigneth."
> (Revelation 19:6 KJV)

The chorus, as the great multitude of voices, represents the glorious picture of all of heaven rejoicing at the victory over the rule of Satan. The Book of Revelation is the classic story of the final battle of good versus evil. The word "revelation" comes from the Greek "Apocalypse," meaning "an uncovering"; in this case it refers to a revelation from God to the apostle John on the island of Patmos concerning the extraordinary events that would herald the end of the present age. The victory is God's as He ushers in His kingdom.[4] The words preceding this passage are, "Then the seventh angel blew his trumpet, and there were loud voices in heaven saying, 'The kingdom of the world has become the kingdom of our Lord and of His Christ, and He shall reign forever and ever.'"

Charles Jennens found this reference to the trumpet and wanted to include these powerful words in his text for Handel's composition. Handel decided not to have the chorus sing *about* trumpets; instead, he added trumpets to the score at this very moment, foreshadowing the great piece that is to come, "The trumpet shall sound," found later in chapter forty-eight.

The blast of the trumpet is followed by an outburst of joy in heaven. Revelation 11:19 (RSV) describes the glorious scene, "Then God's temple in heaven was opened, and the ark of his covenant was seen within his temple; and there were flashes of lightning, loud noises, peals of thunder, earthquakes, and heavy hail."

---

4 Lynn Harold Hough, "The Revelation of St. John the Divine," *The Interpreter's Bible*, Vol. XII (New York: Abingdon Press, 1956), 506.

The audience's pulse quickens with the explosion of chords and instruments on these words. Van Camp enthuses, "The Hallelujah Chorus is a crowd-pleaser, due to its vocal and instrumental fireworks. The music sings of a victorious Lord, with his host of people carrying banners and shouting the triumphal outburst of 'Hallelujah.'"[5]

The words of the chorus move directly back to Revelation 11:15; and now Handel introduces a slower paced tempo, changing the mood dramatically, only to swell again soon after that.

> The kingdom of the world has become
> the kingdom of our Lord, and of his Christ:
> And he shall reign forever and ever.
> (Revelation 11:15 RSV)

"The kingdom of this world" refers to the rule of Satan, also exemplified by the Roman Empire. Their rule has now been boldly crushed and will soon be replaced by the eternal kingdom of our Lord.[6] We hear powerful melodic phrases sung in octaves by the tenors and basses on the words, "For the Lord God omnipotent reigneth," which is in contrast to the rhythmical theme of "Hallelujah." Within a few measures, the two phrases combine in double counterpoint (four independent melodies sung simultaneously). Handel was a genius in moving from polyphonic (many voices) to chordal (sounding as one voice) texture in a very short space.[7] Observe the counterpoint of the four separate voices in the following score:

5 Van Camp, 124.
6 Hough, 507.
7 Van Camp, 125.

In his book entitled *Harmony and Melody*, Elie Siegmeister explains, "The evolution of the relationship between harmonic motion and verbal meanings forms a large part of the history of music from the 16th through the 19th centuries. Expressive imagery may reflect more than a word or a phrase; it often illustrates the basic idea of a text."[8] In this example of one of Handel's most dramatic moments, the words, rhythm, melody, and harmony unite in depicting an awesome scene.

Siegmeister goes on to say, "Conversely, musical form does not depend solely on the text. Vocal composition has its own special musical structures, characteristics, and requirements, and often imposes itself on the words. Some words influence the rhythmic patterns of melody, are accented, or suggest verbal inflection, thus suggesting melodic inflections."[9] Such is the case with the word "Hallelujah."

The last phrase of the Hallelujah Chorus is taken from Revelation 19:16 (RSV), which declares, "On his robe he has a name inscribed, King of kings and Lord of lords." The sopranos boldly confess His kingship as they climb higher and higher on their notes, with all the other singers agreeing "forever and ever."

We now hear the basses fearlessly declare, "And He shall reign forever and ever." The tenors agree, followed by the altos and sopranos (hitting a high A), who join in professing "King of Kings" as the men sing "forever and ever." These powerful words proclaim that our Lord reigns . . . forever. Can you fathom how long that is? It is eternity to the max! The kingdom of this world is now the kingdom of our God and of His Messiah, and His rule is without end!

Let us compare these three significant verses chosen by the librettist in the user-friendly terms of the *Contemporary English Version*:

> Then I heard what seemed to be a large crowd that sounded
> like a roaring flood and loud thunder all mixed together.
> They were saying, "Praise the Lord! Our Lord God All-Powerful
> now rules as king."
>
> (Revelation 19:6)

> At the sound of the seventh trumpet, loud voices were heard
> in heaven. They said, "Now the kingdom of this world belongs to
> our Lord and to his Chosen One! And he will rule forever and ever!"
>
> (Revelation 11:15)

---

8 Elie Siegmeister, *Harmony and Melody*, Vol. 1 (Belmont, California: Wadsworth Publishing Company, 1965), 415.
9 Ibid., 423.

And on the part of the robe that covered his thigh was written,
"KING OF KINGS AND LORD OF LORDS."

(Revelation 19:16)

The music builds to a great climax as enthusiasm mounts toward the last "Hallelujah" shouted by every singer and instrument, including the blaring brasses, the trilling violins, and the rolling drums. Suddenly in the penultimate measure, everything stops for a collective breath as if all the world is waiting. Machlis and Forney say, "What may seem like a split-second in this chorus, may be suspended for an eternity in God's big scheme of things."[10] A pause in a musical composition is highly effective, even though some people are uncomfortable with silence. Look at the following music:

Sunday, September 6, 1741

The chorus is singing four "Hallelujahs," with momentum building on each. Then . . . halt! Two quarter rests indicate to stop immediately before singing the final "Hallelujah." These rests specify a span of time in which there is silence, only to magnify the final word. The immense popularity of the Hallelujah Chorus undoubtedly stems from its exultant message and velocity.

Notice above that the date of completion for this chorus was written on the original score as Sunday, September 6, 1741. The final "Hallelujah" is a thrilling moment as the last chord hangs in the air while both the audience and performers experience a shared sense of exaltation that only great music can bring.

---

10 Machlis and Forney, 168.

Machlis and Forney continue, "The triumphal outburst of the Hallelujah Chorus has been compared to the finale of Beethoven's Fifth Symphony, [or, I would submit, to the cannons arriving in Tchaikovsky's "War of 1812"]. Handel has achieved a grand effect in the sustained 'King of Kings' and 'Lord of Lords' in the upper voices against the jubilant 'Hallelujah' and 'forever' of the lower voices. The drums beat, the trumpets resound. This music sings of a victorious Lord, and His host is an army with banners."[11] Milton Cross and David Ewen, in their *Encyclopedia of Great Composers and Their Music,* call the Hallelujah Chorus "one of the miracles of polyphonic writing."[12]

Legend has it that King George II leapt to his feet when he heard the Hallelujah Chorus during one of the world's first performances in London. Because no person could remain seated while the king stood, the entire audience rose with him. Even to this day, it is customary for audiences to stand throughout the singing of this chorus. Standing as a group in the name of tradition unites the audience with the performers in a very energizing way as we are all giving tribute to the Almighty God.

George Frideric Handel was a musician who was fortunate to be popular during his own lifetime. A fellow musician, Joseph Haydn, stood with King George II at a performance of *Messiah* in Westminster Abbey. It is said that Haydn wept and proclaimed of Handel, "He is the master of us all." Mozart, too, admired the work of Handel, declaring, "When he chooses, he strikes like a thunderbolt."[13]

Few words take root in us like "Hallelujah." What does "Hallelujah" mean to us individually? To what cause or purpose can we respond, "Hallelujah"? Alfred Mann admonishes us that, "We cannot just leave the reason for our being to Handel. We must grab it for ourselves, and for our souls."[14] Can you join with all humanity and say, "Hallelujah" or "yes" to God today? Can you respond with the collective shout of "Hallelujah" or "Praise ye the Lord"?

This crowd-pleasing chorus lasts almost four minutes. Perhaps due to the haste with which Handel composed the entire oratorio (just twenty-four days), there are two peculiarities in the original score of this chorus that are interesting to note. Handel was in such a hurry that in a few instances, he used a shorthand

---

11 Ibid., 458.

12 Milton Cross and David Ewen, *An Encyclopedia of the Great Composers and Their Music,* Vol. I (New York: Doubleday & Co., 1953), 342.

13 George Lucktenberg, *Handel: An Introduction to His Keyboard Works* (Van Nuys, California: Alfred Publishing Co, 1966), 8.

14 Alfred Mann, ed., *Handel's* Messiah in Full Score (New York: Dover Publications, 1989), 181.

symbol to signify the word "Hallelujah," almost like a "ditto," and even in the next to last measure, he accidentally misspelled it as "alleluja."[15]

Clifford Bartlett, editor of the book entitled Messiah: *The Full Score,* says:

> Handel himself was a marginally religious man, but what counts more in *Messiah* is his understanding of how to express a vast range of instantly recognizable emotions in memorable music, an understanding refined in his course of writing forty operas. Handel was primarily a dramatic composer, and it shows from *Messiah*'s first chord to its final Amen. If he did "see the heavens open" as he told his manservant upon finishing the masterwork, perhaps it was because he was overwhelmed by the power of his own music.[16]

The Hallelujah Chorus is the end of "Part the Second" of *Messiah*, expressing the theme of the passionate sacrifice of Christ, recounting the events leading to His death and resurrection, telling of the mighty work of redemption by His sacrifice, and ending with the triumphant resurrection expressed in this mighty chorus. This "Part the Second" lasts forty-seven minutes. Now on to . . . the rest of the story.

---

15 Mann, 224.
16 Clifford Bartlett, ed., Messiah: *The Full Score* (New York: Oxford University Press, 1998), v.

HANDEL'S *Messiah*

PART THE THIRD

CHAPTER FORTY-FIVE

"*I know that my Redeemer liveth*"

(ARIA FOR SOPRANO)

*This chapter is Job's powerful proclamation of faith.
He trusts solely in the power of God,
proclaiming Protestant dogma unshakeable!
This is beautiful music that soars
with its ultimate message of redemption.*

W hew! We've just studied the magnificent "Hallelujah Chorus." If you think Handel can't surpass such beauty, wait until you hear this *aria*. Milton Cross and David Ewen declare, "It is incredible that the concluding part of *Messiah* should not seem anticlimactic after all the immensity that preceded it. We have only to hear the opening soprano *aria*, 'I know that my Redeemer liveth,' with its ineffable serenity, to realize that Handel is still capable of further elevation."[1]

If you have read this book all the way through, and have reached this "Part the Third," as Handel called it, congratulations! Hopefully, you will find that these musical melodies and texts fit together and tell a story, and you will have learned more about *Messiah*, which has become the best-loved and best-known work of sacred classical music ever.

---

1 Milton Cross and David Ewen, *An Encyclopedia of the Great Composers and Their Music,* 342. Vol. 1 (New York: Doubleday & Co., 1953), 342.

Handel's creative genius came swiftly, even when writing his operas. Although Handel wrote *Messiah* during a particularly low point in his career, it took him just twenty-four days to compose the oratorio, an undertaking we can barely imagine today. *Messiah* became Handel's favorite composition, and one that has lasted for well over two centuries, performed for audiences over and over.

Beginning with March 23, 1743, Handel annually performed *Messiah* for awaiting audiences. German composer and conductor Max Spicker says, "In the course of time he made various alterations in certain musical numbers, set several new ones to music, transcribed a few *arias* for different voices, but left the work as a whole unchanged, both vocally and instrumentally, from its original form. This bears witness that, despite its limitations, this primitive conception of the work was the enduring one."[2]

"Part the Third" continues with the effect of the resurrection of Jesus, extending this ultimate defeat of death through faith to ALL people, and ends with a thanksgiving hymn for the final overthrow of death. This *aria* for soprano begins with the orchestra introducing the main melody in F major, followed by the soprano soloist singing her beautiful and memorable line, the text of which is taken from the Book of Job:

> I know that my Redeemer liveth,
> and that he shall stand at the latter day upon the earth:
> and though worms destroy this body,
> yet in my flesh shall I see God.
> (Job 19:25-26 KJV)

This tremendous expression of faith is sung with the lilting comfort of a *larghetto* (slowly). The form of the piece is in two sections, "A" and "B," with a recurring refrain. The conviction of the text is expressed in the very first phrase, with the highest musical note emphatically placed on the word "know," creating a huge vocal expression and declaration of faith. Observe the opening part of the score written in E major, with its long introduction by the violins:

---

2 Max Spicker, *Score of* Messiah (New York: G. Schirmer Publishers, March 1912), iii.

HANDEL'S *Messiah*

Part the Third

No. 45 ARIA

The listener is acquainted with these well-known words, "I know that my Redeemer liveth." Few words have the power to stir, provoke, and even transform lives. These words are those of a man named Job whose faith cannot be denied and/or be dismissed.

In his book in the Old Testament, Job described the character of humankind's relationship as he vividly represents estrangement from God. Throughout the biblical book, he has asked God for recognition of his *worth*—but not for mercy, and therein lies his problem. In his exegetical commentary on Job, Samuel Terrien says, "Of course, the text is no witness to the Christian mystery of the Incarnation, but it prophetically proclaims, through some 'via negative,' the necessity of a Christ. God is God and forever above man (Job 9:32). If only there were a mediator who could bring God and man face to face."[3] He later speculates, "If only the abyss between the transcendent God and impure humanity could be spanned. If only some being, at once God and man, could affect reconciliation."[4] We are reminded that we, as believers, should not feel hopeless, for our hope is grounded in the overall purpose and direction of God's work.

Terrien goes on to suggest:

> Israel at this time of Job's misery was standing at the crossroads, and it was no longer possible for either the nation or the individual to hold fast to the balanced simplicities of the traditional faith in that holy will which with an equal hand, according to the oracles of the prophets, weighed out to man for his rebellion terrible and sure disaster, and for his obedience, peace and power and measureless bounty.[5]

Job says, "I know that my Redeemer liveth." The term "redeemer" is taken from ancient family law in which the redeemer, as the nearest male relative, is under an obligation to guarantee family solidarity. Thus, when a kinsman has been sold into slavery, the redeemer pays a sum of money to purchase him back. Similarly, if the family's blood has been shed, the redeemer must avenge it. Yahweh performs the duties of the redeemer by paying the ransom for his people ("ransom for many," Mark 10:45). He avenges himself upon those who have violated what belongs to Him.[6]

This redemption is inward and spiritual. Yahweh acts for the comforting of His people, wiping out their sins and forgiving them. He redeems them because He is powerful to redeem, for He is Israel's Mighty One, the Lord of hosts, the coming conqueror.[7]

---

3 Samuel Terrien, "The Book of Job," *The Interpreter's Bible,* Vol. III (New York: Abingdon Press, 1955), 900.
4 Ibid., 901.
5 Ibid., 907.
6 R. B. Y. Scott, "The Book of Isaiah," *The Interpreter's Bible,* Vol. V (New York: Abingdon Press, 1955), 400.
7 Terrien, 901.

It is at this point in the story that Job utters his words and the text of our soprano's *aria*, "For I know that my Redeemer liveth; and at last he shall stand upon the earth." Samuel Terrien says, "Job has reached the climax of his struggles, and affirms that his vindicator or mediator (Go'el) God will live beyond Job's death, and will restore him to fellowship with God. The word 'Go'el' could be translated high priest, or even 'hero.' Job now surrenders all claim and trusts solely in the power of a heavenly high priest to present him before the holy of holies."[8]

Terrien goes on to say that "the Book of Job conveys the poetry of pure religion because Job understands, almost as well as Paul, that righteousness is not the work of humankind, but the gift of God. The Book of Job is not just at the fringes of Old Testament literature. Like the prophecy of Isaiah, it asks the most profound question of Hebraism, and it leads directly to the New Testament."[9]

The *Contemporary English Version* of the Bible paraphrases the Job passage as follows:

> I know that my Savior lives,
> and at the end he will stand on this earth.
> My flesh may be destroyed,
> yet from this body I will see God.

The next section of the *aria*, taken from Paul's first letter to the new Christians in Corinth, defends the certainty of the resurrection of believers:

> For now is Christ risen from the dead,
> the first fruits of them that slept.
> (1 Corinthians 15:20 KJV)

The score paraphrases these words as "Christ himself being the first-born from the dead . . ." Faith in God's love, power, and redemptive purpose for those new Corinthian Christians and for all humankind is historically based on the resurrection. A God of love and power who cares for humankind to the extent that He would send Christ to the cross, where His redemptive purpose is revealed, will not let His care for them end with death. The cross itself, for that reason, becomes the most profound assurance of the resurrection and what it implies for the Christian faith.[10]

---

8 Ibid., 902.
9 Ibid., 901.
8 John Short, "The First Epistle to the Corinthians," *The Interpreter's Bible*, Vol. X (New York: Abingdon Press, 1953), 232.

Jesus is the "first fruits of all others who believe in Him. This is an Old Testament image of the first installment of the first sheaf of the harvest—which in Paul's time was brought to the temple on the first day following the Passover celebration—which anticipates and guarantees the ultimate offering of the entire harvest, given by God and consecrated to Him. Because Christ rose from the dead, those who are asleep in Christ have a guarantee of their own resurrection. The raising of Christ by God's power portends the resurrection of all persons belonging to Him."[11]

The soprano's compelling theme ascends stepwise as she sings these words, "For now is Christ risen," just as the word "risen" implies, until it cannot reach any higher than its climatic G sharp. The height of the note reflects the ultimate message of the entire oratorio, and proclaims Protestant dogma unshakeable…."For now is Christ risen." Look at the ascending scale in the music below, beginning on the words "for now."

In their book, *The Enjoyment of Music*, Machlis and Forney say, "This rising line depicts Christ's ascension, reaching fearlessly for the truth."[12] The strings, likewise, raise their plaintive voices, and we hear the oboe sighing. It is beautiful music that soars with its ultimate message of redemption.

The soprano soloist has an important role in interpreting this *aria*. She must take command of her tone, attack, and support if she is to convince the audience that she believes in what she sings. She must display confidence as her voice effortlessly traces the elegant and voluptuous phrasing of the melody in one arc after

---

9 Note taken from *Nelson's New King James Version Study Bible*, copyright ©1997 by Thomas Nelson, Inc. Used by permission, 1938.

10 Joseph Machlis and Kristine Forney, eds., *The Enjoyment of Music*, 6th edition (New York: W. W. Norton & Co., 1990), 170.

HANDEL'S *Messiah*

another. She must be convincing, as she is taking her listeners on a journey that she has already experienced. As her voice rises into the stratosphere with the notes, we know, too, that "our Redeemer has risen."

Handel has a great gift of melodic architecture. In a piano keyboard score edited by George Lucktenberg, Professor Paul Henry Lang is quoted as saying:

> Melodic construction is the most difficult component of composition, the bold, broad, widely arching melody, the one with the "long breath" being of particular difficulty. Handel, the melodist, is fascinatingly powerful. His wondrous melodies, refined as though passed through fire a thousand times, give the impression of simple improvisation, but their simplicity hides an artfully magnificent structure that cannot be improvised.[13]

In most of "Part the Third," the majority of the texts are drawn from Paul's first letter to the Corinthians, Romans, and Revelation; but the third and final section of *Messiah* has begun with this declaration in the Book of Job. Handel is able to reinterpret biblical words into a musical narrative as he paints a large canvas of an epic drama. In Handel, we see an enlarged spirit of a man who has learned to reach out with his soul and understand the drama of humanity, and then turn about and express it in music that we all can understand.[14]

Machlis and Forney observe, "The oratorios of Handel are choral dramas of overpowering vitality and grandeur; and as vast murals, are conceived in grand style. Their soaring *arias* and dramatic *recitatives*, stupendous *fugues* and double choruses consummate the splendor of the Baroque."[15]

1 George Lucktenberg, *G. F. Handel: An Introduction to His Keyboard Works*. (Van Nuys, California: Alfred Publishing Co, 1966), 4.
2 Jay Welch, jacket cover to Columbia Records album, Handel's *Messiah*, The Philadelphia Orchestra, Mormon Tabernacle Choir, Eugene Ormandy, Conductor, n.d.n.p.
3 Machlis and Forney, 166.

CHAPTER FORTY-SIX

"Since by man came death"

(CHORUS)

This chorus is a theatrical interplay of text and music with two distinct melodies, expressing the difficult concept of being "in Christ," and explaining how we can share in His redemption.

George Frideric Handel

Liturgically, the oratorio continues in Paul's first letter to the Corinthians:

Since by man came death,
by man came also the resurrection of the dead.
For as in Adam all die,
even so in Christ shall all be made alive.

(1 Corinthians 15:21-22 KJV)

Evidence of Handel's interpretative genius is his use of musical "word-painting as the melodic line mirrors the meaning of the words. In this oratorio, there is a great use of contrasts between light and dark, ethereal and commonplace, symbolic and literal, and accompanied and unaccompanied. 'Since by man came death' is very theatrical. Handel deliberately made the music move chromatically as the chorus begins its haunting melody. When the chorus sings *a cappella* (with no accompaniment), the depth of the vertical harmony is particularly poignant with its movement and relationship of intervals and chords to one another."[1]

---

4 G. H. Eric Schmid, *George F. Handel* (New York: C. F. Peter Corporation, 1979, originally Henry Litolff's Verlag, 1977), 50.

The words, taken from Paul's first letter to the Christians in Corinth, expose the anxiety of the time. The apostle Paul speaks directly from the experience of his conversion on the road to Damascus. In Acts 26:8-18 he admitted how difficult it was for him to yield himself to the truths of the gospel, since formerly, until his conversion, he was a persecutor of Christians. He was not easily won to the Christian faith, but the resurrection of Jesus was born into his mind and heart with terrific force on the Damascus road in his dramatic conversion. (Read Acts 9.)[2] Look at the following music in which the chorus enters, barely audible and unaccompanied. It is written in a broadly expansive *grave* (solemn) tempo:

5 Clarence Tucker Craig, "The First Epistle to the Corinthians," *The Interpreter's Bible,* Vol. X (New York: Abingdon Press, 1953), 223.

Erich Schmid calls this chorus a "special level of music." He goes on to warn, "When a choir is singing *a cappella* in a 'grave' piece, intonation can be quite difficult. The sopranos must watch their leap of a 4th on the word 'man' (and moving up to a C) so as not to be flat or under the pitch, and bring the entire chorus down in pitch. All the singers must pay close attention to the conductor."[3]

The first four measures of the score show considerable changes that resulted in an intensification of the entire opening of the *a cappella* phrase. These measures originally looked like this:[4]

The beginning theme is highly contrasted by the following explosive response, "By man came also the resurrection of the dead," which is sung *allegro* (or moderately fast), in "a tempo driven hard, almost relentless, as if we are being rushed forward to our final judgment."[5] (Observe the opening score on the preceding page.) With these decisive entrances, Handel highlighted the text as an "event."

The second major statement of the text is also sung *a cappella* (with no instrumental accompaniment) and slowly on the words:

> For as in Adam all die, even so in Christ,
> shall all be made alive.
> (1 Corinthians 15:22 KJV)

The apostle Paul is telling the people in Corinth that they could share in redemption by becoming "in Christ." This meant a union with Him that was so complete the believer could be nothing less than a "member

6 Schmid, 50.
7 Alfred Mann, ed., *Handel's* Messiah *in Full Score* (New York: Dover Publications, 1989), 224.
8 Joseph Machlis and Kristine Forney, eds., *The Enjoyment of Music,* 6th edition (New York: W. W. Norton & Co., 1990), 230.

of the body of Christ." Those "in Him" were therefore certain of being raised at His coming. Believers were already living in the new age by the power of the Spirit, which Christ had given them.. The Messiah and His people comprised "one body." To be "in Christ" was both an eschatological and a mystical fact; it is impossible to separate the two aspects of the apostle's meaning in which he used this phrase.

What does this say to us today? In his exegesis on 1 Corinthians for *The Interpreters Bible,* Clarence Tucker Craig remarks, "There are two methods concerning how people become part of the 'body of Christ'; one is through faith, and the other is through baptism. Faith is acceptance of the salvation which God has provided in Christ, and baptism is the method by which believers are made into one body with Christ. Both are expressions of relinquishing one's will to be in God's will."[6]

This *a cappella* section again is followed by the *allegro,* "Even so in Christ shall all be made alive." These melodies are smoothly joined together; although totally opposite in nature, there is symmetry but still a dichotomy. It is as if two different personalities are expressing tremendous eternal truths. Observe the lively music accompanying these words:

9 Craig, 9.

In the text "Even so in Christ shall all be made alive," we are told that God gives us the victory over sin today and over death later in the hereafter. The "resurrected body" will be a new body that God will provide, which is *not* perishable and *not* physical.[7]

This is a wonderful passage for Jennens to have chosen at this particular stage in the development of the oratorio. Every part of the letter in First Corinthians deals with some aspect of the New Testament theme of a high Christology of the Resurrection, which is central to the message of salvation and paramount to the motif of the third movement of *Messiah*.

The *Contemporary English Version* of the Bible paraphrases this text into "user-friendly" language:

> Just as we will die because of Adam,
> we will be raised to life because of Christ.
> Adam brought death to all of us,
> and Christ will bring life to all of us.

The Message Bible is not very subtle with its version of this passage:

> There is a nice symmetry in this:
> Death initially came by a man,
> and resurrection from death came by a man.
> Everybody dies in Adam; everybody comes alive in Christ.
> But we have to wait our turn: Christ is first,
> then those with him at his Coming,
> the grand consummation when, after crushing the opposition,
> he hands over his kingdom to God the Father.
> He won't let up until the last enemy is down—
> And the very last enemy is death!

The significance of the resurrection is supremely important. If Christ had not been raised, there can be no faith in Him as the savior of the world. Sin was defeated, and its power was broken for those who have faith to believe it. Because Christ rose from the dead, one's human spirit can—if one believes—be free

---

1 Ibid., 223.

forever.[8] The words the chorus sings, "Since by man came death," are a vivid reminder of humankind's sinful nature and our tremendous need for a redeemer. In contrast, the words "In Christ all shall be made alive" are indeed "lively" and extremely hopeful! Although we still face physical death, we have the assurance of eternal life as well as His promise to raise our bodies up in the resurrection.

2 Ibid.

CHAPTER FORTY-SEVEN

"Behold, I tell you a mystery"

(ACCOMPANIED RECITATIVE FOR BASS)

George Frideric Handel

The beginning of the end of the oratorio . . .

This *recitative* begins the collective climax of the entire oratorio. Again, the definition of a *recitative* is the "half-sung, half-spoken dialogue that occurs between the *arias* . . . whose main purpose is to move the story forward."[1] This is a crucial time in the overall text of the oratorio, for the next seven musical pieces will all confirm the overcoming of death and the reign of God, bringing Handel's *Messiah* to an end.

In his first letter to the Corinthians, the apostle Paul divulges a secret that had been revealed to him in some mystic fashion, which bears insight into God's secret purposes. The text says:

> Behold, I shew (tell) you a mystery:
> we shall not all sleep,
> but we shall all be changed in a moment,
> in the twinkling of an eye,
> at the last trump (trumpet).
> (1 Corinthians 15:51-52 KJV)

---

3 Willi Apel, ed. *The Harvard Dictionary of Music,* 2nd edition (Cambridge, Massachusetts: Harvard University Press, 1964), 629.

Here the term *mystery* is used, not so much to mean a "secret," as to signify something that is "difficult to explain, or even a mystery we'll probably never fully understand." This *mystery* is a divine revelation or religious truth revealed through Christ, to be told to all. The use of the word "sleep" is a euphemism for "die," just as we hear people today use the similar term "passed on."[2]

The music, beginning in D major, is the only accompanied *recitative* in the oratorio in which Handel uses the full string orchestra from the outset.[3] Notice the D major *arpeggio* in the following piece, (which is shown here in its entirety.) The *arpeggio* consists of the 1-3-5-8 tones on the beginning words, "Behold, I tell you a mystery," a hint of the bass "trumpet" *aria* to follow.

No. 47 ACCOMPANIED RECITATIVE

---

4 Clarence Tucker Craig, "The First Epistle to the Corinthians," *The Interpreter's Bible,* Vol. X (New York: Abingdon Press, 1953), 250.

5 Alfred Mann, ed., *Handel's* Messiah *in Full Score* (New York: Dover Publications, 1989), 224.

Notice two specific things in the piece on page 249: first, the mysterious B minor chord on the word "mystery." Second, in measure 5, the introduction of the sixteenth notes on the words "in a moment" anticipates a pattern of repeated notes in the next bass *aria*, "The trumpet shall sound," and accelerates the pace of the *recitative*. This hint of the trumpet is a warning not to blink, because it will all be over. This piece ends in A major, which is the dominant fifth (up five notes) of the key of D major, making ready for "The trumpet shall sound." (For variety and interest, composers will often modulate to another key usually based on the dominant V, as in this case.)[4]

The *Contemporary English Version* of the Bible interprets the mystery this way:

> I will explain a mystery to you.
> Not every one of us will die, but we will all be changed.
> It will happen suddenly, quicker than the blink of an eye.
> At the sound of the last trumpet the dead will be raised.
> We will all be changed, so that we will never die again.

The transformation will be sudden. This phrase "changed in a moment" comes from the Greek *atmos*, meaning "that which cannot be cut or the smallest portion of matter," from which is derived the word, "atom." Greeks had no trouble in conceiving of the immortality of the soul, but the idea of the raised body was difficult. Paul's point is that there are many kinds of "bodies." The resurrected body will be a new body (not physical or perishable) that God will provide.[5] The dead in Christ will be raised first, then the living believers will be instantly transformed into their immortal bodies when Jesus returns.[6]

In the twinkling of an eye—or in the nanosecond that it takes the eye to blink, we will have missed it, Paul reminds us. We will all be changed. These phrases emphasize the suddenness of the change.[7]

---

1 Leonard Van Camp, *A Practical Guide for Performing, Teaching and Singing* Messiah (Dayton, Ohio: Lorenz, Roger Dean Publishing Co., 1993), 216.

2 Herbert G. May and Bruce M. Metzger, eds., *The Oxford Annotated Bible* (New York: Oxford University Press, 1965), 1395.

3 Note from *Nelson's New King James Version Study Bible*, copyright ©1997 by Thomas Nelson, Inc. Used by permission, 1940.

4 Charles Pfeiffer, *Wycliffe Bible Commentary*, 1258. (Nashville, Tennessee: Moody Bible Institute, 1962), 258.

The Message Bible is so clear in its paraphrase:

> But let me tell you something wonderful, a mystery I'll probably never fully understand. We're not all going to die—but we are all going to be changed. You hear a blast to end all blasts from a trumpet, and in the time that you look up and blink your eyes—it's over. On signal from that trumpet from heaven, the dead will be up and out of their graves, beyond the reach of death, never to die again. At the same moment and in the same way, we'll all be changed. In the resurrection scheme of things, this has to happen: everything perishable taken off the shelves and replaced by the imperishable, this mortal replaced by the immortal. Then the saying will come true:
>
> > "Death swallowed by triumphant Life!
> > Who got the last word, oh, Death?
> > Oh, Death, who's afraid of you now?"

Never again shall humankind ever have to question the power of God. The giver of life is the Almighty Conqueror of death! Through His gift of grace, God permits us to share in the resurrection of Jesus. Through the purpose of God, our bodies will be transformed, imperishable, and free from decay.[8]

In his letter to the Corinthians, Paul anticipates the imminent return of Christ in triumph to the earth using vivid apocalyptic imagery. The end may be soon, or *it may be delayed.* But whether it occurs now or later, we must be ready for the sound of the trumpet and for the instantaneous transformation that will transpire for those who live in the Spirit of the Lord. This distinctive Christian dogma is part of the doctrine of the resurrection; and at the sound of that trumpet, Christians will have that assurance and participate in Christ's victory. This *recitative* connects immediately with the following well-loved *aria* for bass, "The trumpet shall sound," which heralds God's resurrection power.[9]

---

5 Craig, 233.
6 Ibid., 250.

CHAPTER FORTY-EIGHT

"The trumpet shall sound"

(ARIA FOR BASS)

History's grand finale.
This is a well-loved aria heralding in God's resurrection power!

George Frideric Handel

This *aria* for bass is another wonderful example of "tone-painting" in which Handel uses the human voice as if it were an instrument, making the most of its rich tone color. Scoring a composition instrumentally is at the discretion of the composer, and Handel certainly knew what effect he was after, for he chose certain instruments that were available which would be the most effective in the context.

The trumpet, rarely highlighted in *Messiah*, begins with its statement of the main theme; then the bass soloist enters. In this *aria*, the trumpet and singer imitate one another brilliantly. The bass soloist gives the effect of being a trumpet as he sings his dazzling passage work; and the orchestration itself rouses the trumpet in its pompous performance. The original tempo marking for the *aria* was *andante ma non allegro*, but Handel replaced *andante* (in a walking manner) with *pomposo* (pompous)[1], and it certainly is! Both trumpet and bass powerfully attack their notes.

---

7 Alfred Mann, ed., *Handel's* Messiah *in Full Score* (New York: Dover Publications, 1989), 225.

The text of this famous *aria* expresses these familiar words:

> The trumpet shall sound,
> and the dead shall be raised incorruptible,
> and we shall be changed.
> For this corruptible must put on incorruption,
> and this mortal must put on immortality.
> (1 Corinthians 15:52-53 KJV)

In his exegesis of this text in *The Interpreter's Bible*, Clarence Tucker Craig says, "The blowing of the trumpet was a regular part of the temple liturgy, but this reference is to the eschatological trumpet (of Isaiah 27:13), which will call the dispersed believers back to the worship at Jerusalem. Here the trumpet is the signal for the twin events of the resurrection of the dead in Christ, and the transformation of the living members of the church."[2] This exegesis of the text is colored by vivid apocalyptic imagery, especially the expectation of an imminent return of Christ in triumph to the earth. Not only will the dead undergo a transformation in the resurrection, but with the final coming of Christ, the living will also be changed.

Paul explains the distinction between the perishable and the imperishable by distinguishing the resurrected body as a new body (not perishable, not physical, which God will provide). God will give us the victory over sin now, in this life, and hereafter victory over death.

Craig goes on to say:

> The Hebrew Old Testament contains no equivalent for the word "immortality," as Jewish thought conceived of man as essentially mortal. But the word "immortality" was a part of Hellenic thought. When Paul uses the word here, it is in a quite different sense beyond the Greek idea of immortality. His distinction is that immortality is not something which belongs to humans by nature; instead, it is "put on" when God raises humans from the dead.[3]

---

8 Clarence Tucker Craig, "The First Epistle to the Corinthians," *The Interpreter's Bible,* Vol. X (New York: Abingdon Press, 1953), 250.
9 Ibid., 251.

The Living Bible explains this phenomenon extremely well:

> For there will be a trumpet blast from the sky and all the Christians who have died will suddenly become alive, with new bodies that will never, never die; and then we who are still alive shall suddenly have new bodies too. For our earthly bodies, the ones we have now that can die, must be transformed into heavenly bodies that cannot perish but will live forever.[4]

Craig declares, "This consummation of the redemptive process begun on earth will be the final demonstration of God's love and power and his abiding victory."[5] Let's look at two more versions of this passage. 1 Corinthians 15:52-53 in the *Contemporary English Version* of the Bible reads:

> It will happen suddenly, quicker than the blink of an eye.
> At the sound of the last trumpet, the dead will be raised.
> We will all be changed, so that we will never die again.

The Message Bible paraphrases 1 Corinthians 15:52-53 as follows:

> But let me tell you something wonderful, a mystery I'll probably never fully understand. We're not all going to die—but we are all going to be changed. You'll hear a blast to end all blasts from a trumpet, and in the time that you look up and blink your eyes—it's over. On signal from that trumpet from heaven, the dead will be up and out of their graves, beyond the reach of death never to die again. At the same moment and in the same way, we'll all be changed. In the resurrection scheme of things, this has to happen.

This certainly sounds as if it is history's grand finale. Let us look at the musical score. The separate notation of the violin I is discontinued after the initial upbeat for the first seven measures with the notation marked "unis. colla tromba," meaning "unison with the trumpet."[6] Look at the long introduction at the top of the following page. Again, the musical motif is an arpeggio (1-3-5-8) as in the preceding recitative, "Behold, I tell you a mystery."

---

10 *The Living Bible, Paraphrased* (Wheaton, Illinois: Tyndale House Publishers, 1971), 574.
11 Craig, 249.
1 Mann, 225.

HANDEL'S *Messiah*

No. 48 ARIA

Musicologist Alfred Mann says, "Handel's original setting of the word 'incorruptible' appears to have been changed as early as 1760. That it remained unaltered in the earlier sources may be due to the fact that the bass part was sung by the same German singer, Thomas Reinhold, from the first London performance until his death in 1751."[7] Look at the score below of measures 33-39, which shows alternate ways of singing the phrase, "raised incorruptible":

As we have learned before, in a *da capo aria*, the vocalist sings all of the musical material and then returns to the first section, as in this case. Harold Schonberg explains, "On the return, or repeat, the singer was expected to show off his or her bag of vocal tricks, embellishing, adorning, and ornamenting the melody."[8]

---

2 Ibid., 225.
3 Harold C. Schonberg, ed., *The Lives of the Great Composers,* 3rd edition (New York: W. W. Norton & Company, 1997), 55.

Handel was "the Great Bear," a lusty man. A naturalized British subject who spoke English with a heavy accent, he was a man with an explosive temperament; and, in contrast to the deeply religious Johann Sebastian Bach, Handel was a man with a simple, uncomplicated faith. Milton Cross and David Ewen tell us, "He had a direct and masterful personality. In *Messiah*, his greatest masterpiece, he took a few well-worn harmonies, sequences and points of imitation between the human voice and instruments, and put them together with an unerring sense of balance into mighty choruses, duets, and solos that have appealed for centuries to English-speaking peoples just because they are so direct and masterful."[9]

Cross and Ewen later state:

> Bach and Handel—these two giants dominated the music of the first half of the eighteenth century. They were born in the same year (Handel was four weeks older); they came from the same region in central Germany, yet they never met. Bach was provincial; Handel was the cosmopolitan who had traveled extensively. Musically, too, they were poles apart. Handel was the product of Italian musical culture; Bach represented and glorified the German. Handel was the genius of dramatic and lyrical expression; Bach was the genius of religious thought. Handel interpreted human experience, whereas Bach idealized it. Handel wrote for an audience; Bach wrote only for his conscience[10] [or, I suggest, his God].

Handel's own generation knew him as a brilliant composer, for he was even famous during his own lifetime. Yet, "Handel guarded his privacy and went out of his way to keep his public life divorced from his private life."[11] In his book, *The Lives of the Great Composers*, Harold Schonberg says, "Handel was religious, but not fanatically so, and he told Hawkins of his delight at setting the Scriptures to music."[12] In his book entitled *Music and Its Makers*, Dale Cunningham notes, "In a curiously Baroque way, Handel was the greatest of the international composers, a German steeped in Italian tradition who created an English style which influenced all music well into the 19th century."[13]

---

4 Milton Cross and David Ewen, *An Encyclopedia of the Great Composers and Their Music*, 340. Vol. 1 (New York: Doubleday & Co., 1953), 340.

5 Ibid., 337.

6 Harold Schonberg, ed., *The Lives of Great Composers*, 3rd edition (New York: W. W. Norton & Co., 1970), 57.

7 Ibid., 58.

8 Dale Cunningham, *Music and Its Makers* (New York: Sterling Publishing Company, Inc., 1963), 36.

Handel's *Messiah*

Handel continued to appear in public, conducting the oratorios he had written and displaying his legendary powers of improvisation on the organ. Even though he was becoming totally blind in 1752, at the age of sixty-seven, he didn't want to stop his composing (or conducting). Handel was working on his last oratorio, *Jephtha*, when midway his eyesight failed completely. On January 27, 1753, the *Theatrical Record* reported, "Mr. Handel has at length unhappily quite lost his sight." He was operated on several times, once by the surgeon who had tried to save Bach's eyesight, and with no greater success than in Bach's case.[14]

Handel continued composing by dictating his last works, which were mainly revisions of earlier compositions. Before Handel died in 1759, he had created forty-six operas, thirty-two oratorios, many cantatas, and lots of smaller works, including the music to which we sing Isaac Watt's famous Christmas carol, "Joy to the World." *Messiah* itself has doubtlessly been heard by the largest audiences and the greatest number of people than any other sacred music ever composed.

Handel—sharp entrepreneur though he was—could never have dreamed of *Messiah*'s enduring place in music history when he completed the oratorio almost 270 years ago. By the end of the eighteenth century, *Messiah* was an international hit. This oratorio has become standard fare for church choirs, choral societies, and many other singing ensembles ever since.[15]

9 Cross and Ewen, 337.
10 Joseph Machlis and Kristine Forney, eds., *The Enjoyment of Music*, 6th edition (New York: W. W. Norton & Co., 1990), 165.

CHAPTER FORTY-NINE

"Then shall be brought to pass"

(RECITATIVE FOR ALTO)

George Frideric Handel

"It's a fact....it's going to happen!"

The trumpet is now silent so that the alto soloist may declare her bold statement from 1 Corinthians 15:54 (KJV), "Then shall be brought to pass the saying that is written, 'Death is swallowed up in victory.'" The biblical excerpt preceding these words is, "So when this corruptible shall have put on incorruption, and this mortal shall have put on immortality…"

The *Revised Standard Version* declares:

> When the perishable puts on the imperishable,
> and the mortal puts on immortality,
> then shall come to pass the saying that is written . . .

The *Message* Bible explains, "This has to happen . . . then the saying will come true." In *The Living Bible*, the text goes even further: "When this happens, our earthly bodies, the ones we now have that are weak and can die, must be transformed into heavenly bodies that cannot perish but will live forever."

In his letter to the church in Corinth, the apostle Paul quotes from two Old Testament Scriptures: the first quote is from Isaiah 25:8, which says, "Death is swallowed up in victory"; and the second is a question from Hosea 13:14 which asks, "O death, where is thy victory? O death, where is thy sting?"[1] These verses are explained in the next chapter of this book that discusses a duet for alto and tenor, but this alto *recitative* is so connected to the following duet that it is hard to even discuss them separately. Both quotes illustrate just how glorious the future event will be. So we find here in his letter to the Corinthians that Paul is citing these Old Testament Scriptures with strong conviction, since for the people to whom he is quoting these words, there can be no doubt that death was a fearful calamity.[2]

The Message Bible explains this phrase as:

> "Death swallowed by triumphant Life!
> Who got the last word, oh, Death?
> Oh, Death, who's afraid of you now?" Whew!

Observe the short *recitative* here:

No. 49 RECITATIVE

Handel intended for this entire oratorio to be a Lenten event, and he surely didn't envision audience "sing-alongs" at Christmastime. He had collaborated with his librettist on other oratorios, including *Saul* and *Belshazzar*, in which there is plenty of evidence of an interaction between the librettist and composer. Unfortunately there is no comparable direct evidence of any pre-composition collaboration over *Messiah*, and

---

1 Clarence Tucker Craig, "The First Epistle to the Corinthians," *The Interpreter's Bible*, Vol. X (New York: Abingdon Press, 1953), 252.
2 Ibid., 249.

circumstantial evidence suggests that there was no contact between the two during the period that Handel drafted the score. It is thought that Handel took Jennen's work as it was given to him.[3]

As mentioned earlier in this book, even though Jennens was considered a friend of Handel's, he was a pompous and conceited aristocrat who had the nerve to write to another friend:

> I should show you a collection that I gave Handel, called "Messiah," which I value highly, and he has made a fine entertainment out of it, though not near so good as he might and ought to have done. I have with great difficulty made him correct some of the grossest faults in the composition.[4]

In another letter, Jennens wrote to Edward Holdsworth:

> I hope he will lay out his whole genius and skill upon it that the composition may excel all his former compositions, as the subject excels every other subject. The subject is Messiah.[5]

What an understatement. As mentioned before, in concerts, conductors sometimes pick and choose specific *recitatives*, *arias*, and choruses from *Messiah* for their choirs to perform. This particular alto *recitative*, "They shall be brought to pass," is frequently omitted. To fully enjoy a long composition such as *Messiah*, which can last up to three hours long, the listener should do his homework and know the entire story in advance. Otherwise, he or she may miss a great deal of the beauty and poignancy of the piece. Now, on we go to the only duet in the oratorio.

3 Donald Burrows, *Handel:* Messiah (Cambridge, England: Cambridge University Press, 1991), 10.
4 Jay Welch, jacket cover to Columbia Records album, Handel's *Messiah*, The Philadelphia Orchestra, Mormon Tabernacle Choir, Eugene Ormandy, Conductor, n.d.n.p.
5 Burrows, 11.

HANDEL'S *Messiah*

CHAPTER FIFTY

"O death, where is thy sting?"

(DUET FOR ALTO AND TENOR)

*The only duet . . . declaring,
"Death, you've lost the battle!"*

This piece, the only duet in *Messiah*, features the alto and tenor who appear to be batting phrases back and forth from one to another, as in a tennis match. John Tobin suggests that, "The evenly flowing quavering movement of the *basso-continuo* in the duet is an excellent foil to the broken and syncopated vocal theme. The broken iambics of the repeated 'O Death' and the syncopation caused by placing the questioning 'Where' on the second beat create a fitting musical expression of the text."[1]

> O death, where is thy sting? O grave, where is thy victory?
> The sting of death is sin, and the strength of sin is the law.
> (1 Corinthians 15:55-56 KJV)

The apostle Paul is quoting from the Old Testament passages in Isaiah 25:8 and Hosea 13:14. Back in the Old Testament days when the prophet Hosea asked these questions, "Shall I ransom them from

---

6 John Tobin, *Handel's* Messiah: *A Critical Account of the Manuscript Sources and Printed Editions* (London: Cassel & Co., 1969), 154.

the power of Sheol? Shall I redeem them from death?" The answer, of course, is no. These words from the prophet, in this context, actually contain a terrible pronouncement of doom.

Paul now uses these same words in his letter to the Corinthians written approximately AD 80-90, in which he quotes from Hosea and repeats the word "death." But due to Paul's new confidence in Christ's resurrection, he has put a fresh spin on the words, achieving a completely different tone. Paul speaks of the ultimate destruction of death, and for him, death has totally lost its power.[2] Observe the "tennis match" in the following score:

As an interesting sidebar to this chapter, we are told that in his original version of *Messiah*, Handel wrote this duet in a considerably longer form. In the longer version, the alto part beginning in measure 5

7 Clarence Tucker Craig, "The First Epistle to the Corinthians," *The Interpreter's Bible*, Vol. X (New York: Abingdon Press, 1953), 253.

HANDEL'S *Messiah*

used to be followed by seventeen measures, which have been omitted. Measure 5 was reworked by Handel to connect with the new measure 6, which we see in the score on the previous page. The original copy of the score, preserved in the library of St. Michael's College, Tenbury, shows a "pasting over" of these seventeen measures and some alterations in both the handwriting of Handel and his copyist, John Christopher Smith.[3]

These are powerful words: "Oh, Death, where is thy sting?" Before the resurrection, death was still operative; it retained its "sting," or power. Paul's teachings declare, "It is the law which strengthens the destructive power of sin." It was sin that made death so frightening. Paul views sin as "death's weapon to destroy man" and the law as "increasing the power of sin" rather than correcting it.[4] Laws make us aware of what sin is and aware of our own sinfulness and guilt.

All three words, *sin, law,* and *death,* appear in this same verse:

> The sting of death is sin,
> and the power of sin is the law.
> (1 Corinthians 15:56 RSV)

Sin, guilt, and death are now gone. Clarence Tucker Craig, in his exegesis in *The Interpreter's Bible,* explains that:

> They have all been overcome by "Christus Victor." The word "victory" appears only three times in Paul's letters, all of them in this one paragraph. Here we are reminded of the extreme results of sin. One might ask, "How did sin enter the world in the first place?" and "How did it gain such power?" Through our limited knowledge, we understand that sin entered the world through Adam; and sin introduced into our human life the principle of decay, and death was its outward result. Paul thinks of sin as more than transgression, as having demonic power, which has reduced man to a kind of slavery.

> Just as in Adam, the head and symbol of the old natural humanity, by his *disobedience* involved all humans in guilt, bondage, and death, so Christ by his *obedience* qualifies as the head of a new humanity—a new creation—in which are justification, redemption from the power of sin, and victory over death.

---

8 Alfred Mann, ed., *Handel's* Messiah *in Full Score* (New York: Dover Publications, 1989), 225.
9 *The Interpreter's One-Volume Commentary on the Bible* (New York: Abingdon Press, 1971), 812.

Paul is certainly not suggesting that sin and the law are equal. In creation, we were given "free will" which, due to our selfish interests, has become the natural law of our sinful nature. When Moses brought the law, there emerged a deep understanding of sin. The law was necessary in order to teach humankind what God required. In a sense, the law was educative; it trained the conscience, it sharpened the sense of sin, and it taught those who were capable of learning the lesson that neither its resources nor their own strength could enable them to fulfill its demands. The law awakened the conscience; through the law comes knowledge of sin. The law teaches us where we stand in relation to the demands of God. With the law came the beginning of moral consciousness; we became aware of God's high moral requirements.

The human problem is that our knowledge of right is invariably greater than our power to perform it. We know what is good and right, and we want to act accordingly, but we fail. The law can reveal the nature of sin, but it is powerless to overcome it. God in His mercy has intervened to use this natural law for our salvation. The principle was always there; we turned it into destruction. The mighty act of God has now turned our sinfulness around and now uses it for His reason for the gift of salvation.[5]

The *Contemporary English Version* of the Bible paraphrases these verses as follows:

> When this happens, then at last the Scriptures will come true,
> "Death has lost the battle!
> Where is its victory?
> Where is its sting?"

The Message Bible helps us to understand the text with these words:

> Death is swallowed by triumphant Life!
> Who got the last word, oh, Death?
> Oh, Death, who's afraid of you now?

In Joyce Meyer's *The Everyday Bible,* the text is explained as, "Now sin is the sting of death, and sin exercises its power (upon the soul) through (the abuse of) the Law."[6] *The Message* Bible continues to explain, "It was sin that made death so frightening and the law-code guilt that gave sin its leverage, its destructive

---

1 Craig, 254.
2 Joyce Meyer, *The Everyday Life Bible, Amplified Version* (New York: Warner Faith, 2006), 1879.

HANDEL'S *Messiah*

power. But now in a single victorious stroke of Life, all three—sin, guilt, and death—are gone, the gift of our Master, Jesus Christ. Thank God!" *The Living Bible* says, "For sin—the sting that causes death—will all be gone; and the law, which reveals our sins, will no longer be our judge."

The tone of this duet reinforces the words and carries us along in its own sweet time. The alto and tenor have been chasing each other all throughout the relatively short piece, only to merge at the very end, segueing into the next chorus. Notice in the score in the following chapter the directive words, "segue Chorus," found underneath the music. Handel intended this duet to be "attached" to the next chorus, "But thanks be to God."

CHAPTER 50 *O death, where is thy sting?*

CHAPTER FIFTY-ONE

"But thanks be to God"

(CHORUS)

George Frideric Handel

All Christendom joins in thanking God for His victory!

It is fitting that the chorus follows the duet in affirming the victory over death. This chorus, symbolizing all humankind, is a "giddy *fugue*"[1] sung as if all the people are nodding their heads in agreement and thanksgiving. The text for the chorus is as follows:

> But thanks be to God
> > who giveth us the victory
> > > through our Lord Jesus Christ.
> > > > (1 Corinthians 15:57 KJV)

As mentioned earlier, this chorus is meant to follow immediately after the previous duet that Handel marked "segue Chorus" (continue to chorus). Observe the ending of the duet on the word "law," followed by a double bar line, which is then followed by the "But thanks," sung by the following chorus:

---

3 Leonard Van Camp, *A Practical Guide for Performing, Teaching and Singing* Messiah (Dayton, Ohio: Lorenz, Roger Dean Publishing Co., 1993), 235.

266

It is surprising that this chorus is not as widely known as many of the others; it is rather long, as well as joyful, which is suggested by the cheerful sixteenth notes on the word, "giveth," in the score that follows:

As the text says, all Christendom is thanking God for His victory over death.[2] For believers, death is not the end because in Christ, we live forever. Since this chorus is connected to the previous duet, we feel a response to the question, "O, Death, where is thy sting?" with the antiphonal form of questions and answers. In measure 34, Handel reused the musical theme he had used in the duet:

The *Contemporary English Version* of the Bible triumphantly says:

But thank God for letting our Lord Jesus Christ give us the victory!

Back in his day, Handel's original chorus only totaled twenty-four singers, at the most. Today's choruses tend to be much larger. Singing in a chorus has great therapeutic value, especially for type "A" personalities.

---

1 G. H. Erich Schmid, *Handel's* Messiah: *Introduction and Instruction for Study* (New York: C. F. Peter Corporation, 1979, originally Henry Litolff's Verlag, 1977), 150.

It is a chance to unwind and become part of a group, cooperating with other voices for a common goal. Also, when you sing in harmony, you can feel a strange synergy taking place; the music becomes your own in some essential way that cannot have happened by merely listening to it.

Singing under a conductor who is technically accomplished is a joy. Conductors give the choir members musical and dramatic insights as to what vocal sound they wish to achieve with the blending of their voices. The conductor also helps the singers discern why the composer wrote every note and phrase, or imagined every degree of orchestral color or tone in a particular way. Each conductor uniquely highlights a particular dramatic element of the score; and the best ones unify and inspire their choirs, some even demanding and achieving excellence! Oh . . . and the audience has an interesting perspective of the conductor; if you watch his back muscles, you can actually see his phrasing!

CHAPTER FIFTY-TWO

"If God be for us"

(ARIA FOR SOPRANO)

George Frideric Handel

*As if under a spell, Handel feverishly composes Messiah in just 24 days . . .
actually believing that God had visited him.*

To be a Christian in the first century was both difficult and dangerous.[1] Likewise, for Christians in the twenty-first century, it is also challenging. The text of this *aria* for soprano is taken from Romans 8:31, 33, and 34, in which we return to Paul's letter written to the Christians in Rome. In this passage, he assures them of the believers' hope of salvation:

> What shall we then say to these things?
> If God be for us, who can be against us?
> Who shall lay anything to the charge of God's elect?
> It is God that justifieth, who is he that condemneth?
> It is Christ that died, yea rather, that is risen again,
> Who is even at the right hand of God,
> who also maketh intercession for us.
>
> (Romans 8:31, 33-34 KJV)

---

1 Note taken from *The Oxford Annotated Bible,* 1368.

This lovely *aria* begins in G minor with a long twenty-four measure introduction by the violins. The soprano enters on the words, "If God be for us, who can be against us?" imitating the melodies that the violins have just played. She confidently sings, "Who can be against us?" which is repeated by the violins, exhibiting a touching interplay between voice and instruments. The mood of the piece is one of strength.[2] If God is on our side, how can we lose? Observe the following score:

This particular commanding *aria* had some minor problems that Handel worked out after a few performances. He reworked the placing of the text, making it easier for the words to flow with the vocal line. Another change was the word "be" to "is," (not so in this example, however). According to arguments about musical consistency and preferences in prosody, the "revised version may have been suggested by one of Handel's soloists, possibly the famous contralto, Mrs. Susanna Cibber, who sang the *aria* transposed to C minor in the first performance. It is conceivable that the altered text setting was accepted by Handel."[3]

As mentioned earlier in this book, we understand from music historians that Handel was not a particularly religious person. He had rejected a career solely in church music and went off to compose operas in the Italian form. Even *Messiah* was meant to be performed in the commercial concert hall by this bankrupt impresario-composer eager to recoup his losses.[4]

But we all agree that he must have been profoundly moved and inspired to have written such a masterpiece.[5] Milton Cross and David Ewen tell us:

2 Joseph Machlis and Kristine Forney, eds., *The Enjoyment of Music,* 6th edition (New York: W. W. Norton & Co., 1990), 168.
3 Alfred Mann, ed., Handel's *Messiah in Full Score* (New York: Dover Publications, 1989), 8.
4 Machlis and Forney, 168.
5 George Lucktenberg, *Handel: An Introduction to His Keyboard Works.* (Van Nuys, California: Alfred Publishing Co., 1973), 8.

From the moment he started working on *Messiah* he was under an uninterrupted spell, in a kind of trance. He did not leave his house; he allowed no visitors to disturb him. The food that was brought to him was usually left untouched, and when he did eat something he would munch on a piece of bread without stopping his work. He did without sleep, too. When his housekeepers tried to get him to rest or eat, he would answer them with ill-tempered and sometimes even incoherent retorts—his eyes blazing with a wild fury—so that they sometimes thought he was losing his mind.

Again and again his servant found him in tears as he put to paper an awesome phrase or a devout passage. Day and night he kept hard at his task, living wholly in the realm where rhythm and tone reigned supreme. As the work neared an end, he was increasingly inspired, increasingly tortured by the fury of inspiration. He had become a captive of himself, a prisoner within the four walls of his study; he strummed on the harpsichord; he sang, then, sitting at his worktable he worked and worked until his fingers gave out. Never had he experienced such a frenzy of creation. Never before had he so lived and fought with music.[6]

Cross and Ewen go on to say:

> Never a religious man in the same sense as Bach, Handel became a God-intoxicated man while writing *Messiah*. When he completed the score he cried, "I did see heaven." His comment upon completing the score leads us to assume that he was himself moved by the religious significance of the text and inspiration. He said he "did see all Heaven before me and the great God himself." Finally, after the last monumental Amen had been written, he confided simply to a physician, "I think God has visited me." The exaltation with which *Messiah* was created is found on every page of the score.[7]

The Revised Standard Version of the text for this soprano's *aria* in Romans is much easier to understand:

> What then shall we say to this?
> If God is for us, who is against us?
> Who shall bring any charge against God's elect?
> It is God who justifies; who is to condemn?
> It is Christ Jesus, who died,

6 Milton Cross and David Ewen, *An Encyclopedia of the Great Composers and Their Music*, Vol. 1 (New York: Doubleday & Co., 1953; quote from "Tides of Fortune" by Stefan Zweig, New York: Viking Press, 1936), 341.
7 Ibid., 342.

yes, who was raised from the dead,
who is at the right hand of God,
who indeed intercedes for us?

These confident words are written from the standpoint of Paul's dramatic Christian conversion and experience. He therefore ascribes the whole process of his salvation to God's action. The introduction, "What then shall we say to this?" is a favorite formula of Paul's (which was omitted by the librettist as unnecessary) and prepares us to hear his following argument: "Since God is for us, who is against us?" Paul is confidently proclaiming, "Since God's power is supreme, all other forces challenge it in vain; therefore, we should have no fear of the outcome, yet we shall not be free from opposition, but we shall be confident."[8]

Paul poses the question, "Who shall bring any charge against God's elect?" Here the apostle uses a metaphor taken from the courts of law. In effect he is saying, "Sin will bring a charge, even against God's elect." We know we have "offended against God's holy laws." We are truly conscious of our unworthiness and the seriousness of our wrongdoing, yet Paul continues, "If it is God who justifies, who is to condemn?"[9]

Gerald Cragg, in his exegesis of Romans in *The Interpreter's Bible,* explains:

> Paul means, "The first challenge to our assurance of salvation has already been met; though we are sinners we have been acquitted." It is God who intercedes for us. The only One who could condemn us is actively involved in defending us. We have a new standing with God, and this gives us our security. These verses are quoted in the Anglican Prayer Book in creedal form and are called the doctrine of "Justification by Faith." Both the mystery and the finality of death have been destroyed.[10]

Cragg later says, "If God is supreme and if his creation is responsive to his will, nothing he has made can obstruct his merciful purpose. The ultimate power for good—a power indestructible and undefeated—is love. Its final victory is assured because it is the active expression of the essential nature of God Himself. This love, which is the whole meaning of the Christian life, is primarily the love of God, or God's specific and incredible love. This love was poured out in and through the life, death, and resurrection of Jesus."[11]

---

8 Gerald Cragg, "The Epistle to the Romans," *The Interpreter's Bible,* Vol. IX (New York: Abingdon Press, 1956), 528.
9 Ibid., 533.
10 Ibid., 529.
11 Cragg, 534.

The Message Bible expresses these verses in user-friendly terms:

> So, what do you think? With God on our side like this, how can we lose?
> Who would dare tangle with God by messing with one of God's chosen?
> Who would dare even to point a finger?
> The One who died for us—who raised to life for us!—
> is in the presence of God at this very moment sticking up for us.

In November 1741, Handel set off for Ireland to begin what was to become an incredibly successful series of productions. *Messiah*, intended to be the grand finale of his Dublin visit, was premiered at a benefit concert during Holy Week. The following year, on April 13, 1742, *Messiah* was presented in London by a professional men and boys choir accompanied by a sparse string orchestra, with oboes and bass added, and joined by trumpets and kettledrums on a few pieces. It was presented in a secular hall during Lent, with the soloists singing along with the chorus.[12]

Now American audiences were eager to hear *Messiah*. After it was performed in Boston in 1770, many other performances were soon heard in Charleston, Philadelphia, and Baltimore. In these later performances, there was an expanded amount of performers as well as instruments, including flutes, clarinets, horns, and trombones. As more and more performances of *Messiah* are taking place today, some purists are insisting on a minimal orchestra as being "authentic" and most representative of the one intended by Handel himself and used at the oratorio's premiere in Dublin.

This masterpiece that Handel wrote in a few days has lasted a lifetime. Recently, I heard *Messiah* at Riverside Church in New York City, and the sound from the Westminster Choir of Princeton, New Jersey, reverberated around the cathedral walls, invoking glory upon glory. Imagine being an eyewitness to such glory! Surely, this is a piece loved by all.

---

12 Leonard Van Camp, *A Practical Guide for Performing, Teaching and Singing* Messiah (Dayton, Ohio: Lorenz, Roger Dean Publishing Co., 1993), 7.

HANDEL'S *Messiah*

Chapter Fifty-Three

"Worthy is the Lamb"

(Chorus)

After twenty-four grueling days,
Handel writes his final scene of universal praise,
a triptych of treasures in this last chorus,
ending with S. D. G. for Soli Deo Glorio!
To God be the glory!

George Frideric Handel

This last chorus begins a "triptych of treasures" in this wondrous score and provides an overwhelming conclusion to the oratorio. Again Handel wisely uses the technique of the *fugue*, thus establishing its role in musical composition for years to come. The use of the *fugue* is particularly effective as the finale in large-scale sacred vocal works as it builds layer upon layer of sound involving all the performers.[1] This chorus reaches fearlessly to proclaim the essential truth as found in the text:

> Worthy is the Lamb that was slain,
> and hath redeemed us to God by his blood,
> to receive power, and riches, and wisdom, and strength,
> and honour, and glory, and blessing.
> (Revelation 5:12-14 KJV)

The scene is one of universal praise to the Creator-Redeemer as the elders and angels pay homage and worship Him. The gospel message that was introduced first in this "Part the Third" by the soprano's *aria*, "I

---

1 Leonard Van Camp, *A Practical Guide for Performing, Teaching and Singing* Messiah (Dayton, Ohio: Lorenz, Roger Dean Publishing Co., 1993), 240.

know that my Redeemer liveth," is the ultimate message of the entire oratorio. Here in this last collection of three choruses, this magnificent thought triumphs as Christ the Lamb is worthy to be praised. Observe the beginning of the following chorus:

Handel highlights this feeling of grandeur and awe from the very beginning with his use of trumpets and timpani in the "A" section of this chorus, "Worthy is the Lamb." Famed composer Erich Schmid suggests, "Due to the majestic character of the piece, every note should sound 'chiseled.' The piece shows an extreme compactness of the voices, and in the orchestra as well. From here on, until the end of this triptych, a brilliant *forte* is necessary and is intensified by the attack of trumpets and timpani."[2]

---

2 G. H. Erich Schmid, *G. F. Handel's* Messiah: *An Introduction and Instruction for Study* (New York: C. F. Peter Corporation, 1979, originally Henry Litolff's Verlag, 1977), 55.

HANDEL'S *Messiah*

Countless choral societies and choirs have sung these three final choral sections with a rich, opulent sound. Handel's chorus comprised only about twenty singers, but today's choruses are usually much larger, and therefore produce masses of sound along with the larger orchestras doubling the instrumental parts.

In our score, the tempo of "Worthy is the Lamb" is marked *largo* (slow and solemn), yet we understand that the first tempo marking was changed twice in the original score. Musicologist Alfred Mann says, "It is likely that these tempo changes were made in deciding the sequence of *largo-to-andante* (slow moving to walking speed) for the three sections of the chorus."[3] This majestic tribute to the Lamb of God is strongly punctuated by all the voices, instruments, and even timpani and trumpets, rarely used in *Messiah*.

Following the majestic opening, we now hear the "B" section, which is in sharp contrast in its lively tone and movement. The text follows:

> Blessing and honour, glory and power be unto him,
> that sitteth upon the throne and unto the Lamb.
> (Revelation 5:13 KJV)

The tempo here is marked *larghetto*, or a little faster than the largo of "A." We will see that the piece increases in tempo as it charges toward the end. These words of blessing and honor pay homage to the Lamb and his council. The text is tossed from one voice to another in this extended joyful *fugue*. On the words, "forever and ever" there are downward sixteenth notes by all voices and instruments alike. Then stepwise rising notes are heard in the soprano line.

---

3 Alfred Mann, *George Frideric Handel's* Messiah *in Full Score* (New York: Dover Publications, 1989), 226.

There is a seamless transition to the final section or "C" section, the "Amen" *fugue*, and it should not feel as if it is treated separately. The "Amen" *fugue* begins at measure 72 with an *allegro moderato* (moderately fast) tempo. Handel's original score shows a number of revisions even as he hastily penned the composition. It is thought that Handel may have contemplated two shortened versions of the final chorus. In his original version, he drew large vertical pencil marks in measure 39 and at measure 53, possibly indicating a shortening of the chorus between these measures, which was a development of the "blessing and honour" phrase.[4]

The basses begin the *fugue*, followed by every other voice part. Then there is a ten-measure instrumental violin interlude, followed by another chorus entry with trumpet and timpani. After a whirlwind of "Amens," there is a dignified rest in the music—a beat of silence in which the whole world hangs on edge—and usually a collective sigh in the concert hall. Then we hear the final "Amen" cadence.[5] Look for the *fermata* on the whole rest in the fourth measure from the end in the following score. Also notice Handel's use of accentuated dissonances with the tonic and leading tone, being struck together immediately before the final cadence chord.

This final chorus, the end of the oratorio *Messiah*, concludes with a spacious, exultant "Amen." Stefan Zweig wrote, "These two abrupt and short syllables were to be built into a monument which would reach to the skies. One voice tossed it to another; the syllables became long and protracted, to be re-knit again, and

---

4 Ibid., 226.
5 Van Camp, 241.

HANDEL'S *Messiah*

then rent apart, more glowing. Like God's breath, Handel's inspiration resounded in the concluding work of the sublime prayer, which thus became as wide and as manifold as the universe."[6]

In their book, *The Enjoyment of Music*, Machlis and Forney declare of the final Amen, "One need only say that it meets the supreme challenge of following the Hallelujah Chorus without a sense of anticlimax. With this is consummated a work as titanic in conception as in execution."[7]

It takes almost seven minutes to perform this last major chorus just by itself. "Part the Third" lasts a total of thirty-one minutes. The entire oratorio, if performed in its entirety, would last two hours and twelve minutes. It ends with a flourish; the rush leaves us reeling. At the end of this noble oratorio are the letters "S. D. G." indicating *Soli Deo Glorio,* meaning "To God be the Glory." The completion of the work, indicated by *Fine dell'Oratorio,* was on September 12, 1741 (twenty-four days from its beginning).

In 1759, shortly after his seventy-fourth birthday and with his health failing, George Frideric Handel began his usual oratorio season, conducting ten major works in little over a month to packed houses. *Messiah* always closed the series. Handel collapsed in the theater at the end of the last performance that he conducted and died some days later on Good Friday, April 14, 1759.[8]

Prior to his death, Handel had added a codicil to his will, requesting burial in Westminster Abbey, which was granted.[9] The nation he had served for half a century accorded him its highest honor: burial in Westminster Abbey.[10] Phil Goulding says, "Tour guides today claim him as an Englishman, pointing out his monument and grave in the Poet's Corner of the Abbey, guarded by a stone tablet bearing a portion of the *Messiah* score."[11]

Author Marshall Cavendish says, "At his funeral 3,000 Londoners were present, and the funeral anthem was sung by the combined choirs of the Chapels Royal, St. Paul's, and Westminster Abbey. Upon his death, Handel willed the autographed score to his favorite charity for which it was written, London's Foundling Hospital. At the time of his death, he had quite a substantial fortune and was highly respected by his music-

6 Milton Cross and David Ewen, *An Encyclopedia of the Great Composers and Their Music,* Vol. 1 (New York: Doubleday & Co., 1953, quoting from Stefan Zweig's *Tides of Fortune,* New York: Viking Press, 1936), 343.

7 Joseph Machlis and Kristine Forney, eds., *The Enjoyment of Music,* 6th edition (New York: W. W. Norton & Co., 1990), 458.

8 Machlis and Forney, 165.

9 Phil Goulding, *Classical Music: The 50 Greatest Composers and Their 1,000 Greatest Works* (New York: Fawcett Columbine, 1992), 200.

10 Machlis and Forney, 165.

11 Goulding, 200.

loving public."[12] A few years ago while in London, my husband and I had the privilege of visiting Westminster Abbey, standing next to Handel's grave marker, and my eyes flooded with tears. Cross and Ewen tell us, "Marking the grave is a statue by Roubiliac, portraying Handel in front of his worktable. On the table are his quills and the score of *Messiah* open at the passage: "I KNOW THAT MY REDEEMER LIVETH.""[13]

Cross and Ewen go on to say, "In composing *Messiah*, Handel has captured and expressed something that is holy and beyond the power of words to describe. He has transported us where hearts can reach and notes can speak. We are amazed at the fecundity of his mind."[14] When you close this book, I pray that you've felt like you've just witnessed a performance. *Messiah* is much more than an oratorio; it has been a love story. Handel gave us his voice, his personal statement of an epic drama and a passion in the pursuit. He gave us a tremendous gift to unwrap.

Yet God surely was the author of this masterpiece. It is the most widely performed and revered piece of religious music in Christendom. Think of what music means to the human soul and what it can do. It is a means of communicating with God and with one another.

The world weeps through music.

The world worships through music.

The world can touch the hand of God through music.

It is through music that our spirits are united

with His Spirit.

S. D. G.

---

12 Marshall Cavendish, *Great Composers: An illustrated companion to the lives and works of the most celebrated composers* (Secaucus, New Jersey: Chartwell Books, 1989), 38.

13 Cross and Ewen, 337.

14 Ibid., 338.

Tribute to Handel

Let us now praise famous men

and our fathers in their generation.

The Lord apportioned to them great glory,

His majesty from the beginning.

There were those who were wise in their words of instruction.

There are those who composed musical tunes,

and set forth verses in writing.

(Ecclesiasticus 44:1-5 KJV)[1]

---

1 This book of wisdom (written circa 180 BC), is part of the Apocrypha, a collection of 14 or 15 books which stood in the inter-testament period between the Old Testament and the New Testament. The majority of these books came to be included in the Greek version of the Old Testament in the Septuagint, but not included in the Hebrew scriptures as "canonized" by the Council of Jamnia (circa AD 90). The word "Apocrypha" is Greek for "hidden" (books). Its intention was for these books to be kept from the public because of the esoteric wisdom they contained. Most Protestant denominations do not recognize any canonical status for these books. However, the content of this particular passage struck the author as an appropriate salute to Handel.

Closing Prayer

Almighty God
>   Wonderful Counselor
>>   Everlasting Father
>>>   Prince of Peace . . .

With this list of beautiful promises,
>   we are assured that You are everlasting, that You
>>   will be with us to the end,
>>>   And as Prince of Peace, You have
>>>>   given us peace
>>>>>   that no one can understand.

We give You ourselves, our souls and bodies;
>   Yoke us unto You.
>>   And so, with quietness of spirit,
>>>   we end this study of Handel's *Messiah.*
>>>>   We thank You for anointing Handel
>>>>   with this gift.

And we pray this in the name of
>   Jesus, the Christus,
>>   *The MESSIAH.*
>>>   AMEN

Glossary [1]

A

a cappella	sung with no accompaniment
adagio	slowly
ad libitum	giving the performer complete freedom of improvisation
alla breve	cut time, relatively rapid tempo
allegro moderato	moderately fast
andante	in a walking manner
antiphonal	alternating responses sung by two or more groups stationed apart
appoggiatura	an ornamental, dissonant pitch falling on the beat
aria	a lyrical piece expressing an emotion that may be removed from context and performed as a solo
arpeggio	a chord whose pitches are sounded successively, not simultaneously
attacca il Coro	signifying for the chorus to attack, or sing, immediately

B

basso-continuo	thoroughbass, or figured bass; an independent bass line upon which harmonies are extemporized on a keyboard instrument

C

cadence	a progression of chords that creates an end or gives an effect of closing a sentence in music
cantata	an extended choral piece with or without solo voices, and usually with orchestral accompaniment
castrato	a male singer who has a masculine body and lung power, but feminine vocal range
chromatic	as in a chromatic scale, ascending or descending by semitones
coda	a section, or added ending, rounding off the piece
coloratura	a soprano with a high range who uses elaborate ornamentation, or an agile, florid style of vocal music
concertino	a small group of instrumentalists performing together
concerto grosso	a larger group of supporting players, as in *ripieno*
con fagotti	with bassoons (a double-reed bass woodwind instrument)
counterpoint	the simultaneous combination of two or more melodic lines
countertenor	an adult male whose voice range is higher than a regular tenor; a male alto who can sing falsetto
crescendo	a gradual increase in the volume or intensity of sound

---

[1] Definitions adapted from Don Michael Randel's *The Harvard Dictionary of Music*, 4th edition (Cambridge, Massachusetts: Harvard University Press, 2003) and Arthur Jacobs' *A New Dictionary of Music* (Chicago, Illinois: Aldine Publishing Company, 1961).

D

da capo   to return; go back to the beginning and repeat the opening section

da lontano   as from a distance

dissonance   a combination of tones considered to suggest unresolved tension or discord

docetism   a sect which proclaimed that Jesus was totally divine and only appeared human, denying His humanity

dominant   the fifth note, or scale degree, upwards in relation to the keynote

down bow   the motion of the bow of a stringed instrument when pulled by a player

duet   a composition or performance of two musicians

E

eschatology   a biblical term signifying that a great divine event is about to happen to mark the decisive end of times

F

fagotti   an Italian name for two or more bassoons

falsetto   a kind of singing produced by adult males in a register higher than their normal sound; countertenors use only this method of voice production

fermata   a half-moon symbol indicating to hold the note longer than usual; a pause or hold

figured bass   an instrumental bass part to which Arabic numbers (figures) have been added, as a kind of harmonic shorthand. Figures indicate the distance above the bass-note of the tones which are to be sounded

forte   loudly

fortissimo   very loudly

fugue   from the Latin word "fugere," meaning to flee; imitative counterpoint in which the theme is stated in each voice of the polyphonic texture

G

grace note   in 17th century England, a note printed in small type to indicate that its time value is not counted in the rhythm of the bar and must be subtracted from that of an adjacent note

grave   Italian for slow or solemn

H

half-close   imperfect cadence, or ending

homophonic   music in which the parts move together as "one" line of music, with no counterpoint

I

interval   the distance between two notes, in so far as one of them is higher or lower than the other

J-L

larghetto   slowly

largo   more slowly

leading tone   the seventh degree of the major scale, leading to the tonic, a semitone above it

legato   played smoothly with no separation between successive notes

M

major key	a classification of the notes of a scale generally sounding pleasing or happy
marcato	marked, as in a prominent manner
melisma	a group of notes sung to a single syllable; a florid vocal passage
meter	rhythmic beats of a piece
minor key	a classificaiton of the notes of a scale generally sounding melancholy or sad
mordent	a musical ornament of embellishment over a note
motif	a musical theme, or melody

N

natural	an accidental sign used to cancel a previous sharp or flat
Neapolitan sixth	an Italian chord based on a lowered second scale degree

O

octave	an interval considered to be eight notes apart, with the same letter names
opera	a musical drama in which all the characters sing, and the chorus is supportive
oratorio	a musical drama for soloists, chorus, and orchestra, not requiring scenery, costumes, or action

P

parallel fifths	the simultaneous statement of the same melodic interval at five notes apart
perfect fourth	the term used to describe the interval of a fourth (as in from C up to F)
piano	soft
pianissimo	very soft
piffaro	an Italian double-reed woodwind instrument like the shawm, or piva, which is a bagpipe of northern Italy
piu lento	more slowly
polyphonic	a counterpoint, or several melodic lines played or sung at the same time
prestissimo	very fast

Q-R

recitative	a style of text-setting that imitates and emphasizes the natural inflections, rhythms, and syntax of speech, and covers a great deal of territory in just a few lines; conversational singing
recitative secco	a "dry" sung dialogue merely accompanied by a few chords every once in a while
reprise	a phrase of music, or verse, which returns to the original theme

S

senza	without
senza ripieno	a small ensemble of the orchestra playing, as in doubling of the parts; not the entire orchestra
segue il coro	connected to the next piece with no break
siciliana	a late Baroque instrumental movement that evokes a gentle, pastoral mood
staccato	short, detached notes (opposite of legato, or smoothly)
stile rappresent-ativo	the dramatic or theatrical style of recitative used in the earliest operas of the first decades of the 17th century, based on the natural inflections of voice, characterized by the freedom of rhythm and irregularity of phrasing

subdominant	the fourth scale degree; immediately below the dominant fifth degree
syncopation	a change in accent causing one of the weak beats to function as a strong beat

T

tasto solo	to play only the single bass-note written and not the supporting chords which a continuo-player would normally add
tempo	speed or pace of the musical piece
tenor clef	a sign placed on the fourth line at the beginning of a staff to indicate where middle C is located
tessitura	the particular range of a vocal part that is concentrated in one part of the scale
testo	in an oratorio, the narrator who sings recitatives
text painting	the music technique of having the melody mimic its lyrics
thoroughbass	figured bass, or *basso-continuo*, an independent bass line of which its harmonies are extemporized
tied notes	a slur joining two adjacent notes of the same pitch, indicating that the second note is not to be attacked, but its duration is to be added to that of the first note
tierce de Picardie	the Picardy third, or the raised major third of the tonic triad as the final chord in a musical piece otherwise in the minor mode
timbre	tone color, or quality which distinguishes the sound of one instrument over another
timpani	kettledrums
tone-painting	word-painting in which music vividly mirrors the words and ideas expressed
tonic	home key, or first degree of the scale
trill	a musical ornament consisting of the rapid alternation of the written note and the note above, used for decoration
turbe	the Jewish population who spoke in passionate words
turn	a musical ornament consisting of the rapid movement of singing or playing around the written note—the first one above the note, back to the note again, then to the one below, and finally returning to the original note
tutti	indicating all instrumentalists or singers to perform together

U

unis. colla tromba	in unison with the trumpet

V

viola da gamba	a fretted, bowed stringed instrument in use from the 16th to 18th centuries played upright, resting on or between one's legs
virtuoso	a performer of great technical ability
voice leading	the movement of several voices or parts in a polyphonic texture; the laying out of a composition so that each part progresses euphoniously

W-Z

word painting	or text painting; a musical technique in which the music mimics the literal meaning of the lyrics

Meet the Author

Mezzo-soprano Gretchen Brown is a freelance writer, teacher, singer, and lecturer. She is also a private vocal coach and piano teacher, having prepared almost one thousand students for performance. She holds a music education degree from Westminster Choir College of Rider University in Princeton, New Jersey, and a masters of theological studies from Episcopal Theological Seminary of Virginia. While at Westminster, she sang under the batons of Leonard Bernstein, Eugene Ormandy, Herbert von Karajan, and Sir Colin Davis at New York's Lincoln Center for the Performing Arts and Carnegie Hall. She has taught countless Bible studies and directed many Broadway musicals, chorus performances, recitals, and endless Christmas pageants! Gretchen and her husband, The Rev. Rod Brown, have served in churches in Virginia, Maryland, and Delaware since 1976 and enjoy beach life in Rehoboth, Delaware.

Gretchen is eager to hear from you.
To share how Handel's *MESSIAH* has impacted you
or to schedule a speaking engagement,
please feel free to email her at rod.brown@mchsi.com.

Spread the Word!

The Word of God and the gospel of Jesus Christ are elegantly and powerfully portrayed in Handel's *Messiah*—don't miss this annual tradition. Whether you're among those who sing a gusty "Hallelujah!" in the choir, who applaud with the audience at a live performance, or who enjoy the music on CD at home, get into the holiday spirit with Handel's epic masterpiece. This Christmas or Easter, enhance the memories by presenting the music-lovers in your life with a gift they will cherish: Gretchen Simmons Brown's book:

Handel's MESSIAH: *A Musical, Historical & Theological Study*

Help spread the Word. Place your order today!

Fruitbearer Publishing, LLC
P.O. Box 777
Georgetown, DE 19947
(302) 856-6649 • FAX (302) 856-7742
info@fruitbearer.com

www.fruitbearer.com

Inquire about bulk discounts for your church or school fund-raisers.

Breinigsville, PA USA
19 November 2010
249612BV00002B/9/P